Re-Interpreting Curriculum Research: Images and Arguments

Re-Interpreting Curriculum Research: Images and Arguments

Edited by
*Geoffrey Milburn, Ivor F. Goodson
and Robert J. Clark*

The Falmer Press

THE ALTHOUSE PRESS
London, Ontario, Canada

UK	The Falmer Press, Falmer House, Barcombe, Lewes, East Sussex, BN8 5DL
USA	The Falmer Press, Taylor & Francis Inc., 242 Cherry Street, Philadelphia, PA 19106–1906
CANADA	The Althouse Press, Faculty of Education, The University of Western Ontario, London, Ontario, Canada, N6G 1G7

© Selection and editorial material G. Milburn, I.F. Goodson and R.J. Clark, 1989

All rights reserved. No part of this publication may be reproduced, stored in a retrieval system, or transmitted, in any form or by means, electronic, mechanical, photocopying, recording, or otherwise, without permission in writing from the Publisher.

First published 1989

British Library Cataloging in Publication Data

Re-interpreting curriculum research: images and arguments.

1. Schools. Curriculum. Theories.
I. Milburn, G. (Geoffrey), 1932-   . II. Goodson, Ivor, F.
III. Clark, Robert J.

375'. 0001

ISBN 1-85000-504-4
ISBN 1-85000-505-2 Pbk.

Library of Congress Cataloging-in-Publication Data available on request

Canadian Cataloguing in Publication Data

Main entry under title:
Re-interpreting curriculum research
Rev. versions of papers presented at an invitational curriculum conference held in London, Ont. in Oct. 1986.
 Bibliography: p.
 ISBN 0-920354-24-6

1. Education—Curricula. 2. Educational sociology.
I. Milburn, G. (Geoffrey), 1932-   . II. Goodson, Ivor, F.
III. Clark, Robert J., 1936-   .

LB1570.R44 1989   375   C88-095053-6

Editorial Assistants: K. Butson, T. Johnson, S. Talos, J. Calhoun

Jacket design by Caroline Archer
Typeset in 11/13 Bembo by
Alresford Typesetting & Design, New Farm Road, Alresford, Hants.

Printed in Great Britain by Taylor & Francis (Printers) Ltd.

Contents

Preface	*vii*
Introduction *Robert J. Clark, Geoffrey Milburn and Ivor F. Goodson*	1
Cultural Perspectives in Curriculum Research	11
'Chariots of Fire': Etymologies, Epistemologies and the Emergence of Curriculum *Ivor F. Goodson*	13
Curriculum Policy and the Culture of Teaching *Andy Hargreaves*	26
Curricular Change and the 'Red Readers': History and Theory *Bruce Curtis*	41
State Formation and Classroom Practice: Once Again 'On Moral Regulation' *Philip Corrigan*	64
Methodological Alternatives in Curriculum Research	85
Feminism, and the Phenomenology of the Familiar *Madeleine Grumet*	87
The Persistence of Technical Rationality *John Olson*	102
Action Research: A Practice in Need of Theory? *Catherine Beattie*	110
Evaluation as Subversive Educational Activity *Joel Weiss*	121

Teachers and their Curriculum-change Orientations *Dennis Thiessen*	132
An Integrative Function for Teachers' Biographies *Richard L. Butt*	146
How Much Life is there in Life History? *Geoffrey Milburn*	160
References	169
Notes on Contributors	181
Index	183

Preface

We are particularly indebted to Katherine Butson for her secretarial and editorial assistance throughout the preparation of this volume. Tammy Johnston and Steven Talos also made valuable contributions. In the Faculty of Education Library, Anna Holman and Jean Colhoun responded to our requests as generously in this project as they have done in the past. Without the help of these colleagues our task would have been much less pleasant.

The contents of this volume are much revised versions of papers presented at an Invitational Curriculum Conference held in London, Ontario, in October 1986. The authors and editors have benefited from the critical comments of those scholars who attended the Conference. We are indebted to Hugh Stevenson and Frank Harper for financial support both for the Conference and also for subsequent editing of the papers, which was provided by the Faculty of Education at The University of Western Ontario.

Readers will notice that footnotes are listed at the end of each chapter, while references are collected at the end of the book. Figures and Tables are numbered consecutively in the chapters to which they refer. Sections of the chapter by M. Grumet are reprinted, with permission, from *Bitter Milk: Women and Teaching* (Amherst: University of Massachusetts Press, 1988), copyright (c) 1988 by The University of Massachusetts Press.

GM/IFG/RJC
July 1988

Introduction

Robert Clark, Geoffrey Milburn and Ivor Goodson

The chapters in this book all originate in different ways from an acknowledgment of an obvious, yet often neglected, fact. In our reflections on schooling, and particularly in our studies of school curriculum, it is always as well to remind ourselves that we are dealing with social inventions and ongoing social constructions. Once we begin to investigate schooling and school knowledge as a social construction, the unproblematic 'givenness' of much curricular scholarship and educational policy begins to emerge in a clearer light.

Over twenty years ago, Williams (1961) put this central point very clearly in the context of the origins of the school curriculum in England and Wales.

> An educational curriculum, as we have seen again and again in past periods, expresses a compromise between an inherited selection of interests and the emphasis of new interests. At varying points in history, even this compromise may be long delayed, and it will often be muddled. The fact about our present curriculum is that it was essentially created by the nineteenth century, following some eighteenth century models, and retaining elements of the medieval curriculum near its center. A case can be made for every item in it, yet its omissions are startling. (pp. 150–1)

As a social construction, then, the school curriculum involves a set of selections: the criteria for selection are various, ranging from the intellectual to the political. Williams' essay focuses on the selection of *content*, but just as important is the selection of *form*. For instance, 'proper', 'academic' school knowledge in England is normally 'abstract, highly literate, individualistic and unrelated to non-school knowledge' (Young, 1971a, p. 38). This is a selection of *form*.

Tomkins (1986) made a similar argument about the origins of curriculum in Canada in the seventeenth century. In their curricular selections, the Jesuits 'established the tradition of highly centralized curriculum' that 'foreshadowed the "standards" or grades that later became a basic organizing principle for schools in all western systems of education' (Tomkins, 1986, pp. 12–3). Given such premises, scholars have begun to investigate the nature of the social construction of curriculum, and the relationship of the school curriculum to changing patterns of economic, social and political power. In their different ways the substantive and methodological pieces in this volume try to further this scholastic endeavour.

Such curricular investigations are linked to recent advances in the sociology of knowledge, in which the relationship between knowledge and control has been a principal feature. This was particularly the case in the 'new sociology of education' movement in the 1960s and 1970s. However, the world's changing aspirations of this intellectual genre plainly receded after the *annus mirabilis*, 1968. Whitty (1985), one of the early exponents, warns us that 'in the current conjuncture the school curriculum has itself become an important site of ideological struggle, even though it almost certainly lacks the overwhelming significance that "the new sociology of education" sometimes seemed to attribute to it' (p. 38). The collective view represented in this volume would, we think, share this sense of perspective and humility.

Given this perspective in curriculum studies, however, the task of the researcher assumes a different form. New problems and new questions demand new methodologies and new methods of reporting. Traditional methods of curriculum research related to management or teacher effectiveness are ill-adapted to exploring cultural or social relationships. Yet alternatives to these traditional forms are not easy to articulate and the usefulness of such alternatives is subject to dispute.

The authors in this book are interested in both the substantive questions and also in related methodological problems in the historical, sociological and cultural analyses of curriculum. In sum, they offer a series of images and arguments on the social interpretation of curricular research, intended to extend current debates on the nature and contribution of such a perspective.

The first part of this volume consists of four chapters grouped together under the title of 'Cultural Perspectives in Curriculum Research'. Although each chapter deals with a different subject, the four authors share a common purpose: to relate an important curricular question to the society of which it is a part. In particular, they try to show how changes in curriculum definitions, inservice education, reading texts for students, and official guidelines are influenced by, or caused by, social and economic changes within political systems. Thus these authors offer interpretations of curricular phenomena, and insights into educational practice, that differ from those dominated by the assumptions of traditional curricular research.

The usefulness of such cultural analysis is illustrated by Goodson's analysis of the term 'curriculum'. His focus is on the original meaning of 'curriculum' and on the changes that have occurred in the period since it was first used. This search for an historical context for curriculum stands in stark contrast to contemporary usage in which the term is constricted (and restricted) to satisfy the needs of managers and administrators interested simply in technical matters. This purposeful constriction has served to disguise the origins of the term and to suppress previous meanings that were ascribed to 'curriculum' in earlier times.

It is these suppressed meanings—the 'etymology' and 'epistemology'—of 'curriculum' that Goodson examines in this volume. He points out that scholars have located the first uses of the term in Calvinist Europe in which new types of rulers were attempting to build a new theological and social order. From that period dates the identification of curriculum with new forms of approved knowledge for social control. Goodson also finds a link between the notion of the 'elect' and the implementation of a class-based curriculum that eventually led to the development of different forms of schooling for different classes of students in nineteenth-century England. His comments on the role of 'subjects' as school disciplines in this transformation add to our growing knowledge of the role of academic power groups in forming the contemporary curriculum. In sum, Goodson outlines an historical ground against which the figure of contemporary educational discourse takes on a new character. It is not a prospect that will give much solace to either curriculum theorists or practitioners.

Although Hargreaves examines a familiar problem, why teachers resist curricular change, his method of analysis and his final recommendations do not follow conventional patterns. He examines in some detail two widely adopted strategies for change and finds both of them wanting. Current attempts to transform teaching by transforming the ways in which teachers talk or think about their work—which he labels 'cultural interruption'—perish, he argues, on the conservatism of classroom practice, primarily because such reforms ignore the powerful conditions that sustain the culture of teaching. On the other hand, contemporary efforts to reform the curriculum through 'subject' renewal seem to reinforce rather than redesign existing structures. Consequently, Hargreaves uses the term 'structural reinforcement' to describe curricular reforms in Britain and several other countries, reforms that seem to be waxing rather than waning in some of the latest pronouncements of government policy.

Hargreaves thus picks up some themes that Goodson identified as part of the social construction of curriculum. He argues for a view of curriculum change as a social process that encourages teachers to confront existing power relationships, especially those embedded in subject-specialist differentiations in schooling. His criticism of familiar patterns of curriculum renewal, and his recommendations for alternative procedures and practices, reflect his interest in examining curriculum as a socially constructed phenomenon.

The last two authors in this section examine examples of government-approved curriculum documents, on the one hand school textbooks in the nineteenth century, and on the other hand a recent government policy document on evaluation. They serve as two case studies in analyzing familiar documents to reveal the nature and purpose of state regulation in curriculum.

First, Curtis examines the change-over in schools in Canada West (now Ontario) from the Irish National Readers (in use from 1846) to the Canadian Series of Readers (the 'Red Readers') in 1866. Although both sets of readers, he argues, were concerned with the dissemination of official knowledge among school populations, the two sets part company on questions of content and pedagogy. The earlier set appears to be more heavily didactic and designed for direct instructional methods, while the later set includes more readings relevant to Canadian concerns and designed to be more pleasing to young learners. Curtis ascribes these changes to the changing nature of a frontier economy; in the earlier period perceived needs for establishing a firmly controlled provincial economic structure encouraged education officials to take a heavier hand in curriculum formation than was the case a generation later when the capitalist system was more certainly founded.

This issue of regulation of the school curriculum by state authorities is examined in a contemporary setting by the final author in the first part of the volume. Corrigan examines a recent Ontario policy document on education to locate its purpose and intent. He notes the ways in which the central authority uses its authority to relate the school curriculum to a particular vision of society. As a consequence, he argues that students will have no alternatives other than being socialized into a consumer society oriented to *the* information age. This document, in short, is a strategic example of the state using its power not only to control the curriculum, but to set a particular agenda for curriculum renewal and change. Rather than encourage schools to examine important issues, the document works from a series of centrally generated givens to which the schools are required to correspond. Curriculum renewal, in consequence, is seen in purely administrative terms in which technical rationality is inevitably victorious.

The first four chapters, therefore, are examples of alternative forms of educational criticism. Rather than discuss such curricular terms as 'effectiveness' and 'impact', they attempt to relate developments within curricula to the cultural contexts of which schools are a part. Their points of departure are more historical and sociological than technical: their interests are in power relationships within the state, and in the pedagogical and curricular results of changes in those relationships. The chapters in the first section of this volume illustrate the force of this type of interpretation, and set the stage for the methodological studies that follow in the second section.

The contributors to the second part of this volume focus upon research methodologies related to the types of cultural analysis illustrated in the previous part. In research style, the studies are qualitative and critical rather than quantitative, and in methodological range, they include phenomenological and autobiographical analyses, as well as field work and life-history approaches. Despite this diversity, however, common theoretical strands are woven throughout the section. The authors, for example, seek to understand the meaning of events and the interactions of teachers and administrators from these persons' points of view in particular curricular settings. In effect, curricular phenomena are construed as socially constructed in particular contexts; in this regard, the contributors are sensitive to theory emerging from the evidence being collected rather than being superimposed on the evidence. Their concern is identification of the ideological underpinnings of social and political relations located in their curricular studies.

The form and substance of the chapters vary. Some authors are reporting and analyzing a particular body of research evidence, others are critically reflecting about the methodology as well as the social and political meanings attached to different types of qualitative enquiry. Some couch their accounts in narrative form, others rely upon more categorical frameworks to structure their studies. Some more self-consciously disclose the subjectivity that they bring to their investigations, others tend to distance themselves in more formal, analytical fashion. Whatever the variety that exists, all suggest new agendas for researchers in the field of curriculum studies.

Grumet's narrative style provides an example of the extent to which forms of qualitative research have departed from empirical-analytical enquiry. In keeping with her autobiographical approach, she begins by narrating her own growing disenchantment with, and defection from, mainstream social science methodology in favour of a phenomenological perspective. In similar fashion, she ascribes at least a part of her interest in feminism to her awareness of the disregard and denigration of women, even among 'the so-called left in curriculum theory'. Her phenomenological and feminist interests come together in her studies of the significance of reproduction in both teaching and accounts of teaching. In her interpretation of three autobiographical narratives written by a female teacher, Grumet illustrates her focus on the phenomenology and psychoanalytic account of gender in order to better understand how the private and public lives of women are intertwined in their work. The teacher's accounts are vivid in their descriptive detail of personal experiences and replete with reflective musings.

Grumet's analysis of the texts reveal her interpretive, methodological stance. In each autobiographical account she detects an emergent pervasive meaning of the whole text; moreover, she teases out relationships that reveal continuities and discontinuities among the three excerpts. Her interpretation is strengthened by psychoanalytical insights, metaphoric analyses and etymological explanations. In particular, she combines phenomenological and feminist perspectives in keeping with the basic argument at the beginning of her chapter.

Olson, on the other hand, is interested in exploring reasons for the persistent dominance of technical rational ideology in shaping the professional discourse and practices of educational administrators and teachers. The durability of this stance, he maintains, is rooted in administrators' needs to legitimate their work, which is fraught with ambiguity and value conflicts, and constantly subject to public scrutiny. In this regard, he contends that scientific management theories, with their promise of enhanced efficiency and accountability in bureaucratic environments outside of the field of education, prove irresistible as legitimating principles for school administrators and teachers. While this tendency to project an image of the ordered management of change may win some degree of public acceptance and hence reduce career anxieties, he argues that it falsely obviates the need to confront important value issues that permeate curricular phenomena. Olson has no immediate remedy for the situation, but he does suggest that a more self-conscious awareness by educators of their penchant for rationalizing reputational anxieties would lead to a more realistic appraisal of means-ends issues central to curriculum deliberation.

In a similar fashion, Beattie analyzes the extent to which action research, a controversial approach to curricular research, should and can be theoretically justified. She admits that proponents of this form of research traditionally claim a context-dependent, inextricable relationship between theory and practice that defies the building of generalizable propositions. Nevertheless, she points to both logical and political reasons for initiating theory construction. Logically, for example, if action research is to be understood and rationally assessed, then meta-theoretical principles seem to be a prerequisite. Likewise, in a political sense, if this form of research is to gain academic legitimacy, then the devising of theoretical principles is essential.

Next, in dialectical fashion, Beattie presents counter arguments. She claims, for example, that the uniqueness of personal, practical knowledge, and the danger of appropriating meta-theory developed independently of practice, discount a role for traditional social scientific propositions. In a related argument, she asserts that the use of testable propositions would subvert action researchers' aim to enhance practitioners' control and understanding of curricular phenomena. Beattie ends her analysis with a seemingly intractable challenge for academic theorists: to explain how a research style predicated upon strengthening teacher control and empowerment can be sustained in bureaucratic structures in which teachers enjoy very little power.

Like Beattie, Weiss raises perplexing questions about the relationship between theory and practice, but his focus is upon evaluation. He aspires to a political and theoretical realignment of program evaluation to increase its educational potential. This impetus is needed, he contends, because the findings of professional evaluators have been largely ineffectual, for reasons ranging from bureaucratic inertia to evaluators' failure to reflect critically about their enterprise. It is a damning indictment. On a more promising note, Weiss detects harbingers of a renewed focus upon the educative potential of evaluation emanating from a shift toward qualitative research in education, reinforced, in particular, by questions of agency associated with action research, and conceptions of emancipation raised by critical theory.

In advancing his argument to lend educative import to evaluative endeavours, Weiss re-casts the role of evaluation within the context of curricular principals: the teacher (evaluator), evaluative paraphernalia and interactions (curriculum materials), the audience (student) and evaluative conditions and context (media). This culminates in his delineation of an educational agenda for evaluators. The policy imperatives he identifies include a call for more deliberate self-reflection by evaluators about their current methodologies and ideological predispositions. He also sees a need for bridging professional boundaries and seeking greater collaboration with other academic colleagues in the field of curriculum studies. In sum, Weiss envisions a complete reappraisal of typical conceptions of evaluation and their application in curricular settings.

In the following chapter, Thiessen reports on his research designed to identify curriculum-change orientations that emerged from interviews of selected Ontario teachers and administrators. The interviewees were asked to provide a retrospective view of curriculum change as it pertained to the development and implementation of a curriculum guideline for the study of English.

Thiessen illustrates his research strategy by providing excerpts from his interview transcripts, followed by his interpretive analysis of the comments of two groups of teachers working for the same board of education. Initially, he identifies commonalities that emerge in establishing the meaning of curriculum and curriculum change, the role of the teacher and the indication of important value positions on the part of the interviewees. When he turns next to assess the views of particular individuals, significant variations in meaning and emphasis become apparent.

Thiessen labels the two dominant stances he identifies as a 'teacher-centered-adaptation orientation', and a 'professional-renewal orientation'. He explains that those who espouse the former view are willing to adjust, but not significantly alter their practices; whereas the latter are more open to change, depending upon collaborative discussion and critical debate about what they consider to be personally and socially important in the classroom. Apart from these two positions, he briefly notes two additional orientations that characterized interviewees working for four different school boards included in his study: a 'structured-direction', top-down, technical-management position, and a 'strategic-influence orientation' which attributes the shaping of curriculum change to key educators in a particular school jurisdiction. *In toto*, Thiessen's research appears to detect conceptions of curriculum change that cannot be readily accommodated within existing models and perspectives in this field.

Butt amplifies the importance of the personal and biographical aspects of teachers' knowledge raised in Thiessen's study, and in the theme of life histories which courses its way through the various chapters of this volume. What is distinctive about Butt's contribution is his deliberate description and reflective analysis of his graduate-education course emphasizing autobiographical accounts that reveal aspects of the personal and experiential nature of teaching.

Butt describes his course, including assignments intended to encourage students to construct different forms of documentation such as daily journals or tapes of lessons with reflective concern for emergent themes and patterns. He stresses that careful modelling and mutual participation by the instructor are essential to encourage a co-operative, non-judgmental relationship among students, both to promote understanding of classroom phenomena, and to negotiate comfortable levels of personal disclosure. It would appear to require a delicate *modus operandi* by an instructor with heightened personal and ethical sensitivities.

Butt's justification for his course centers upon the need to assist teachers to understand the sources and nature of their personal, practical, knowledge. In turn, he hopes that the generation and status enhancement of more authentic professional knowledge will enrich scholarly enquiry in the field of curriculum studies. In the context of a collaborative, autobiographical enterprise of this nature, he argues that the multiple functions of teaching, learning, professional development and research can be integrated for the personal and academic benefit of both the students and the instructor. In particular, Butt contends that this type of study is particularly conducive to research and professional development. In this regard, it supplants the outsider-insider, theory-practice dichotomies of technical-rational approaches with a form of investigation that enhances teachers' understanding, and potentially, their control of their future professional growth and study. Probably the most significant long-term value of the graduate-course approach, however, is the collegiate nature of relationships between professor and students as co-learners and co-researchers.

In the final chapter in this section, Milburn departs from the preceding contributors' advocacy of different forms of qualitative or ethnographic research by offering caveats about theoretical and applied aspects of life-history research. Using a particular case study, he begins by questioning the meaning of the term 'life history', and suggests that conventional definitions betray ambivalently uncomfortable attempts to straddle, on one hand, humanistic, historical biographies and, on the other hand, social scientific studies of collectivities. To illustrate this lack of consensus about a clear investigative focus, he cites a bewildering array of terminology in a variety of authors.

Next, the data underpinning life-history accounts is subjected to scrutiny. In essence, Milburn advises caution in investing credence in generalizations scantily supported by a quotation or series of quotations excerpted from field notes. The difficulties are carefully delineated: the frailty of subjects' recollections, the potential distortion of the meaning of subjects' spoken words in the editing of transcripts, and the denial of corroboration stemming from the anonymity necessarily accorded to the subjects. Milburn also attests to being unsettled by the dominant sociological categories that characterize life-history research, despite claims to the contrary. In this regard, he also contends that authors should prudently note the interpretive rather than objective quality of their findings produced by their social scientific methodology. In the end, he queries the appropriateness of reporting life-history research within the framework of traditional academic papers. While several of the contributors to this section admit to limitations in their research styles, Milburn's account at the end of the book reminds us of the complexity and difficulty of embarking upon alternative research endeavours in the field of curriculum studies.

In sum, then, this book contains a series of essays and case studies that re-interpret curriculum research from a particular perspective: the relationship of school curricula to the political and social systems of which they are part and product. The intellectual traditions from which the contributors draw are not those with which many curriculum designers and practitioners may be familiar; but they supply the background for a series of substantive and methodological investigations that approach familiar questions from a different perspective. The authors try to uncover some of the mystifications that cloud our understanding of the invention, selection and social construction of school curricula, and to debate some of the ways in which that uncovering may be accomplished by students and scholars.

Nevertheless, it should be emphasized that the studies in the following chapters offer images and arguments, not irrefutable propositions, provide opportunities for further research and debate, not final statements on basic questions facing curricular theorists at the present time, and prompt readers to reflect upon the issues under discussion, rather than suggest facile solutions to complex or intractable curricular problems.

Cultural Perspectives in Curriculum Research

'Chariots of Fire': Etymologies, Epistemologies and the Emergence of Curriculum

Ivor F. Goodson

The problem of reconceptualizing our study of schooling can be partially illustrated in the basic etymology of curriculum. The word curriculum derives from the Latin word *currere*, which means to run, and refers to a course (or race-chariot). The implications of etymology are that curriculum is thereby defined as a course to be followed, or most significantly, presented. As Barrow (1984, p. 3) notes, 'as far as etymology goes, the curriculum should be understood to be "the presented content" for study'. Social context and construction by this view is relatively unproblematic for by etymological implication the power of 'reality-definition' is placed firmly in the hands of those who 'draw up' and define the course. The bond between curriculum and prescription then was forged early; it has survived and strengthened over time. Part of the strengthening of this bond has been the emergence of sequential patterns of learning to define and operationalize the curriculum as prescribed.

From its Latin origins it is important to trace the emergence of curriculum as a concept which began to be used in schooling. According to Hamilton and Gibbons (1980, p. 15), 'the words class and curriculum seem to have entered educational discourse at a time when schooling was being transformed into a mass activity'. But the origins of the class/curriculum juxtaposition can be found earlier and at the higher education level. From Mir's analysis of the origins of 'classes' as first described in the statutes of the College of Montaign we learn:

> It is in the 1509 programme of Montaign that one finds for the first time in Paris a precise and clear division of students into *classes* .... That is, divisions graduated by stages or levels of

increasing complexity according to the age and knowledge required by students. (Cited in Hamilton and Gibbons, 1980, p. 7)

Mir argues that the College of Montaign actually inaugurated the Renaissance class system, but the vital connection to establish, however, is how organization in classes was associated with curriculum prescribed and sequenced for stages or levels.

The Jesuits were one of the first religious groups to establish a tradition of highly centralized curriculum control in their schools. The *Ratio Studiorum* was 'arguably the most systematic course of study ever devised. This carefully graded curriculum organized into classes foreshadowed the "standards" or grades that later became a basic organizing principle for all western systems of education' (Tomkins, 1986, p. 13). The Jesuits carried their systems to many countries. In Canada, for instance, in 1635 they founded the Jesuit College in Quebec (a year before Harvard College was founded in Massachusetts). The curriculum (French was the language of instruction) comprised Latin, Greek, the teaching of grammar, rhetoric and philosophy, as well as history, geography and mathematics.

The *Oxford English Dictionary* locates the earliest source of the word 'curriculum' in 1633 in Glasgow. The annexation of the Latin term for a race-course is clearly related to the emergence of sequencing in schooling, but the question 'Why Glasgow?' remains. Hamilton and Gibbons (1980) believe that:

> the sense of discipline or structural order that was absorbed into curriculum came not so much from classical sources as from the ideas of John Calvin (1509–1564). As Calvin's followers gained political as well as theological ascendancy in late sixteenth-century Switzerland, Scotland and Holland, the idea of discipline — 'the very essense of Calvinism' — began to denote the internal principles and external machinery of civil government and personal conduct. From this perspective there is a homologous relationship between curriculum and discipline: curriculum was to Calvinist educational practice as discipline was to Calvinist social practice. (p. 14)

We have then an early instance, if these speculations carry weight, of the relationship between knowledge and control. This works at two levels with regard to curriculum definition. First, there is the social context in which knowledge is conceived of and produced. Secondly, there is the manner in which such knowledge is 'translated' for use in particular educational milieux, in this case classes but later classrooms. The social context of curriculum construction must take account of both levels.

Etymologies, Epistemologies and the Emergence of Curriculum

The evidence of Paris and Glasgow in the sixteenth and seventeenth centuries has been summarized in the following quote, in which we can see the interlinked nature of the emerging mode of curriculum and patterns of social organization and control:

> the notion of classes came into prominence with the rise of sequential programmes of study which, in turn, resonated with various Renaissance and Reformation sentiments of upward mobility. In Calvinist countries (such as Scotland) these views found their expression theologically in the doctrine of predestination (the belief that only a preordained minority could attain spiritual salvation) and, educationally, in the emergence of national but bipartite education systems where the 'elect' (i.e., predominantly those with the ability to pay) were offered the prospect of advanced schooling, while the remainder (predominantly the rural poor) were fitted to a more conservative curriculum (the appreciation of religious knowledge and secular virtue). (Hamilton, 1980, p. 286)

This quote sets up the unique significance of curriculum as it developed. For soon after as its power to designate what should go on in the classroom was realized, a further power was discovered. Alongside the power to *designate* was the power to *differentiate*. This meant that even children who went to the same school could be given access to what amounted to different 'worlds' through the curriculum they were taught.

The general connection between 'class' pedagogies and a curriculum based on sequence and prescription is clear but to move towards the 'modern' duality of pedagogy and curriculum involves the transition from class to classroom system. In analyzing the historical transition from 'class' to classroom system, the shift in the initial stages of the Industrial Revolution in the late-eighteenth and early-nineteenth century 'was as important to the administration of schooling as the concurrent shift from domestic to factory production was to the management of industry' (Hamilton, 1980, p. 282). Indeed, as Smelser (1968) has shown, the two were intimately related:

> In the pre-industrial family of a craftsman, the parents themselves are responsible for teaching the child minimum occupational skills, as well as for his emotional molding during his early years. When a growing economy places demands for greater literacy and more technical skills, the pressure is for this multi-functional family to give way to a new, more complex set of social arrangements. Structurally distinct educational institutions appear and the family

> begins to surrender some of its previous training functions to these new institutions; having lost these functions, accordingly, the family becomes more specialized, focusing relatively more on emotional conditioning in the early childhood years and relatively less on its former economic and educational functions. (p. 79)

In the 'domestic putter-out' system, then, the family unit remained at home, and education, albeit rather more in the guise of training and apprenticeship, could therefore take place in the home. With the triumph of the factory system, the associated break-up of the family opened up these roles to subsequent penetration by state schooling and to their replacement by the classroom system where large groups could be adequately supervised and controlled. Hence 'the change from class to classroom reflected a more general upheaval in schooling — the ultimate victory of group-based pedagogies over the more individualized forms of teaching and learning' (Hamilton, 1980, p. 282).

If we specifically turn to the development of schooling in England, at this stage the intersection of pedagogy and curriculum begins to resemble more 'modern' patterns. As Bernstein (1971, p. 47) has argued, pedagogy, curriculum and evaluation considered together constitute the three message systems through which formal educational knowledge can be realized, in this sense they constitute a modern epistemology. In the 1850s the third prong was pioneered with the founding of the first university examination boards. The centennial report of the University of Cambridge Local Examinations Syndicate (1958, p. 1) reports:

> The establishment of these examinations was the universities response to petitions that they should help in the development of 'schools for the middle classes.'

Also at this time the feature of curriculum mentioned earlier, the power to differentiate, was being institutionalized. The birth of secondary *examinations* and the institutionalization of curriculum *differentiation* were then almost exactly contemporaneous. For instance the Taunton Report (1868) classified secondary schooling into three grades depending on the time spent at school. Taunton (1868, p. 587) asserted:

> The difference in time assigned makes some difference in the very nature of education itself; if a boy cannot remain at school beyond the age of fourteen it is useless to begin teaching him such subjects as required a longer time for their proper study; if he can continue till eighteen or nineteen, it may be expedient to postpone some studies that would otherwise be commenced earlier.

Etymologies, Epistemologies and the Emergence of Curriculum

The Taunton Report (1868, p. 587) noted that 'these instructions correspond roughly but by no means exactly to the gradations of society'. (This statement could, as we shall see, be equally well applied to the Norwood Report [1943] nearly a century later.) In 1868, schooling until eighteen or nineteen was for the sons of men with considerable incomes independent of their own exertions, or professional men, and men in business whose profits put them on the same level. These received a mainly classical curriculum. The second grade up to sixteen was for sons of the 'mercantile classes'. Their curriculum was less classical in orientation and had a certain practical orientation. The third grade till fourteen was for the sons of 'the smaller tenant farmer, the small trades-men, (and) the superior artisans'. Their curriculum was based on the three 'Rs' but carried out to a very good level. These gradations cover secondary schooling. Meanwhile most of the working class remained in elementary schools where they were taught rudimentary skills in the three 'Rs'. By this time the curriculum functioned as a major identifier of and mechanism for social differentiation. This power to designate and differentiate established a conclusive place for curriculum in the epistemology of schooling.

By the turn of the century the epistemology, with which we are familiar, was emerging. Thus:

> By the twentieth century, the batch production rhetoric of the 'classroom system' (for example, lessons, subjects, timetables, grading, standardization, streaming) had become so pervasive that it successfully achieved a normative status—creating the standards against which all subsequent educational innovations came to be judged. (Hamilton, 1980, p. 282)

The dominant epistemology which characterized state schooling by the beginning of the twentieth century combined the trilogy of pedagogy, curriculum and evaluation. The last of the pieces in the trilogy was the establishment of university examination boards, and here the side-effects on curriculum were to be both pervasive and long-lasting. The classroom system inaugurated a world of timetables and compartmentalized lessons; the curriculum manifestation of this systemic change was the school subject. If 'class and curriculum' entered educational discourse when schooling was transformed into a mass activity in England, 'classroom system and school subject' emerged at the stage at which that mass activity became a state-subsidized system. And in spite of the many alternative ways of conceptualizing and organizing curriculum the convention of the subject retains its supremacy. In the modern era we are essentially dealing with the *curriculum as subject*.

Whilst this system was inaugurated in the 1850s, it was established on the present footing with the definition of the Secondary Regulations in 1904 which list the main subjects followed by the establishment of a subject-based 'School Certificate' in 1917. From this date curriculum conflict began to resemble the existing situation in focusing on the definition and evaluation of *examinable* knowledge. Hence the School Certificate subjects rapidly became the overriding concern of grammar schools and the academic subjects it examined soon established ascendancy on these schools' timetables. The Norwood Report (1943, p. 61) stated that:

> a certain sameness in the curriculum of schools resulted from the double necessity of finding a place for the many subjects competing for time in the curriculum and the need to teach these subjects in such a way and to such a standard as will ensure success in the School Certificate examination.

The normative character of the system is clear and as a result of 'these necessities' the curriculum had 'settled down into an uneasy equilibrium, the demands of specialists and subjects being widely adjusted and compensated' (Norwood Report, 1943, p. 61). The extent to which university examination boards thereby influenced the curriculum through examination subjects is evident. The academic subject-centered curriculum was in fact strengthened in the period following the 1944 Education Act. In 1951 the introduction of the General Certificate of Education allowed subjects to be taken separately at the Ordinary ('O') level (in the School Certificate blocks of 'main' subjects had to be passed); and the introduction of an Advanced ('A') level increased subject specialization and enhanced the link between 'academic' examinations and university 'disciplines'. The academic subjects which dominated 'O' and especially 'A' level examinations were then closely linked to university definitions; but even more crucially they were linked to patterns of resource allocation. Academic 'subjects' claiming close connections to university 'disciplines' were for the 'able' students. From the beginning it was assumed that such students required 'more staff, more highly paid staff and more money for equipment and books' (Byrne, 1974, p. 29). The crucial and sustained link between 'academic' subjects and preferential resources and status was therefore established.

But if this system was predominant with regard to staffing and resources for academic subjects in grammar schools, the implications for the other schools (and styles of curriculum) should not be forgotten. Echoing Taunton, the Norwood Report (1943, p. 2) had discovered that schooling had created distinctive groups of pupils each of which needed to be treated 'in a way appropriate to itself'. This time the social and class basis of differentiation remained the same but the rationale and mechanism for differentiation was significantly different. Before, the argument had focused on time spent at school: now the emphasis was on different 'mentalities' each recognizing a different curriculum. First, 'the pupil who is interested in learning for its own sake, who can grasp an argument or follow a piece of connected reasoning'. Such pupils 'educated by the curriculum commonly associated with grammar schools have entered the learned professions or have taken up higher administrative or business posts' (p. 2). The second group whose interests lie in the field of applied science or applied arts were to go to technical schools (which never developed very far). Thirdly, the pupils who deal 'more easily with concrete things than with ideas'. Their curriculum would 'make a direct appeal to interests, which it would awaken by practical touch with affairs' (p. 4). A practical curriculum then for a manual occupational future.

We see then the emergence of a definite pattern of *prioritizing* of pupils through curriculum; what emerged I have called elsewhere 'the triple alliance between academic subjects, academic examinations and able pupils' (Goodson, 1983 a, p. 33). Working through patterns of resource allocation, this means a process of pervasive 'academic drift' afflicts sub-groups promoting school subjects. Hence subjects as diverse as woodwork and metalwork, physical education, art, technical studies, book-keeping, needlework and domestic science have pursued status improvement by arguing for enhanced academic examinations and qualifications. Likewise, schools defined as different from grammar schools, the technical schools and secondary modern schools also were ultimately drawn into the process of academic drift, both ending up competing for success through academic subject-based styles of examination.

In a way, the evolution of each subject reflects in microcosm a struggle over alternatives over time which is not dissimilar to the overall pattern discerned as state schooling is established and defined. Hence Layton (1972) sees the initial stage as one where 'the learners are attracted to the subject because of its bearing on matters of concern to them'. At this point the teachers are seldom trained as subject specialists but do 'bring the missionary enthusiasms of pioneers to their task'. Significantly at this stage, 'the dominant criterion is relevance to the needs and interests of the learners'. However, as the subject 'progresses' (a subject at any point in time resembling a coalition which veneers a sub-set of warring factions) the role of the universities becomes more and more important. This is not least because subject groups employ a *discourse* where they argue increasingly for their subject to be viewed as an 'academic discipline' (thereby claiming the financial resources and career opportunities which accrue). The corollary of this claim is that the university scholars must be given control over defining the 'discipline' (the aspiration to the rhetoric of 'the discipline' is related to acceptance of this hierarchical pattern of definition so in this sense the discursive formation is critical). Jenkins and Shipman (1976, p. 102) have noted that:

> one detects a certain embarrassment in teachers who not unnaturally feel the difference between forms, disciplines and subjects are in part differences of status.

In effect, the differences are over *who* can define 'disciplines' — essentially this is presented as the characteristic activity of university scholars.

The progressive refinement of an epistemology suited to state schooling then embraces the trilogy of pedagogy, curriculum and examination. Until recently, the 'triple alliance' of academic subjects, academic examinations and able students has been able to enjoy a clear hierarchy of status and resources. Thus our understanding of curriculum has to focus mainly on analyzing the dominant convention of the school subject and the associated examination by university boards. The linking of resources to 'academic' subjects places a priority on subjects that can be presented as 'academic disciplines' and this places further power in the hands of the universities. Not that the power of the universities over curriculum is unchallenged, the challenges are recurrent. Reid (1972) has noted that a major area of conflict is between the external constraints arising from university requirements and the internal pressures which have their origins in the school:

> Schools are, however, poorly equipped to resist university pressures. To a large extent they allow the legitimacy of the university demands, and have evolved an authority structure which is linked to them. (p. 106)

Such recurrent conflict is of course likely as the school subject 'progresses' away from Layton's (1972) early stage where 'the dominant criterion . . . is relevant to the needs and interests of the learners' (p. 11). But as we have seen, an epistemology has been institutionalized and resourced which places the academic 'discipline' at the top of the curriculum apex. Not surprising, the culminating stage in the establishment of an 'academic' subject celebrates the power of scholars to define the 'disciplines' field. In this culminating stage, however, Layton argues that related to this change in who defines school knowledge 'students are initiated into a tradition, their attitudes approaching passivity and resignation, a prelude to disenchantment' (p. 11).

This final stage of Layton's (1972) model comments upon the kind of political 'settlement' with regard to curriculum, pedagogy and evaluation in operation. Plainly however, there are recurrent conflicts and the 'achievement' of this 'settlement' has been a painstaking and deeply contested process. It is important when assessing the contribution of scholars of education to establish how their work resonates with the contested nature of education generally and curriculum specifically. As always there is a danger of accepting that which is worked for and achieved as a *fait accompli*. Nothing could be further from the truth.

Antecedents and Alternatives

The epistemology and institutionalized system of state schooling briefly described above was in sharp contrast to antecedent forms of education and to the involvement of the State in schooling at this earlier stage. Rothblatt (1976), for instance, describes education in Georgian England as follows:

> The State was not interested in 'national education' — indeed the idea had not yet occurred. The Church, which was interested in education, because of its continuing rivalry with Dissent, still did not have a firm policy and left the direction of studies to local or personal initiatives, or to the forces of the market. The demand for education and the demand for particular levels of education varied radically from period-to-period and from group-to-group, depending upon social and economic circumstances, occupational distributions and cultural values. Countless persons, lay as well as clerical, opened schools, tried out various educational experiments and programmes in an effort to retain a fickle or uncertain clientele. And home tuition, where adjustments in curricula could be made quickly and easily according to the learning ability of the pupil, certainly remained one of the most important means of elementary and secondary education throughout the nineteenth century. (p. 45)

Such a personal and local mode of educating could well have allowed response to the experience and culture of the pupils even in situations less ideal than home tuition 'where adjustments could be made quickly and easily according to the learning ability of pupil' (Rothblatt, 1976, p. 45). But among working-class groups certainly, in the sphere of adult education such respect for life experience in curriculum was a feature at this time and later. This contribution can be summarized as: 'the students' choice of subject, the relation of disciplines to actual contemporary living and the parity of general discussion with expert instruction' (Williams, 1961, p. 144). Above all, there is the idea of curriculum as a two-way *conversation* rather than a one-way *transmission*.

Likewise, different patterns of education and attendance characterized the working-class private school, which thrived in the first half of the nineteenth century and continued into the second half in many places even after the 1870 act. Harrison (1984) has described these schools and the views which state inspectors held of them:

> Government inspection and middle class reformers condemned such schools as mere baby-minding establishments. They noted with strong disapproval the absence of settled or regular attendance. The pupils came and went at all times during the day. School hours were nominal and adjusted to family needs — hence the number of two- and three-year olds who were sent to be 'out of the way' or 'kept safe'. The accommodation was over-crowded and sometimes stuffy, dirty and unsanitary. The pupils were not divided into classes, and the teacher was a working man or woman . . . . (p. 290)

As well as not being arranged in classes, the curriculum was often individualized rather than sequential. Harrison (1984, p. 290) describes 'Old Betty W's School' where 'on fine days the little forms were taken outside her cottage and placed under the window. The children had their books, or their knitting and the old lady, knitting herself incessantly, marched backwards and forwards hearing lessons and watching work'.

These working-class schools were effectively driven out by the version of state schooling which followed the 1870 Act. Thompson (1968) has argued that the watershed for such schools, certainly such styles of working-class education, were the fears engendered by the French Revolution. From now on the State played an increasing role in the organization of schooling and of curriculum:

> Attitudes towards social class, popular culture and education became 'set' in the aftermath of the French Revolution. For a century and more, most middle class educationalists could not distinguish the work of education from that of social control: and this entailed too often, a repression or a denial of the life experience of their pupils as expressed in uncouth dialect or in traditional cultural forms. Hence education and received experience were at odds with each other. And those working men who by their own efforts broke into the educated culture found themselves at once in the same place of tension, in which education brought

with it the danger of rejection of their fellows and self-distrust. The tension of course continues. (p. 16)

The disjuncture then between common cultural experience and curriculum can be estimated, for working-class clienteles, as developing after the moral panics associated with the French Revolution. From this date the school curriculum was often overlaid by social control concerns for the ordinary working populace.

For other classes at the time this overlay of closely structured, sequenced and presented curriculum was not always deemed necessary. We learn that the public schools 'followed no common pattern of education, though they agreed on the taking of Latin and Greek as the main component of the curriculum. Each evolved its own unique forms of organization with idiosyncratic vocabularies to describe them' (Reid, 1985, p. 296). In so far as the curriculum depended on a learning of texts, it was not judged essential that the teacher taught the text—a highly individualized form of curriculum. Moreover 'where students were divided into "forms" (a term referring originally to the benches on which they sat) this was done in a rough and ready manner for the convenience of teaching and not with the idea of establishing a hierarchy of ability or a sequence of learning' (Reid, 1985, p. 296).

Hence coherent alternative forms of education and curriculum developed in a wide range of schools for all classes prior to the Industrial Revolution and even after industrial transformation were retained in the public schools for the 'better classes' (and indeed for the working class were retained and defended in pockets such as 'adult education'). The model of curriculum and epistemology associated with state schooling progressively colonized all educational milieux and established itself some time in the late-nineteenth century as the dominant pattern. The subsequent linking of this epistemology to the distribution of resources and the associated attribution of status and careers stands at the center of the consolidation of this pattern. The assumption that the curriculum should be primarily academic and associated with university disciplines has been painstakingly worked for and paid for. We should beware of any accounts which present such a situation of 'normal' or 'given'.

At root such a hierarchical system is often seen as denying the dialectic of education, the notion of dialogue and flexibility which some viewed (and view) as central to the way we learn. This mutuality is deliberately denied if 'subject matter is in large measure defined by the judgments and practice of the specialist scholars' and 'students are initiated into a tradition; their attitudes approaching passivity and resignation'. The rhetoric of the 'discipline' and the academic subject might therefore be seen as characterizing a particular mode of social relations.

Educationalists concerned with establishing a more egalitarian practice and curriculum are driven to assert the need for dialogue and mutuality, and with it to argue for 'reconstruction of knowledge and curriculum'. For if the opinions cited are right, the very fabric and form of curriculum (as well as the content) assumes and establishes a particular mode of social relations and social hierarchy. Seen in this way, to argue only for changing the teaching method or the school organization is to accept a central mystification of hierarchical structure through curriculum which would actively contradict other aspirations and ideals. Hence, where pockets of alternative practice exist, they present a similar case for egalitarian practice. In liberal adult education the following argument is presented:

> All education which is worth the name involves a relationship of mutuality, a dialectic: and no worthwhile educationalist conceives of his material as a class of inert recipients of instruction — and no class is likely to stay the course with him — if he is under the misapprehension that the role of the class is passive. What is different about the adult student is the experience which he brings to the relationship. This experience modifies, sometimes subtly, and sometimes more radically, the entire educational process: it influences teaching methods, the selection and maturation of tutors, the syllabus: it may even disclose weak places or vacancies in received academic disciplines and lead on to the elaboration of new areas of study. (Thompson, 1968, p. 9)

By this view then, the disciplines cannot be taught as final 'distillations' of knowledge unchallengeable and unchanging and should not be taught as incontestable and fundamental structures and texts. This would provide a deeply-flawed epistemology, pedagogically unsound and intellectually dubious, for in human scholarship 'final distillations' and 'fundamental' truths are elusive concepts. We are back with the dual face of socially contexted knowledge — both because knowledge and curriculum are pedagogically realized in a social context and are originally conceived of and constructed in such a context.

The alternatives to such a dominant view continue to surface. In recent debates we can find certain radical teachers pursuing the comprehensive schooling ideal seriously and arguing that in such a milieu knowledge and curricula must be presented as provisional and *liable to reconstruction*. Armstrong (1977, p. 86) writes that this 'contention is that the process of education should imply a dynamic relationship between teacher, pupil and task out of which knowledge is reconstructed, for both teacher and pupil, in the light of shared experience'.

Conclusion

In this chapter some of the origins of curriculum have been speculatively scrutinized. In particular we have seen that the notion of curriculum as structured sequence or 'discipline' derived a good deal from the political ascendancy of Calvinism. From these early origins there was a continuing juxtaposition between curriculum and discipline. Curriculum as discipline was allied to a social order where the 'elect' were offered the prospect of advanced schooling and the remainder a more conservative curriculum.

Out of these origins we have seen how the concept of curriculum became appended at a subsequent stage to a new notion of discipline. This time (so we are to believe) 'fundamental' disciplines of 'the mind'. The juxtaposition of curriculum with (newly-defined) 'discipline' intersects with a remarkably similar social configuration. This time the 'elect' are recruited by their capacity to display a facility for those academic 'subjects' allied to the 'disciplines'; their 'election' is signified by going on to study the 'disciplines' in the universities where they are defined and institutionalized.

Curriculum Policy and the Culture of Teaching

Andy Hargreaves

This chapter is concerned with curriculum change. It starts from the central precept, advanced by Stenhouse (1980), that curriculum development is ultimately about teacher development. Change in the curriculum is not effected without some concomitant change in the teacher. After all, it is the teacher who is responsible for presenting or 'delivering' the curriculum at classroom level. What the teacher thinks, what the teacher believes, what the teacher assumes — all these things have powerful implications for the change process, for the ways in which curriculum policy is translated into curriculum practice. Some of these patterns of thinking, belief and assumption are so widely shared among the community of teachers that they amount to what might be called a broad occupational culture of teaching. This culture of teaching, I shall argue, seriously inhibits practical curriculum change at school and classroom level.

Two widely adopted strategies of curriculum change — *cultural interruption* and *structural reinforcement* — at best ignore and at worst merely shore up this existing culture of teaching, thereby frustrating the achievement of substantial curriculum innovation. It is only through a third strategy, I shall propose — one of *structural redefinition* — that the culture of teaching can be successfully reshaped and the practical school curriculum be improved.

The Cultural Reproduction of Teaching

It is now over half a century since Waller (1932) investigated what teaching did to teachers. Since that time, several writers have puzzled at length over that same issue. As a result of their studies, some of the dominant features of the culture of teaching are now reasonably well known, even if their range, consistency and origins remain matters of dispute.

Teachers, it seems, are present-oriented, conservative and individualistic. They tend to avoid long-term planning and collaboration with their colleagues, and to resist involvement in whole school decision-making in favour of gaining marginal improvements in time and resources to make their own individual classroom work easier (Lortie, 1975). This classroom-centeredness is indeed one of the overriding characteristics of the teaching profession (Jackson, 1968); a characteristic which arises from and is in turn fed by the daily, recurring experience of classroom isolation. That isolation is itself a product of what Lortie (1975) called the 'egg crate structure' of schooling; the fact that schools are segmented into isolated and insulated classroom compartments which divide teachers from one another and make comparison and collaboration between them difficult.[1]

Add to this general orientation the necessities of coping daily with classroom constraints of low resources, poor buildings and large class sizes (A. Hargreaves, 1978; Sharp and Green, 1975; Westbury, 1973; Woods, 1977), along with the strains that arise from the conflict-based character of the teacher-pupil relationship (Waller, 1932), and one can understand why teachers become not just concerned with but also confined to classroom life and its problems. In such circumstances, it is hardly surprising that most teachers show little interest in becoming involved in extra-classroom activities such as whole curriculum planning or union activity.

For those seeking increased teacher involvement in school-wide curriculum change, the reproduction of this culture of teaching has a depressingly circular quality about it. The classroom isolation of teachers cultivates a preoccupation with classroom affairs, with those matters over which teachers have direct and immediate control and which consume the major part of their time and energy. This, in turn, discourages their involvement in school-wide decision-making. Moreover, on the occasions when they do make occasional forays into that wider sphere, teachers' inexperience and unfamiliarity with many of the issues and procedures is likely only to reinforce their view that their competence and expertise really resides in their own classroom, and that other matters are ultimately best dealt with in the principal's office (Burlingame, 1981; Hanson, 1981).

The culture of teaching, then, is a culture in which classroom experience is exalted above all else in collective discussions of educational matters. It is a culture whose material conditions of existence in the pressing and recurring immediacy of classroom work and in the isolated context of classroom performance make sustained and shared reflection of a rigorous nature difficult. And it is a culture whose material conditions in the allocation of time to different areas of the teacher's task, place the classroom at the center and all else at the periphery of this work. Once in motion, the culture of teaching is reproductive and self-generating, but only as long as the material conditions of its existence — the isolation and constraints of the classroom, the limited opportunities for reflection, the minimal allocation of statutory time to non-classroom work — persist and continue to sustain it.

This relationship between the culture of teaching and the material conditions of its existence can be further illustrated by examining one more feature of that culture — its division and fragmentation, especially at the secondary or high school level, along academic subject lines. School subjects are more than just groupings of intellectual thought. They are social systems also. They compete for power, prestige, recognition and reward within the secondary or high school system. As both Goodson (1983 a) and Cooper (1985) point out, the subject department provides one of the major routes for improved prospects, pay and promotion within the secondary sector. It is one of the major avenues for the pursuit of teacher self-interest, for the improvement of status, and the maximization of economic reward. As such, it is likely to act as a powerful source of resistance to any school-wide innovations which threaten its position through attempts to disband it, to amalgamate it with other departments, or to reduce its timetable allocation and thereby the size and scope of its influence on the curriculum along with the promotion prospects of its teachers. In such vipers' nests of vested interest, it is scarcely likely that attempts to secure an agreed whole school curriculum policy will meet with anything more than paper success (Her Majesty's Inspectorate, 1983).

A second contributory factor to this process of conflict and division among secondary or high school teachers in particular resides in the fact that even at their point of entry to teaching, the identities of many teachers have already been formed predominantly on subject lines. This socialization of teachers into subject loyalty stretches back to their own experience as successful pupils, is reinforced through the specialist pattern of most undergraduate education, and is virtually completed with exposure to a subject-divided and also subject-biased pattern of teacher-training (Bernstein, 1971; Lacey, 1977). This again has implications for the creation of loyalties and attachments among teachers to separate communities of interest within a school rather than to the school community as a whole.

Thirdly, membership of subject communities, of different subcultures within the more general culture of teaching, usually carries with it a set of beliefs, assumptions and practices shared with other members of that subculture about how that subject is best delivered in the classroom. Subject subcultures therefore serve as a grounding for pedagogical subcultures. Classroom pedagogy, assumed best ways of teaching and relating to children, therefore tends to vary on subject lines (Ball, 1981; Barnes and Shemilt, 1974). This has been found to make teachers' experiences of teaching outside their subject difficult. Not only have they had to come to terms with different subject matter, but different ways of teaching too (Hargreaves, 1986).

These subject divisions, along with the differences they embody in attitudes to children and learning and in approaches to pedagogy, further reinforce those tendencies towards conservatism and individualism that characterize the culture of teaching more generally. When curriculum policy is intended to transform curriculum practice, it is this culture of teaching that strikes wedges through that relationship. Curriculum policy does not correspond with curriculum practice. The intended curriculum is cast adrift from the curriculum-in-use. The implication for anyone seeking to bring about radical curriculum reform is that they must therefore face the formidable challenge of fundamentally reshaping this culture of teaching, and therefore of interrupting its reproductive processes. In what follows, I want to examine how well various curriculum-change strategies have met that particular challenge.

Cultural Interruption

The first strategy for breaking the cultural reproduction of teaching is that of cultural interruption. This is a process designed to develop, refine and transform the language and categories in which teachers think about their work. It seeks to infuse the teaching profession with a new set of insights and understandings about the schooling process. It proposes to lay the conceptual groundwork for a new, more educationally worthwhile, and enlightened culture of teaching. There are two broad ways in which this can be done.

The traditional version of this strategy in teacher education can be found in academic, award-bearing programs that draw widely on the educational sciences of sociology, psychology and philosophy and, more recently, of management theory. Undoubtedly, in a personal sense, many students and in-service teachers have found such courses invigorating and exciting. The evidence available, however, suggests that on their entry or re-entry to practical classroom teaching, those teachers have quickly pushed aside or 'forgotten' these more general aspects of their educational studies (Bolam, 1982; Hanson and Herrington, 1976; Lacey, 1977). However enlightened they may be, individual teachers are in a weak position to combat the wider culture of teaching with all its resistance to educational theory and school-wide change that persists among those colleagues whose company they must keep when they return to school.

Academic programs of initial training, taught courses of in-service training, and the stated aims and objectives of curriculum policy documents have therefore tended to expose teachers to theories, categories and principles which have often struck them as unhelpfully remote and disconnected from the particular needs of their immediate classroom and school situation. The gap between presented theory and experienced practice has commonly seemed too great.

In this context, movements towards school-centered innovation have offered a most attractive alternative (A. Hargreaves, 1982). Such patterns of innovation have adopted a more pragmatic and appreciative stance towards teachers and their thinking. The advocates of school-centered innovation recognize that teachers already possess a wide range of categories for theorizing about their work (Elbaz, 1983; Olson, 1982 b). This existing knowledge and awareness lays the basis for researchers and evaluators to collaborate with teachers in extending that ability still further. Relevant theory is not introduced somewhat imperialistically from the outside, though, but is based on and built upon the already existing organizing categories or 'craft knowledge' of the practising teacher (Ashton and Merritt, 1979; Brown and McIntyre, 1985). The act of theorizing practice or eliciting craft knowledge is consciously related to the immediate practical needs of the classroom, and to that extent is seen to be superior to the formal teaching of educational theory as an already constituted body of knowledge.

This principle of working *with* teachers and not just preaching *at* them may well be vital to the task of securing effective curriculum development in any particular school. It is sensible that curriculum research should treat teachers with seriousness and get a sense of the classroom and school world as they see it — of the meanings and frameworks of their actions (Clandinin, 1986). For without that understanding, it is likely that curriculum developments will be misconceived for want of knowing how teachers will interpret, transform or resist them at classroom level. But the difficulty with all this is that while the existing qualities of teacher thinking are certainly received much more warmly by the school-centered pragmatists than by their more traditional academic counterparts, there is a strong tendency for theory to be applied and developed only to those things which teachers already value — to practical classroom issues. Given what we know about the culture of teaching, the use of teachers' present experience as the mainstay of explanations of classroom practice raises serious doubts about whether it will be possible to move beyond the bounds of existing practice to construct critical and collective revisions of the nature of teaching, still less to develop school-wide, state-wide or nation-wide policies of change. The likely consequence of school-centered innovation, then, is that in the main it will endorse and gloss what teachers already think and do. It will reinforce and rationalize the existing culture of teaching, not transform it.

Admittedly, there is in principle no reason why the process of collaboration and engagement between teachers and researchers should not extend to enquiring into issues of power and constraint and their effects upon the classroom process. In principle, the consciousness of teachers can be heightened in relation to such issues as assessment constraints, subject-status hierarchies, the dynamics of managerial domination, the effects of cutbacks in educational expenditure and so on, just as easily as it can be raised in connection with more specifically 'micro' questions to do with the development of listening skills, pupil-centered group work and the like (Pollard, 1984). In practice, though, the policy initiatives and practical recommendations of curriculum collaborators tend to run in one of these directions only — the one most immediately and practically amenable to *individual* teacher intervention. The work of such writers as Olson (1982 b) exemplifies this tendency and the pragmatic, humanistic approach towards changing curriculum practice, on which it rests.

Olson draws upon his research into how teachers respond at classroom level to the principles and intentions built into the British Schools Council Integrated Science Project (SCISP), to point to the recurrent failure of curriculum developers to take account of the language and daily working problems of teachers. He also refers briefly to the difficult constraints and dilemmas with which teachers have to cope during the course of their work — with examination constraints, for instance — but overall, he seems much less interested in the nature of those constraints, or in their tractability, than in how teachers *perceive* them. This leads to some intriguing policy recommendations. For after noting that, for example, science teachers twist SCISP material to suit the constraints and demands of the existing examination system, Olson does not then advocate the reform, still less the abolition of those examinations. Instead, he notes only that 'the person who wishes to communicate ideas to teachers is going to have to understand the network of beliefs that teachers hold and what particular terms mean within such networks' (Olson, 1982 b,

p. 20). The language of innovations, that is, 'is in need of translation into practitioner language' if the 'innovative ideas are to be understood' (p. 27). The basic problem of teacher reception of innovation, then, is ultimately perceived not as one of social constriction and constraint which might suggest a contentious need for organisational and structural reform of the education service, but as essentially one of language and communication.

Important as this analysis is in emphasizing the need to understand teachers' own perspectives on innovation and classroom life, it has to be said that in stressing the importance of teachers' own language and thinking on curriculum matters, it does not really deal with the conditions and constraints which sustain that culture of teaching. If indeed this emphasis on teachers' existing language truly is the prime course of action being recommended by Olson, he would do well to recall the debate which took place in connection with another kind of language use, that of working-class pupils in classrooms, some twenty years ago.

Like Bernstein's widely known early work on working-class children's use of what he called restricted linguistic codes (1971–1977), many curriculum packages of a mechanistic kind, employing a model of technical efficiency, have been predicated on a deficit view of teachers' language and thinking (Apple, 1979, 1982 a). This sometimes led to curriculum developers specifying their curricular and pedagogic instructions to teachers in insultingly laborious detail, to try and make their packages as 'teacher proof' as possible. As Apple (1982 a) has pointed out, though, the untenability of this position is demonstrated by the fact that teachers using such packages have stubbornly insisted on going on thinking for themselves all the same — adapting, reshaping and redefining the package materials to suit their own continuing purposes in ways that the package developers could scarcely have predicted.

Writers in the humanistic tradition (Clandinin, 1986; Elbaz, 1983; Olson, 1982 b) have tried to remedy the defects of this approach by pointing to the rich store of personal constructs and forms of practical reasoning which teachers possess, constructs which, in their own way, are every bit as sophisticated (if not quite so pretentious) as the forms of reasoning expounded by curriculum developers and academic educationists. To put it another way, humanistic writers seem to be saying that teachers do not use a 'restricted' form of theoretical language compared to the more 'elaborate' forms of their academic counterparts, but that both teachers and academics employ forms of reasoning that are appropriate to the respective contexts in which they operate. The two groups are in that sense neither better nor worse than one another — merely different. It is therefore incumbent upon the academic educator to evaluate teachers' language and thinking on its own merits, in terms of the practical contexts for which it is best suited, rather than measuring it by the yardsticks of intellectual coherence more appropriate for the university seminar.

All this is reminiscent of the responses made by cultural difference theorists (e.g., Labov, 1973) to Bernstein's 'deficit' model of working-class language in the early 1970s—for they, too, insisted it is possible to identify a richness, worthwhileness and inner coherence in the language used by hitherto sociologically stigmatized groups (in their case working-class and ethnic-minority pupils) if trouble is taken to evaluate it in its own terms and in terms of its appropriateness for the context in which it is normally used.

In either case—pupils' language and culture, or teachers' language and culture—much time and energy has in my view been needlessly wasted on the polarized questions of deficit and difference; on the issue of whether the language and culture of teachers or of working-class/ethnic-minority pupils is really worthwhile or not. The really important point is not that language and thinking are appropriate to social context, but that they are fundamentally shaped by the *particular kinds* of context which people routinely experience on a day-to-day basis. For working class and black people these are most commonly ones of informality or powerlessness. The contexts of power, assertiveness and rational argument calling for the exercise of 'elaborated codes' are not a routine part of working-class life. A change in the language would therefore require changing the contexts that call for its use.

So it is with teachers. Their language and thinking is indeed usually appropriate to the social contexts in which it is applied. But to understand and intervene in that relationship we clearly need to study not only the language and the thinking, but the context too. The influence of examinations or standardized testing on classroom pedagogy, the effects of tightly bounded subject communities on attempts to implement cross-curricular change, the heavy imbalance in teachers' timetable allocations towards classroom duties and responsibilities as against non-classroom ones, and the limited amount of statutory time available for rigorous, sustained and collective reflection about educational issues—all these things are indispensable items on any agenda for substantial innovation. Since it is conditions of just this kind that confine teachers' concerns to the realm of the classroom, sustain their pedagogical conservatism and make collaboration between them difficult—that, in short, help reproduce the existing culture of teaching—it is precisely these conditions, and not just the cultural responses to them that should, perhaps, be made the prime target of curriculum reform.

Consequently while sustained, rigorous reflection and the opportunities to engage in it are necessary for transforming the culture of teaching, there would also be much to be gained by transferring much of our innovatory energies away from the individual teacher in the individual classroom towards creating school-wide, state-wide and even nation-wide structures of an enabling kind which would provide a more welcoming and supportive environment in which a reshaped culture of teaching could grow and prosper. Currently, there are a number of far-reaching structural changes already under way in the official policy sphere which are reshaping the context of teaching in important ways, and whatever we might think of the directions in which these changes are moving, it seems to me important that we begin to engage with them on their own level, and not just focus our energies on helping teachers cope with their effects in the classroom.

Structural Reinforcement

Towards the close of the 1980s, some of the major patterns of educational reform across a range of western societies seem to be creating educational structures which look likely to reinforce rather than reshape the existing culture of teaching. This pattern of structural reinforcement can be evidenced by considering one national case in detail: Great Britain. In British society, recent years have witnessed educational policy changes of national scope and significance which have reinforced the existing culture of teaching in three ways: through the entrenchment and extension of the academic subject-based curriculum; through the intensification of pressure and constraint upon teachers' work which has bound teachers more closely to the immediacy of the classroom environment; and through reduction of teachers' in-service opportunities for extended reflection about the fundamental purposes and parameters of educational change, in exchange for short-term programs of non-reflective training designed to adapt the teaching force to the efficient technical delivery of programs and purposes decided elsewhere. For reasons of space, I shall discuss only the first of these in detail.

In the case of the subject-based academic curriculum, it is interesting that following what amounted to something of a hegemonic crisis in the early-1980s, that kind of curriculum has emerged strengthened, reconstructed and refurbished. Until the late-1970s, in Britain, as indeed in many other countries, the pre-eminence of the high status subject-based academic curriculum was virtually unquestioned. As in many other countries, the academic, subject-based curriculum was the hegemonic

Curriculum Policy and the Culture of Teaching

curriculum (Connell, 1985). Few doubted its worth. Publicly, politically, professionally, subject-based academic knowledge was the most highly prized form of educational knowledge in society.

Yet in a hierarchical society of continuing social and economic inequality in which educational credentials played an important selective role, subject-based academic knowledge was also the currency of educational and social selection and opportunity. To possess this kind of knowledge was also to possess a kind of cultural capital that could be cashed in for educational credentials which in turn could purchase social and occupational opportunities and advancement (Bourdieu, 1977).

So entrenched was this hegemonic understanding of curricular worth, that when social democratic aspirations brought about attempts at educational and social improvement through comprehensive school reform in the 1960s and 1970s, the intention was not to *redefine* cultural capital but to *redistribute* it; to make the fruits of the hegemonic, academic curriculum more easily available to everyone; middle-class and working-class children alike. Grammar schools for all! For many social democratic educational reformers, this *redistribution* position still indeed remains the key strategy for effecting improvement in working-class opportunities through education (e.g., Halsey, Heath and Ridge, 1980). By the late-1970s, the widespread adoption of this redistribution strategy through the extension of the academic curriculum and public examinations to most of the secondary school population right up to age sixteen, had created what many perceived as a fundamental crisis in the curriculum. The conventional academic curriculum was seen as the source of widespread boredom and disaffection amongst the young (Joseph, 1984; D. Hargreaves, 1982).

As this hegemonic crisis intensified, the curriculum became a matter of political and professional contestation. Some promoted an agenda of educational entitlement — a way of *redefining* and not simply *redistributing* worthwhile educational knowledge. Her Majesty's Inspectorate (1977, 1983) advocated a policy of providing *all* young people, as a matter of entitlement, with a broad and balanced range of educational experiences. And an influential committee in the Inner London Education Authority (1984) challenged existing definitions of achievement as being too confined to the academic domain only, and as therefore discriminating against working-class children. A wider definition of achievement, the Committee argued, which embraced social and personal and practical achievements as well as cognitive-intellectual ones would maximize opportunities for success among all young people, but especially among many working-class ones who had traditionally not fared well in the narrowly interpreted academic domain.

The radical and professional end of curricular contestation seemed to be embracing a redefinition of cultural capital as a way of improving educational achievement and increasing opportunity and responsiveness among working-class pupils. Such a strategy, had it been implemented successfully, would also have led to fundamental redefinition of one major aspect of the culture of teaching: its division and fragmentation on academic subject lines. Part of the material base for a widespread review and reconstruction of whole school arrangements for curricular provision would thereby have been created.

Against this agenda of entitlement for all that would create a new curricular hegemony where educational value and worth would extend beyond the academic domain, has been counterposed an alternative agenda, however. In this second agenda, educational differentiation has been dominant. Entitlement has been on the ebb. It has been an agenda promoted by Conservative politicians and educational civil servants within the Department of Education and Science, where the place of academic learning and subject specialization within the school curriculum has been significantly reconstructed and reasserted. This modern reconstruction of the traditional academic curriculum has further buttressed those definitions of cultural capital which have long been the currency of educational selection, a currency in which the middle classes have held a substantial investment.

At the time of writing, the British Conservative Government proposes to introduce a centrally presented national curriculum into schools. This curriculum is unambiguously subject-based. There is not even the mildest flirtation with broader conceptions of areas of educational experience which Her Majesty's Inspectorate has for many years attempted to place at the center of curriculum planning. The core of this subject-based curriculum, to occupy 30 per cent to 40 per cent of the secondary timetable, is to be mathematics, English and science. The majority of the remaining time is to be taken up with a set of foundation subjects which will comprise a modern language, history, geography, creative arts, physical education and technology (the one innovatory concession). Academic subjects are in the ascendant. Little time, status or importance is to be given to aesthetic, practical or social and personal subjects, still less to forms of learning that have no clear subject designation at all. In the ten per cent or so of the curriculum remaining after the core and foundation subjects have been accounted for, there will be little time or space for social and personal education, political education, environmental education, development education, integrated studies, social studies, peace studies and the like.

The British national curriculum will therefore be an unarguably

Curriculum Policy and the Culture of Teaching

academic curriculum. In the place of extended entitlement to a broad range of educational experiences and achievements, the Conservative Government and the Department of Education and Science are substituting compulsory confinement to a narrow band of subject-based academic ones. Cultural capital and its place in educational and social selection is being neither redefined nor redistributed, but reinforced. With the support and stimulus of benchmark testing in the core subjects at seven, eleven and fourteen, whose results will be made publicly available to parents, schools and Local Education Authorities, this national curriculum will enhance the process of educational differentiation on academic, subject lines.

Only when the work of educational differentiation has been done, on the basis of narrowly defined academic criteria that favour middle-class inclination and inheritance, will more imaginative curricular innovations beyond the bounds of the academic, subject-based curriculum then be permitted. From the age of fourteen, a wider optional range of curriculum experiences will be tolerated, including special lower-attainer initiatives for the bottom 30 per cent or 40 per cent of the ability range. Prototypes for such initiatives involving strong emphases on practical achievement, social and personal education, community service and residential experience have already been widely experimented with in the United Kingdom, within a Department of Education and Science pilot scheme (Weston and Harland, in press). Such innovations suggest not a redefinition of cultural capital, nor even a redistribution or reinforcement of it. In effect, they amount to a *resignation* of cultural capital; a writing off of its accessibility and relevance to those groups of pupils on whose futures the sad fate of educational differentiation will already have been firmly etched.

If the structural reinforcement of the hegemonic curriculum has strengthened its role in the business of educational and social differentiation, it has also reinforced the existing culture of teaching and its subject-divided character. The academic, subject-based emphasis of the national curriculum reasserts the priorities of that culture. The establishment of benchmark testing in the core subjects increases the likelihood that in order to protect images of their own competence, teachers will adhere to these priorities. Retention of public examinations at sixteen through the development of the General Certificate of Secondary Education, along with required publication of the results of these examinations, adds to that likelihood. Proposals mounted by the Department of Education and Science (1983) to improve the 'match' or closeness of fit between the subjects in which teachers are specifically qualified and those which they are required to teach, will almost certainly lead to further strengthening of the attachment and loyalty that teachers have to their subject (A. Hargreaves, in press). And new regulations that have been imposed on initial teacher training which require trainee teachers to devote at least 50 per cent of their training to the study of a mainstream academic subject, will further enhance the development of early subject loyalty and identification among the teachers of the future (Rudduck, in press).

It is clear that Britain is therefore undergoing major structural reinforcement of the academic subject-based curriculum through the development of a national curriculum, and a series of related initiatives. It is a strategy which is simultaneously fostering earlier educational differentiation on academic criteria and, by reinforcing the fragmented subject base of the existing culture of teaching, also defusing potential sources of opposition to that process.

Important as it is, though, national curriculum reform is not the only means by which the existing culture of teaching is being structurally reinforced and reproduced. Mounting pressures and constraints on teachers' work are further assisting that reproductive process by reducing, still more, the opportunities that teachers have for sustained and systematic reflection about wider curriculum developments. Teachers are being subjected to escalating pressures and expectations at a time of only marginal improvements in the teacher-pupil ratio. Many of the simultaneously mounted innovations to which teachers are being asked to respond, require time-intensive commitment to extended preparation, individualized learning, and more personal counselling and reviews of individual pupil progress. The intensification of these pressures, expectations and constraints promises only to bind teachers ever more tightly to the non-reflective immediacy of the classroom. So too do newly favoured government strategies of professional development among the teaching community. Tighter government control of expenditure on teachers' in-service development has virtually put an end to extended, award-bearing courses of in-service education in which careful and systematic reflection of a critical and questioning kind is possible, in favour of short, pragmatic programs of in-service training related to particular government initiatives (Harland, 1987). This signals a shift in emphasis from rational and critical deliberation designed to help teachers mount development programs of their own, to training in the skills required for uncritical implementation and delivery of programs and purposes decided elsewhere.

In Britain, then, politically generated changes in relation to curriculum development, classroom constraints and in-service training have led and are leading to structural reinforcement of the culture of teaching. Perhaps this is the political intention. Perhaps it is intended that teachers are denied the reflective resources and opportunities to criticize and contest government educational policy. Perhaps it is intended that teachers be withdrawn from the process of curriculum development and review. But even if this is the case, those who seek to reinforce the subject-segregated and classroom-centered character of the culture of teaching, perhaps ought to appreciate that in doing so, they are almost certainly also sowing seeds of failure and frustration in relation to their wider educational objectives. The culture of teaching can be as resistant to centrally imposed curricular initiatives as to any others. Where these initiatives call for substantial changes in classroom approach, the culture of teaching can supply powerful sources of classroom resistance.

Conclusion: The Case for Structural Redefinition

I have focused on the apparent intractability of the culture of teaching, its effects upon the processes of teaching and learning, and the resistance it poses to school-wide innovation. Attempts to transform that culture and create opportunities for innovation through processes of *cultural interruption*, I have argued, are unlikely to succeed unless they are linked with policies directed towards changing the existing material *structures* of subject specialization and the like to which the culture of teaching is a response and upon which it feeds. Accordingly, I have advocated some shift in academic emphasis and practical intervention from a concern with individual teachers in individual classrooms and their capacity to reflect upon their own teaching—towards giving greater consideration to the educational *structures* that support and help reproduce the language, thinking and action of teachers. This structural level is precisely the one at which much of the future of schooling is now being shaped. The development of centrally initiated policies of curriculum reform, I have suggested, will most certainly lead to a *structural reinforcement* of the existing culture of teaching and its preoccupation, amongst other things, with subject-specialist concerns. It is important therefore that we engage with them; that we try to redefine the structural base of the culture of teaching.

A possible content for such a structural redefinition should now have become clear:

(i) A widening of educational experiences and achievements for all pupils beyond the predominantly subject-based academic domain, to include ones in the social and personal, aesthetic and practical domains also. Why should these not be included in the new basics? This redefinition of worthwhile knowledge and cultural capital for *all* pupils would not only enhance educational fairness and opportunity for pupils; it would also redefine the curricular basis of the culture of teaching, reducing its fragmentation on subject lines and making collective, whole school planning more feasible.

(ii) More generous staffing policies, not to facilitate marginal overall improvement in teacher-pupil ratios, but to release teachers for collective planning, deliberation and review in school time, and to allow greater pedagogical flexibility and experimentation in terms of small group work, individual counselling and so forth. Such policies would not only raise the status of teachers' work outside the classroom, and provide the necessary support for pedagogical innovation; by providing such support it could also breach that classroom isolation that is the very core of the culture of teaching.

(iii) A shift in patterns of professional development from an almost exclusive emphasis on training, to a balanced and coherent mix of training and education of a more reflective, critical and questioning sort.

A possible content for a structural redefinition of the culture of teaching is relatively easy to sketch; an estimation of the political likelihood of its realization is not. In Britain, the signs are that following something of a hegemonic crisis in curricular provision from the mid-1970s to the mid-1980s, the academic curriculum is being reasserted with considerable force and success through national curriculum reform. Developments in the United States seem not all that dissimilar (Apple, 1986). For those with visions of broader educational entitlement, wider educational opportunity and a reshaped culture of teaching, the short-term probabilities do not look promising. Educational probabilities are never absolutely certain, though. Possibilities are never completely foreclosed. For that reason, if no other, it is important that arguments about alternatives persist.

Note

1 Possibly this assessment applies more closely to the US elementary school teachers studied by Lortie (1975), Waller (1932), and Jackson (1968), than, say, to high school teachers or to teachers in other nations. But it is interesting to note that writers on the culture of secondary school teaching in Britain have reached conclusions not all that dissimilar from those of their American colleagues (e.g., D. Hargreaves, 1982).

Curricular Change and the 'Red Readers': History and Theory

Bruce Curtis

In 1866, the Council of Public Instruction in Canada West appointed a committee of four to revise school textbooks. The Council was responding, on the eve of Confederation, to mounting criticism directed at the quality of the reading books in use in the elementary schools, at the reputedly monopolistic Educational Depository and its policies of distribution, and at the alleged bias of the Chief Superintendent of Education in supporting some domestic textbook publishers, over others.

The four committee members—Drs McCaul, Ormiston and Barclay, and the Reverend Mr Grasett—compiled a new series of reading books to replace the Irish National Series, in use in the schools since 1846. The *Red Readers*—from the colour of their binding, not their political content—or more formally, the Canadian Series of Reading Books, were officially authorized for use in the provincial schools in 1866, and remained the standard reading books until the next major textbook revision in 1883.[1]

With the curricular reform of 1866, the nature of state-sanctioned knowledge was transformed in several remarkable ways. My concern here is to detail and explain this change in official knowledge, and this will involve three tasks. First, I will describe the conflicts which led to reform of the curriculum in Canada West, insofar as these can be reconstructed from archival sources. I will then describe and contrast the content of the reading books in use before and after 1866. My third task is of a different order. I will attempt to place the curricular reform of 1866 in Canada in its more general context. A remarkably similar reform took place in England in this same period—yet the empirical circumstances of the English curricular reform were quite different from those obtained in Canada. This phenomenon leads me to investigate more general and abstract forces influencing the nature of school knowledge. I will conclude with the argument that in Britain and America curricular reform took place in the context of a two-fold (and still contested!) process of *normalization*: a normalization of capitalist relations of production and a normalization of a particular kind of pedagogic relations of production.

Criticism of the Irish curriculum in Canada West

The Irish National Series of schoolbooks was authorized for general use in the common schools of Canada West by the (second) General Board of Education in 1846, and again by the Council of Public Instruction in 1850.

The series had been reprinted by the Montreal firm of Armour and Ramsay in 1845, and its adoption had been urged upon the Education Office by school superintendents before this date, although competing series of schoolbooks — both British and American — also existed. The Irish books were recommended in Egerton Ryerson's *Report on a System of Public Elementary Instruction for Upper Canada (1846)* as 'imbued throughout with the purest principles' and as containing 'a great variety of information which is as interesting and useful for the common reader, as it is appropriate for the Common School'.[2] The General Board of Education undertook both to arrange for the cheap importation and reproduction of the series and to secure the support of local educational authorities for its use. Reform party opposition to the School Act of 1846 was partly focused on this 'despotic' power of the General Board and Superintendent over school books.[3]

However, from quite an early period the books produced complaints and dissatisfaction from practising teachers, school trustees and school supporters. Complaints about the Irish series concerned the physical quality of the books, the quality of the reproductions, the methods of instruction they demanded, and their content. Teachers complained that publishers were 'flooding the country with *badly bound* books' which 'fall to pieces before the eyes'.[4] John Hughes of Brantford complained that in his school 'hundreds of books have gone to pieces in this way before they have become in the least worn or soiled'. Worse still in his view were errors in the books, which frustrated teachers and discouraged students. Page 92 of Brewer and McPhail's edition of the arithmetic for 1849 contained twenty-one questions and gave at least five wrong answers, and Hughes claimed it was typical. Indeed, he remarked, 'the small arithmetic is so full of errors and misprints of every kind that with many it has got the book into such disrepute that teachers do all they can to keep it out of their schools'.[5]

School supporters and some teachers opposed the reading methods associated with the Irish texts. Here reading instruction involved a detailed examination of meaning.[6] The utility of the Irish lessons was predicated upon their being 'understood' by the student, and this implied a pedagogy heavily dependent upon the interrogation of the student by the teacher. Teachers were taught to interrogate in the Normal School, and to a certain extent in prefaces to the books themselves, but some of those who adopted the practice encountered local opposition. John Carson's attempts in section two of Tecumseh Township to replace the 'memory-work' of his predecessor with interrogation and drill were opposed by supporters of the school.[7] William McCullough complained that his employers wanted him to teach 'dialogues', in contrast to the emphasis upon silent reading in the Irish series.[8]

T.W. Lillie, a teacher in South Crosbie township in the 1850s, complained that the Irish readers were useless for any but beginning readers. He urged a return to Lindley Murray's *English Reader* which he held 'preferable to learn to read'.[9] School trustees and supporters in some parts of the province claimed that the use of the Irish series retarded the progress of students in learning to read. This was because the Irish series did away with oral methods, with a beginning spelling book, and because their use was tied to collective methods of instruction, which were seen to result in fewer daily lessons for young students.[10] In this context, many teachers simply avoided the intent of the Irish methods. School superintendents repeatedly informed the education office that the methods of instruction prescribed in the Irish series, and urged by statute and circular, were ignored by many teachers.[11]

By the middle 1850s, however, an increasing number of school supporters, teachers, and later, school administrators, began to argue that the Irish series was simply unpleasant and for that reason should be revised or abandoned. J. Cooper, the local superintendent for Woodstock, wrote that the *Fourth Book of Lessons* was 'very heavy with an overabundance of hard names'. One of the town schools had abandoned the Irish series altogether, and there was 'nothing of which the parents complain more than' the *Fourth Book*.[12] John C. Butts, a teacher, wrote that 'as children are fond of variety', reading books should contain material 'calculated to please as well as instruct'. He too urged the abandoning of the Irish readers.[13] The superintendent of Bruce County complained that the 'lessons in the National Books are found to be very "dry". Some of us have thought that the introduction of a more interesting work would be of service'.[14]

In the 1860s, Normal School graduates joined the chorus of complaint. Some claimed to have long regarded the Irish books as 'Deficient and unsuitable'.[15] County school conventions began to call for textbook revision, and even the flagship Hamilton Central School began to modify the official curriculum.[16] Local school administrators began to abandon the official texts,[17] and xenophobic sentiments were increasingly expressed. One correspondent claimed that American texts were often more suited to Canadian students than the

> .... great national Series, for instance in the *First Book of Lessons* we find such as this 'Jack rode a mule or a fine ass. Pat or Sam and Ned & Bog' and now such trash might suit to learn young Irish but we do not want such teaching in Canada....[18]

Egerton Ryerson, the Chief Superintendent of Education, tirelessly defended the Irish texts against all these attacks. Teachers, for instance, were told their own incompetence, and not the texts, was at fault if students found schooling unpleasant.[19] The books were defended as 'amusing as well as instructive' and Ryerson declared himself unable to 'deviate from the catalogue so well considered and so long tried and used'.[20] But Ryerson was already considering the necessity of some revision in the late 1850s, even while defending the series.[21]

In 1865, the Chief Superintendent engaged in a debate over the Irish curriculum which ultimately led to its reform. His opponent, Otto Klotz of Preston, was an influential public educator in Waterloo County who had been involved in 'improvement' since the 1840s. During his term as superintendent of schools for Preston, the town board of school trustees moved to introduce the American Sanders' Series of schoolbooks. This was done explicitly in opposition to the Irish series, which Klotz attacked in a lengthy communication to Ryerson:

> I cannot withold expressing my surprise that notwithstanding the unparalleled progress which Canada during the last twenty years, has made in her System of education...no Canadian Reading Books have yet been introduced and the public is bound by law to use books which in respect of geography and science are out of date, void of interest in reference to subjects they contain....that have many paragraphs which instead of being instructive tend to mislead the pupils; that are entirely silent on the history of Canada, but abound in a multitude of names of persons notorious for their vices and in point of morality are not pure....

Klotz insisted the books were exceptionally dull:

> And since it is a well known fact that books which contain an abundance of stale articles and are barren of interest and of spirit, cannot either instill life or vigour nor give pleasure while reading them; but will produce apathy and displeasure, it follows as a natural consequence that such books as the Irish National Readers are now only read....because the School Act makes it compulsory to read them....[22]

Klotz was on solid ground. Even the compilers of the Irish texts had justified them on the basis of their supposed ability to instruct *and* please.[23] But Klotz observed that 'children very seldom and voluntarily read in the Irish national readers while at home, though they frequently take up and study such other books within their reach'.[24]

Ryerson responded heavy-handedly. Having successfully threatened the Guelph school board in 1859 with penalties for the use of illegal books,[25] he concluded a lengthy defense of the texts in a letter to Klotz with a threat to withhold the school grant if the Preston trustees adopted American books.[26] But Klotz was not cowed. He replied with detailed criticism of the Irish texts, dissecting and criticising particular passages. He remarked that Ryerson was ridiculous to suppose that the loss of the staggering sum of $13—the Preston school grant—would seriously influence the Board of Trustees.[27] At Klotz' urging, the Waterloo County Board of Public Instruction published a Memorial to the provincial Council of Public Instruction and distributed it to all County Boards in the province. Here Klotz' criticisms were reiterated. The Irish books were out of date, clearly intended for use in Ireland, and inadequate in respect of Canadian development. Errors in information about the Americas were exacerbated by the shoddy quality of reprints. The lessons in history, 'instead of illustrating its subject with captivating and instructive narrations' were 'simply a massing together of long and unpronounceable names'.

Worse still, the lessons smacked of immorality:

> Again, historical incidents of a repulsive character, or suggestive of improper sentiments, which might perhaps be properly perused by the maturer student, are prematurely brought down to the Common School Room, and in such cases are a transgression upon the rules of decorum and modesty. It is not necessary that the teacher should be called upon to explain such words as 'debauchery', 'licentiousness', 'concubine', 'pregnancy', etc. The

narration that Nero murdered his wife Octavia that he might marry an infamous woman named Poppaea, whom he afterwards kicked to death while she was in a state of pregnancy, is only calculated to call up unchaste images and can serve no instructive purpose.[28]

In his annual report for 1865, Ryerson attempted to respond to criticism of the texts. The Irish readers, he argued, were not really 'behind the times' or outdated. They were by far the most popular books in England and Scotland, where a free market in textbooks obtained. Even if the books did contain a few trivial errors in scientific subjects:

> a reader is not intended as a book of science, any more than the Holy Scriptures, which would be regarded on some matters of science, 'quite behind the times' by certain publishers of new books and their agents. The object of a school reader is not to teach science, but to teach the pupil to *read* — and the less the learner is diverted from that one object, while learning to read, the better....

'Diversity in the readers of a school', Ryerson concluded, 'is inadmissible as much as diversity of text-books in a military school'.[29]

This was humbug, of course, and probably spoke to Ryerson's increasing frustration at the mounting attacks by educational officials on the Irish books, combined as they were with increasingly well-organized opposition to the Educational Depository. To argue that readers were *simply* about reading was to renounce all of the arguments made in the 1840s for the necessity of the Irish texts. Still, later in 1866, Ryerson attempted again to defend the Irish books. In a pamphlet on *The Schoolbook Question* — foolishly published by John Lovell, who also had exclusive rights to several books on the list authorized for use in Canada West — Ryerson addressed the publishers who complained that the Educational Depository was monopolistic. The attack on the Depository was led by the publisher James Campbell, vociferously supported by George Brown, and conducted largely in the *Globe* newspaper. Ryerson argued that there were no substantive objections to be levelled against the Irish readers, and hence no need for allowing foreign publishers to sell on the schoolbook market. While it was true that there was a certain lack of Canadian geography and history in the Irish series, the publication of geography and history books by the deputy superintendent of education filled this need. The Irish books were again defended as cheap, and the necessity of uniformity in books for a successful national educational system was emphasized. In any case:

the third, fourth and fifth readers are entirely composed of selections from the standard English poets and prose writers— whose writings will never grow old as long as the English language is spoken.[30]

But Ryerson's capitulation was signalled here in his concession that some cautious revision of the texts might be justified, given the reality of the new dominion. He announced that the Council of Public Instruction had appointed a textbook committee.[31] The revisions were complete quite soon after, and the *Red Readers* were in print by 1868, which leads one to suspect that the process of revision had been in progress even while Ryerson was defending the Irish texts.

From the Irish to the Red Readers

Readers contained officially approved knowledge. Mastery of the information in them was a general condition for the passage of students through the school system. Teachers were required by statute to classify their students according to the gradation of the readers. Normal and model school training consisted in part of the study of the readers by teachers, and the content of readers formed the basis of teachers' licensing examinations. One author has gone so far as to suggest that such school reading books exerted a formative influence on national identity in the Canadas.[32]

In my comparison of school knowledge before and after 1866, I would like to focus on the fourth book in each of the series of reading books. The fourth in these series of five books is arguably the most important. The fourth books were aimed at thirteen-year-olds and hence were commonly the last books read at school for many students.[33] They were the first books in which authors assumed that students had mastered the technical skills of reading and could thus be addressed as a rational audience.

The Irish National readers were first published as such in the mid-1830s. Several of the books had been in existence rather longer, and much of the reading material copied the earlier series of books produced by the Society for Promoting the Education of the Poor in Ireland (the Kildare Place Society).[34] The compilers of the Irish texts aimed at a working-class/peasant audience. They saw the reading books as a form of discipline which would not founder on the barriers of national and religious politics. As J.M. Goldstrom has shown, Irish educational reformers were forced to be particularly innovative by virtue of the political context in which they operated. In attempting to produce a set of readers which would spread morality and 'sound intelligence' among the Catholic/nationalist Irish working class, they hit upon a formula of knowledge presentation which enjoyed an enormous international success.[35] At the same time, the access of the Commissioners to a large state school grant was combined with technological innovation in the printing industry to enable the distribution and sale of the Irish readers on terms which few private publishers could match. By 1846, the *Fourth Book of Lessons* in the Irish series was being sold for 5d to the Commissioners' schools and to Canadian schools as well. Lindley Murray's *English Reader*, the book it replaced in Canada West as the most popular school reader, cost at least three times as much.[36] By 1866, over 60,000 Canadian students were reportedly reading the *Fourth Book of Lessons*.[37]

The first, second and fourth *Books of Lessons* were compiled by the Irish resident Commissioner, James Carlile.[38] Carlile, who was born in Scotland and educated at Glasgow University, came to Dublin as minister of the Scots Church in 1813, joined the Irish Commission at its formation, and served as its chief officer until 1839. He then devoted the 'remaining years of his life to an enterprise for the conversion of Roman Catholics to the protestant faith'.[39] Compiled volumes were considered by the Commissioners as a whole, and all contentious passages were eliminated.[40]

In the *First Book of Lessons*, students were presented with the alphabet and simple lessons, beginning with words of one syllable:

> an ox, my ox, is it an ox,
> it is, is it? it is my ox,
> no ox, is so, is it so? no.[41]

Lessons in which moral instruction was jumbled up with simple statements (such as 'An ant is wise in act; do it no harm/If Tom runs will he pant? ask him/Is it a fact that Ned broke his arm?/*I will do no bad act*'), were completed by a short narrative on the danger of throwing stones.[42]

In the *Second Book of Lessons*, Carlile began the presentation of the kind of material which was most characteristic of the Irish series as a whole: formally non-sectarian christian instruction, and the principles of bourgeois political economy. The reader of the Second Book encountered this as his or her first lesson:

> God made all things. He made the sun to give light by day, and the stars, to give light by night. He made the earth, and the sea,

and all that dwelt in them. The beast that moves on the face of the earth, the bird that flies in the air, and the fish that swims in the sea, are the work of his hands. *Who shall not fear him, and speak of all his works?*[43]

The tenth lesson began the presentation of political economy, with a simplified version of Adam Smith's optimistic view of the division of labour.

What a small thing a pin is; and yet it takes ten men, if not more, to make it. One man draws the wire; the next makes it straight; the third cuts it . . . . and the ninth and tenth stick them in rows. What a heap of pins they will thus make in a day![44]

A typical entry in the *Fourth Book of Lessons* was Lesson IV from the section on political economy, which I reproduce in part as Figure 1.[45]

> The mistake of which I have been speaking, of supposing that the rich cause the poor to be the worse off, was exposed long ago in the fable of the stomach and the limbs:—
>
> "Once on a time," says the fable, "all the other members of the body began to murmur against the stomach, for employing the labours of all the rest, and consuming all they had helped to provide, without doing anything in return. So they all agreed to strike work, and refused to wait upon this idle stomach any longer. The feet refused to carry it about; the hands resolved to put no food into the mouth for it; the nose refused to smell for it, and the eyes to look out in its service; and the ears declared they would not even listen to the dinner-bell; and so of all the rest. But after the stomach had been left empty for some time, all the members began to suffer. The legs and arms grew feeble; the eyes became dim, and all the body languid and exhausted.
>
> "'Oh, foolish members,' said the stomach, 'you now perceive that what you used to supply to me, was in reality supplied to yourselves. I did not consume for myself the food that was put into me, but digested it, and prepared it for being changed into blood, which was sent through various channels as a supply for each of you. If you are occupied in feeding me, it is by me in turn, that the blood-vessels which nourish you are fed.'"
>
> You see then, that a rich man, even though he may care for no one but himself, can hardly avoid benefiting his neighbours. But this is no merit of his, if he himself has no desire or wish to benefit them. On the other hand, a rich man who seeks for deserving objects to relieve and assist, and is, as the apostle expresses it, "ready to give, and glad to distribute, is laying up in store for himself a good foundation for the time to come, that he may lay hold on eternal life." It is plain from this, and from many other such injunctions of the apos-

tles, that they did not intend to destroy the security of property among Christians, which leads to the distinction between the rich and the poor; for their exhortations to the rich to be kind and charitable to the poor, would have been absurd if they had not allowed that any of their people should be rich; and there could be no such thing as charity in giving anything to the poor, if it were not left to each man's free choice to give or spend what is his own. Indeed, nothing can be called your own which you are not left free to dispose of as you will. The very nature of charity implies that it must be voluntary: for no one can be properly said to *give* anything that he has no power to withhold. The Apostle Paul, indeed, goes yet farther, when he desires each man " to *give* according as he is disposed in his heart, and not grudgingly," because " God loveth the cheerful giver."

When men are thus left to their own inclinations to make use of their money, each as he is disposed in his heart, we must expect to find that some will choose to spend it merely on their own selfish enjoyments. Such men, although, as you have seen, they do contribute to maintain many industrious families without intending it, yet are themselves not the less selfish and odious. But still we are not the less forbidden to rob, or defraud, or annoy them. Scripture forbids us to " covet our neighbours goods," not because he does not make a right use of them, but because they are *his*.

When you see a rich man who is proud and selfish, perhaps you are tempted to think how much better a use you would make of wealth if you were as rich as he. I hope you would: but the best *proof* that you can give that you would behave well if you were in *another's* place, is by behaving well *in your own*. God has appointed to each his own trials, and his own duties; and He will judge you, not according to what you think you would have done in some different station, but according to what you *have* done, in that station in which he has placed you.

Figure 1: From *Fourth Book of Lessons*, 1857, pp. 229–231.

The edition of the *Fourth Book of Lessons* used in Canadian schools was 328 pages long and contained 53 pages of direct lessons in political economy. Much of this material was drawn from Archbishop Whately's *Easy Lessons on Money Matters*. In addition to the section on political economy, the volume contained lessons in 'Natural History' (seventy pages), 'Geography' (eighty pages), 'Religious and Moral Lessons' (fifty pages), and a number of 'Miscellaneous Pieces' (fifty-eight pages). 'Poetry' was interspersed among these sections, and the book concluded with an appendix containing affixes, prefixes, Latin and Greek etymology.

These sections of the book were written in the same style as that on political economy. Most of the material presented embodied the natural theological and utilitarian assumptions of early nineteenth-century bourgeois educators addressing a working-class audience. Natural theology aimed at the reconciliation of religion and scientific investigation through the belief that the study of laws of nature—which included the principles of political economy—glorified God. Indeed, as the lesson on rich and poor shows, these two concerns were mutually reinforcing, for the laws of political economy were also held to be of divine origin.

In addition, the material presented in the *Fourth Book of Lessons* embodied a class-inflected Pestalozzianism. By the time the Irish readers were compiled, the works of Pestalozzi were very widely known in middle-class educational circles. The Irish readers attempted to translate the main Pestalozzian precept into practice: education should begin by attracting the interest of the student, and it could do this most effectively by basing itself on familiar objects.[46] But in the Irish case, Pestalozzian precepts were mediated by bourgeois concerns with labour discipline and with utility in politics. The study of 'familiar objects' and the cultivation of 'sound habits of observation' which this entailed were believed by bourgeois educators to be cornerstones in the foundation of 'sound judgement' on political questions and of an 'accurate estimation' of their political duties by members of the working class.[47] The *Fourth Book of Lessons* stressed the utility of objects animate and inanimate, and emphasized the laboriousness of animal species. For instance:

> What an unwearied pattern of unremitting exertion and *fidelity* is that invaluable animal the shepherd's dog! What *humane* and excellent life-preservers are the Newfoundland species; and what sagacious guides and safe conductors are that useful breed trained in the Alpine solitudes to carry provisions to the bewildered traveller . . . .[48]

Again, in the section dealing with birds and insects the student learned:

> By the labour and exertions of the bee, we are provided with stores of honey and wax. The seemingly contemptible little silk worm presents us . . . . with materials for constituting our most costly raiment.[49]

51

The section on geography, described different nations according to 'national character' and emphasized the quaint. The traveller in China, it was argued, would:

> Be pleased with the unequivocal marks of good humour which prevail in every crowd, uninterrupted and unconcerned by the bawling of some unhappy victim suffering under magisterial correction; and he will be amused at the awkward exertions of the softer sex to hobble out of sight when taken by surprise . . . .[50]

The reader's pleasure at viewing the happily oppressed Chinese crowds and the subordination of Chinese women was then directed towards Biblical History. The latter was presented in both prose and poetry. Heber's poem 'Christ's Second Coming', and Cowper's 'God the Author of Nature' were accompanied by more sober prose selections such as 'The Settlement of the Israelites in Canaan' and the history of the Israelites 'From the Revolt of the Ten Tribes Till the Captivity'.

> At length, in the year 602 before the Christian era, when Jehoiakim was on the throne of Judah, Nebuchadnezzar, who already shared with his father the government of Assyria, advanced into Palestine at the head of a formidable army. A timely submission saved the city as well as the life of the pusillanimous monarch.[51]

The miscellaneous pieces contained in the *Fourth Book of Lessons* presented much the same general sort of material: useful knowledge of the natural world, and non-sectarian Christian theology. Here the reader was exposed to items such as 'On the microscope', Chalmers' poem on the 'Insignificance of this World' and 'Mr Pitt's Reply to Horace Walpole', or on the crime of being a young man.

The Canadian Series

The magnitude of the curricular reform of 1866 can be illustrated by comparing the *Fourth Book of Lessons* on 'Rich and Poor', with the *Fourth Reader* in the Canadian Series on 'Fight with a Kangaroo' (see Figure 2).

FIGHT WITH A KANGAROO.

WILD and innocent, however, as the kangaroo looks, to bring him to bay is only half-way towards conquering him. He may take to a water-hole, and standing therein and seizing the dogs as they approach him, thrust them under water, holding this one at the bottom with his hinder feet, and this by the nape of the neck, with his hand-like fore-paws, till death by drowning thins the pack very considerably. Should the hunter bring the kangaroo to bay on land, the animal will fight desperately for his life. Each of his hind legs is furnished with a claw as formidable as a boar's tusk, and woe betide the dog that comes within the range of a lunge of either of them; or, worse still, if the kangaroo should catch his assailant in his fore-arms, there he will hold him till he is flayed from chest to tail. Even man may not attack the kangaroo with impunity, as the following incident, extracted from the *Sporting Review*, will show. The narrator had commenced the attack with his dogs, one of which had been seized and treated in the unceremonious fashion above noticed.

Exasperated by the irreparable loss of my poor dog, I hastened to its revenge, nothing doubting that with one fell swoop of my formidable club my enemy would be prostrate at my feet. Alas! decay and the still more remorseless white ants frustrated my murderous intentions, and all but left me a victim to my strange and active foe.

Figure 2: From Canadian Series of School Books, *Fourth Reader*, 1968, p. 308.

The *Red Readers* were largely compilations from popular magazines, reviews and works of travel and adventure. They were compiled by a committee of four cleric-educators: Dr John Barclay, then pastor of St Andrew's Presbyterian Church in Toronto, the chaplain of the Toronto Curling Club, and an active proponent of 'muscular christianity'; Dr William Ormiston, then pastor of Central Presbyterian Church in Hamilton, but also a former student of Egerton Ryerson's at Victoria

Re-Interpreting Curriculum Research

College, a former Normal School master, Examiner at the University of Toronto, and the Grammar School Inspector from 1853–1863. Ormiston was 'a strong Liberal of the Scotch type'. Dr John McCaul, the principal of University College who was educated at Trinity College in Dublin, married into an old Compact Tory family in Toronto, and had a reputation as a classical scholar, was joined on the textbook committee by the Reverend Henry Grasett. Grasett, then rector of Toronto and about to be appointed dean, was educated at St John's, Cambridge. He was John Strachan's nominee to the General Board of Education in 1846, and he sat on the successor to that Board—the Council of Public Instruction—until it was disbanded in 1875. Grasett was also chair of the Home District Board of Education, and had been chair of both the Canada Tract Society and the Upper Canada Bible Society. He was staunchly low church in orientation.[52]

The compilers of the *Fourth Reader* reproduced some of the material which had appeared in the *Fourth Book of Lessons*. A concluding section of the *Fourth Reader*, sixty-three pages in length and entitled 'Miscellaneous', contained most of the Biblical History and Sacred poetry which was in the *Fourth Book of Lessons*. The rest of the *Fourth Reader*—313 pages—presented material compiled from other sources. The book was divided into sections which presented readings dealing with different parts of the world. In sharp contrast to the Irish Series, which devoted scattered paragraphs to the region, the *Red Readers* devoted 168 pages to America, most of it to various parts of the new dominion. Descriptions of the 'Hudson Bay Company' and the 'Coal Fields of Nova Scotia' were separated by exciting and at times titillating narratives. 'The Skater and the Wolves' described the moonlit pursuit of a skater on a lonely river by a ferocious pack of wolves. 'A Female Crusoe' recounted the discovery, by a white explorer and his native guides, of an independent native woman living alone in the wild. Her ingenuity and adventurousness were praised, but at the end of the narrative, 'they put her up for competition and wrestled in the ring for her—the strongest, after he had overthrown all the rest, having her duly assigned to him'.[53] Added to these adventure stories were short historical narratives, such as 'The Death of Montcalm'.

The sections of the *Fourth Reader* dealing with other parts of the world are remarkable for two other features. First, by far the largest part of this material dealt with stories of war: battles, sieges, conquests, massacres and acts of military heroism abound, some of them intended to be mildly humorous, some of them descriptive. Second, a smaller section of the book presented biographical extracts. The compilers used several sections from *Self-Taught Men*, and also extracted 'The Seige of Delphi' from Smiles' *Self-Help*.

Contrasts

There are three sharp differences between the *Fourth Book of Lessons* and the *Fourth Readers*. These have to do with the form of address and the implied reader, with utility and pleasure, and with religion.

In the *Fourth Book of Lessons*, a direct form of address is adopted to the rational reader. This reader—who seems without exception to be male—is assumed to be especially concerned with political economic relations and social structures. An authoritative voice speaks directly to the reader, explaining, outlining, detailing the operations of social and political structures, and enjoining support for them. The limits of individual activity are explicitly stated and collective activity explicitly discountenanced. Religious structures are treated in a similar way, and the text assumes a deep interest in religious matters. Religious lessons are interspersed with other lessons, and divine sanction is frequently sought for the 'natural' laws of political economy. The reader is frequently invited directly to participate in political economic reasoning—urged to imagine the disastrous consequences of a redistribution of wealth, for instance. The didacticism of the text is direct and frequently heavy-handed.

In the *Fourth Reader* in the Canadian Series, a narrative form of address is adopted to a reader concerned with pleasure. This reader is commonly male, although pointed address is sometimes made to the female reader as well. Where instances of direct address do take place in the *Fourth Reader*, they are largely as literary devices intended to heighten the reader's participation in narrative. The reader here has receded from the text. While the nationality of the implied reader in the Irish Series was generally Irish, the reader of the Canadian Series was British/Canadian. Nationality in the former case is rather subtle: we can see that these works address an *Irish* working-class reader, for instance, by their vindication of the necessary benevolence of the dealer in corn during famines,[54] and by less obvious references to Irish landscape. The Canadian Series, by contrast, focuses heavily on Canadian scenes and events, and on the adventures of explicitly British travellers and adventurers.

The serious emphasis upon laboriousness and utility so evident in the Irish series is largely absent from the Canadian. Explicit lessons on political economic relations are not presented in the latter. The Canadian student did learn about the financial operations of capitalist merchant firms, and read descriptions of the slave-trade in Africa and anti-slavery poems. But that student was never directly addressed about the beneficence, necessity, naturalness or divinity of the existing political order. Interest and pleasure on the part of the student reader were not seen, as in the Irish series, to reside in lessons on objects and natural theology. Narrative and adventure in which the reader was excited, terrified, and subtly instructed prevailed in the Canadian Series. The lesson in the *Fourth Reader* 'Conquest of Peru', presented a woodcut of a bare-breasted woman kneeling beside a scantily dressed Inca chief[55] (see Figure 3). The world of this reading book was one in which adventure, conquest and individual (largely male) prowess were celebrated.

CONQUEST OF PERU.

Figure 3: From Canadian Series of School Books, *Fourth Reader*, 1868, p. 161.

Finally, in the Canadian Series, directly religious instruction had receded considerably from the position it had occupied in the Irish books. While some overlap existed in the areas of sacred poetry and biblical history, in the Canadian Series this material was presented in a separate section. Where the Irish series attempted to present a non-sectarian christianity throughout, and to use this christianity as one of the cornerstones of moral regulation, the Canadian Series was heavily secular in content.

The differences in the content of these two sets of books should not be over-emphasized. The political-economic message delivered is broadly similar; the form of its presentation differs. The female reader learning from the *Fourth Book of Lessons* that it was pleasing to see women hobbling around on bound feet was hearing a similar message in the *Fourth Reader* where independent women were given to strong men. Yet it is significant that the form of presentation of these messages changes. As a hegemonic discourse, curriculum responds to, as well as shapes, shifts in the cultural reproduction of bourgeois society.

Pleasure and Normal Knowledge

In *The Social Content of Education*, J.M. Goldstrom divides the development of school readers in England and Ireland into three phases: from 1808 to the early 1830s a 'religious phase'; from the 1830s to 1863 a 'secular phase'; and after 1863, an 'economy phase'. While I am not entirely happy with the naming of these phases, they do illustrate curricular development in Canada West. In the 'secular phase', the Irish texts became the model for all reading books directed at working-class audiences by the middle classes. Political economy and lessons in christian non-sectarian religion predominated in texts produced by all other British educational societies (with the exception of McCullough's series, approved by the Wesleyan Conference, but used largely in middle-class schools).

In the late 1850s, existing textbooks in English elementary schools came under increasing attack from Her Majesty's Inspectors for their dreariness. 'Those who compiled them seem to think that increase in useful knowledge and the infusion of moral ideas are the only objects for which reading ought to be employed',[56] as one assistant commissioner remarked. This kind of criticism was systematized by the Newcastle Commission which reported in 1861. Criticism fell particularly upon the content of the Irish texts, and upon the ways in which the Committee of Council on Education subsidized texts. Under the existing scheme, the Committee published a list of approved books, which by 1860 included — in response to free trade and Voluntaryist agitation — virtually anything publishers chose to submit, so long as it was 'suitable' for elementary instruction. For fear of accusations of censorship, the Committee did not even comment on the books in the catalogue, but the Irish series predominated in the schools because of its cheapness. To subsidize religious and voluntary societies in the acquisition of books, the Committee was compelled to maintain a large staff of clerks, and to pay about 1000 pounds annually to Longman and Company for packing and distributing books. The Newcastle Commission argued that instruction in political and domestic economy should be improved for teachers in training, and that school readers should be made intelligible to younger readers. They suggested that state grants be made on the basis both of average attendance and performance on tests of reading, writing and arithmetic ability.[57]

A major result of official reaction to the Commission was the Revised Code and the system of 'payment-by-results'. Grants were now to be distributed on the basis of school attendance meeting conditions specified by the Committee of Council, and on student performance on standardized tests. With respect to reading, the standardized tests involved students reading before the examining inspector 'a paragraph from a reading book used in the school'.[58] The Committee of Council no longer sought to specify books to be used in these tests and hence, Goldstrom argues, teachers and local school managers began scouring the market for suitable readers. As Goldstrom put it:

> The religious moralizing, the political economy, the 'useful knowledge' and the moral tales directed so earnestly towards the children of the poor in previous series were dislodged. Commercial publishers ... constructed their Revised Code publications so that they were vaguely religious in tone ... but not patronizing .... They were, above all, extremely easy to read. Certainly, if an inspector was going to open a book at random and examine a child, a child was going to be rather more likely of success with 'The Three Bears' than with the political economy, specific gravity, pneumatics, etc., of the Irish books.[59]

The parallel in the transformation of the content of schoolbooks in England and Canada West is clear. School knowledge was broadly similar in the two contexts, yet the empirical conditions of the transformation as such and the specific conditions under which school knowledge was managed were quite different.

In both cases the transformation involved a movement away from directly didactic reading materials directed at a potentially turbulent and profane working class. Political economy and religious matter were largely abandoned in readers — although increasingly directed at teachers-in-training.[60] Narrative replaced simple didacticism, and an increasing concern with the pleasure of the reader in reading came to the fore.

I suggest that insight into this process of transformation in official knowledge may be gained by considering the political economic and the specifically educational contexts of curricular change. Of course in the Canadian context, the role of developing Canadian nationalism was central to curricular development. Frequent criticism was levelled at the Irish texts for their neglect of a specifically Canadian audience, and readers of the *Red Readers* read about Canadian and American subjects at length. As well, the concentration of the *Fourth Reader* upon tales of battle and warfare was a product of a social context of increasing militarism. In Canada, the American Civil War, the growth of Fenianism, and an awareness of the military extension of the empire undoubtedly contributed to an interest in military adventure.

But Canadian nationalism does not account for the general transformation from political economy to narrative. It seems to me that two things were taking place in the administration of popular education in both Britain and Canada in this period. First, educational administrators were well advanced in the process of making ordinary the kinds of regulated behaviour intended by state schooling. In Canada, although they continued to be contested, the routines and rituals of collective public instruction had been in place for two decades by 1866. The disciplinary regimen of the school was increasingly established as a structural system producing its own internal self-justifications. The explicit political thrust of the categories of state schooling became less obvious as the occupation of those categories by generations of students solidified them.

Didactic forms of address were particularly the concern of writers aiming to *establish* the necessity of certain relations. 'Be a good boy'. 'Mind your book'. 'Love God'. These are injunctions offered in educational structures where the technology of goodness and badness, minding and neglecting, sanctifying and profaning, is little developed. Where this technology exists, these injunctions are displaced from the curriculum and structured into the rituals and routines of schooling. Curricular change must be situated in a dialectic of development, one of whose terms is pedagogical practice.

School inspectors in Britain and Canada noticed that students did not enjoy reading the Irish readers, and for different particular reasons assumed that the pleasure of the reader was a key element in educational success. Yet I would suggest, the pleasure of the student in reading comes to the fore only when the facticity of studenthood is firmly in place. The designers of the Irish schoolbooks *were* concerned with pleasure, but were much more concerned with creating sound political and religious beliefs and habits. It was often argued that these things would be experienced by the student as pleasurable, but pleasant or not, they were *necessary* from a certain class viewpoint for political order. For the Irish Commissioners, the main educational imperative was to get the working class of Ireland into the schools, and to shape their political selves in particular ways. By the 1860s in the Canadas, most 'children' were already (more or less) in the schools. The problem of managing them there came to the fore.

Curricular change, then, may be seen at least in part as a response to the normalization of certain educational relations, a process which makes the reaction of the subject of education crucial to administrators.

At the same time, however, in both Britain and America by the 1860s, capitalist relations of production were increasingly dominant and increasingly accompanied by institutional structures of self-justification. In Canada West/Ontario, the end of the agricultural frontier had been reached by 1850, and many parts of the colony had been under continual agricultural cultivation since the 1790s. The primitive industries of the first half of the nineteenth century increasingly yielded to modern capitalist production techniques, and the scale of production in many industries was growing. The railroad boom of the 1850s stimulated both the growth of heavy industry and capital formation in the country as a whole. The countryside was dotted with small-scale village industry. By the 1870s, organized labour in the cities of Ontario was already engaged in the struggle for the eight-hour-day and a labour press existed.

The normalization of pedagogic relations was accompanied by, encouraged by and contributed to a parallel normalization of capitalist relations of production. Capitalist relations of production, as 'progress' or 'improvement', acquired in cultural representation and (less so) in popular consciousness, a certain inevitability. While this is not to deny the existence of possibilities for social transformation, it is important to recall Norbert Elias' argument[61] that the solidity of certain *forms* of power, of certain social structures, exerts pressure on members of bourgeois society to compete for advantage within those structures. This is crudely put, but I argue that the shift from didactic lessons in political economy and natural theology is in part determined by the increasing solidity of capitalist relations of production in Britain and America (combined with the relative autonomization of public education). Where Irish national leaders in political administration in the turbulent 1830s could see political economic doctrine as necessary medicine for the working class, public educational administrators in the 1860s could assume the dominance of those doctrines and attempt to make the structures underlying that assumption appear pleasing to the student. I do not wish to exaggerate. The removal of political economy from school readers was also in large part tactical. Political economy was displaced from the common schoolroom to the model and normal schoolroom; it was targeted less at students and more at student-teachers. I am certainly not arguing that capitalism's solidity was assured: the Paris Commune; the rise of social democracy; the strikes of the 1880s, 1905, 1917; the North-American soviets of 1919 (and on) tell quite a different story. Yet by 1860 the transition from factory village to industrial town had been accomplished in its main outlines.

I have thus far spoken of reading books as repositories of knowledge. In conclusion, I must stress that hegemonic knowledge is a form of managed political ignorance. The *Red Readers* propagated school ignorance in a pleasant form: 'The Skater and the Wolves' provided narrative excitement, but 'A Battle of the Lachine Strike' or 'Fighting the Red Coats at Polycarpe' could equally have done so. Useful knowledge and political economy propagated ignorance by noise. The *Red Readers* attempted to create ignorance with bliss.[62]

Notes

1. See Education Department, *A Brief History of Public and High School Text-Books Authorized for the Province of Ontario, 1846-1889*. Toronto, Warwick and Sons, 1890.
2. Egerton Ryerson, *Report on a System of Public Elementary Instruction for Upper Canada*. Montreal, John Lovell, 1847, p. 173.
3. cf. B. Curtis, 'The speller expelled: disciplining the common reader in Canada West', *Canadian Review of Sociology and Anthropology*, 22, 3, 1985, pp. 346-68; 'The myth of curricular republicanism: the state and the curriculum in Canada West, 1820-1850', *Histoire Sociale/Social History*, 16, 1983, pp. 305-29.
4. Public Archives of Ontario (PAO) Record Group 2 (RG2) Incoming General Correspondence of the Education Office (C6C), T.J. Grove, Mosa, 18 February 1852.
5. PAO RG2 C6C, J.L. Hughes, Brantford, 7 April 1851.
6. cf. Curtis, 'The speller expelled' (see note 3).
7. RG2 C6C, John Carson, Tecumseh, 11 January 1862.
8. RG2 C6C, W.A. McCullough, Greenwood, 31 December 1856.
9. RG2 C6C, T.W. Lillie, South Crosbie, 15 November 1854.
10. RG2 C6C, Superintendent, Ingersoll, 13 February 1854: Trustees, section 12 Vaughan, 15 February 1853; John Richardson, Trustee, section 10 Caledon, 5 December 1862; William Galt, Scarborough, 14 March 1856; John Barker, Warwick, 17 May 1851; H. Armstrong, Teacher, Matilda, 9 May 1861; T.N. Robertson, Fenelon Falls, 20 July 1858.
11. RG2 C6C, Edward Scarlett. Northumberland, March, 1856; R. Monteath, Superintendent, Reach and Scugog, 9 March 1857; H. McRae, Charlottenburgh, 12 March 1857.
12. RG2 C6C, J. Cooper, Woodstock, 6 February 1856.
13. RG2 C6C, John C. Butts, Ontario Township, 29 April 1857.
14. RG2 C6C, Wm. Gunn, Division 1 Bruce County, 11 November 1856.
15. RG2 C6C, H. McColl, section 4 Lobo, 24 April 1863.
16. RG2 C6C, 'Minutes' School Convention, County of York, 20 February 1860.
17. RG2 C6C, Trustee, section 1 Wilmot, 30 June 1856.
18. RG2 C6C, A.A. Munro, Mallorytown, 10 May 1864.
19. RG2 Outgoing General Correspondence of the Education Office (C1) Letterbrook E, Ryerson to T.W. Lillie, South Crosby, 25 November 1854.
20. RG2 CIT, Ryerson to William Gunn, Bruce County, 3 January 1857.
21. RG2 Draft Outgoing correspondence of the Education Office (C2), Ryerson to president of McGill College, 8 November 1859.
22. RG2 C6C, Otto Klotz, Preston, 4 March 1865.
23. For example, Richard Whately, *Introductory Lessons on Political Economy* (1833), London, J.W. Parker, 1855, pp. 133-4.
24. see note 22.
25. RG2 C2, Ryerson to Rev. Robert Torrance, Guelph, 15 April, 1859.
26. RG2 C2, Ryerson to Klotz, 13 March 1856.
27. RG2 C6C, Otto Klotz, Preston, 12 April 1865.
28. *Memorial to the Council of Public Instruction of Upper Canada, From the Board of Public Instruction of the County of Waterloo*. Galt, Reporter Office, 1865, p. 8.

Notice, of course, the delicious irony in the insistence by middle-class reformers that the reader be taught meaning.
29 *Annual Report of the Chief Superintendent of Education, 1865,* pp. 10-11.
30 Egerton Ryerson, *The School Book Question: Letters in Reply to the Brown-Campbell Crusade Against the Educational Department for Upper Canada.* Montreal, John Lovell, 1866, p. 12.
31 *School Book Question,* p. 12.
32 Sherwood Fox, 'School Readers as an Educational Force', in J.M. Bumstead (Ed.) *Canadian History Before Confederation.* Georgetown, Irwin-Dorsey, 1972, pp. 362-73.
33 cf. M.B. Katz, 'Who Went to School?'; Ian E. Davey, 'School Reform and School Attendance', in M.B. Katz and P.H. Mattingly (eds), *Education and Social Change.* New York: University Press, 1975, pp. 271-73.
34 see J.M. Goldstrom, *The Social Content of Education, 1808-1870.* Shannon: Irish University Press, 1972; *Passim; Annual Reports of the Society for Promoting the Education of the Poor of Ireland.* Dublin: 1813-39; *Report from the Select Committee of the House of Lords on the New Plan of Education in Ireland.* London: 1837.
35 Goldstrom, *Social Content.*
36 D.H. Akenson, *The Irish Educational Experiment.* Toronto, University of Toronto Press, 1971, p. 229.
37 J.G. Hodgins (ed.), *Documentary History of Education in Upper Canada.* Toronto: L.K. Cameron, 1894-1910, Vol. IX, p. 67.
38 Akenson, *Experiment,* pp. 231-8.
39 *Dictionary of National Biography.* London: Smith, Elder and Co., 1887, Vol. IX, p. 100.
40 Goldstrom, *Social Content,* pp. 62-66.
41 Series of National School Books, *First Book of Lessons.* Toronto: McPhail, 1859, pp. 6-7.
42 *First Book,* pp. 16-35.
43 Commissioners of National Education. *Second Book of Lessons.* Montreal: Armour and Ramsay, 1845, p. 5.
44 *Second Book,* pp. 10-11.
45 Series of National School Books. *Fourth Book of Lessons.* Toronto, R. McPhail, 1857. Lesson IV, 'On Rich and Poor'.
46 see J.H. Pestalozzi, *How Gertrude Teaches her Children.* London, George Allen and Unwin, 1915, pp. 80-1; also, Kate Silber, *Pestalozzi: The Man and his Work.* London, Routledge and Kegan Paul, 1973.
47 Elizabeth Mayo, *Lessons on Objects.* London, Seeleys, 1851.
48 *Fourth Book,* p. 22.
49 *Fourth Book,* p. 24.
50 Quoted in Canadian Series of School Books, *Fourth Reader.* Toronto: James Campbell, 1868, p. 330.
51 *Fourth Reader,* Section III, Lesson VI.
52 For Barclay, George Rose (ed.), *Cyclopaedia of Canadian Biography.* Toronto: Rose, 1888, p. 320; for Grasett, H.E. Turner, 'Grasett, Henry James' in *Dictionary of Canadian Biography.* Toronto: University of Toronto Press, 1982, Vol. XI, pp. 367-9; for McCaul, G.M. Craig 'McCaul, John' in *Dictionary of Canadian Biography,* Vol. XI, pp. 540-1; for Ormiston, J.C. Hopkins (ed.),

Canada: An Encyclopedia. Toronto: Linscott, 1898, Vol. IV, p. 85 (photo); pp. 205-6.
53 *Fourth Reader*, pp. 21-3.
54 *Fourth Book*, pp. 235-6.
55 *Fourth Reader*, p. 161.
56 Goldstrom, *Social Content*, pp. 159-60.
57 *Social Content*, pp. 160-1.
58 *Social Content*, p. 163.
59 *Social Content*, p. 167.
60 Ryerson wrote a political economy textbook in the 1870s.
61 Norbert Elias, *The Civilizing Process.* New York: Pantheon, 1978-80.
62 Fred Inglis, *The Management of Ignorance.* Oxford: Basil Blackwell, 1985.

State Formation and Classroom Practice: Once Again 'On Moral Regulation'[1]

Philip Corrigan

Preamble

The social constellation that risks being produced will consist of a vast underclass suitably narcotized by a technological rationality that is highly ideological, and a managerial class equipped and fated to organize the modern version of bread and circuses. That technological rationality will become the solder in the upcoming stratification, justifying the overall patterns of social organization and providing the basis for the dominant (ideological) elite . . . What we are witnessing is once again a subtle redefinition of childhood: the crucial *formative years* become redirected upwards while the years spent in elementary and even secondary school take on the nature of *doing time, but doing it nicely*. Kids are being socialized into the new personality syndromes of mass culture and consumer society, where people, and kids who are people too, are encouraged to assert and develop their autonomy within *accepted parameters* . . . . in practice, alternative experiments have foundered on the ideological elements at its core, namely that state and subjectivity are oppositional categories locked in relationships of repression and liberation . . . It is not surprising . . . that the history of school reforms, like that of the welfare state, has witnessed increasing centralization, as the institutional dynamic of subsequent reforms concentrates decision-making power in the upper and restricted spheres of government bureaucracies.

> Whatever other explanations one might offer for this process, it is clear that the functional outcome of such centralization is the exclusion of alternatives and the inexorable because functional victory of the technocratic rationality. Centralization helps to ensure that even the debate about educational reform is framed within the parameters of the discourse of modernity: progress, welfare, meritocratic equality ... (my additions and emphases).

So says Stephen Schecter (1987, pp. 50-3), writing in 1986. Or, as an alternative preface, I could remark simply how 'triage' (the measured application of the law of thirds) seems so constant in schooling: 33 percent of students in Ontario (*and* the whole of the United States) leave without completion of a high school programme.

I had wanted to extend my work (Corrigan, 1975, 1977 a), 1981, in press-a) on Samuel Smiles—particularly his 1859 book usually known by its short title *Self-Help*, but which ought to be also known for its subtitle which relates 'Achievement' to the 'Lives of Great Men'. It should also be known for its frequent reissues—once in 1967 (Foreword by the then Lord Thomson of Fleet) and again in 1985, with a Preface by Sir Keith Joseph, then Her Majesty's Secretary of State for Education and Science. But what follows is a very preliminary exploration of some issues that arise from two differing (but in my mind, at least, related) bodies of work: with Sayer since 1973, culminating in our recent book, *The Great Arch: English State Formation as Cultural Revolution* (Corrigan and Sayer, 1985); and the work with Curtis, Lanning (Corrigan, Curtis, and Lanning 1987), and Shamai (Shamai, 1986; Shamai and Corrigan, 1987) in our SSHRCC funded project on State Formation in the Canadas. In doing this, I also want to center—and advertise—the Ontario Ministry of Education (1984 b) bulletin, *Towards the Year 2000: Future Conditions and Strategic Options for the Support of Learning in Ontario*. This is a primary document which future historians, I argue, will 'fall upon' as an earlier generation did so with Smiles (or should so do).

Schools do not (only) teach subjects, they inform subjectivities

The important shift accomplished, or at least put on the agenda, by the work of Young (1971 b) and others in the early 1970s, argued that curriculum was, to use Williams' (1961, 1981, 1983) arguments, a selection from selective traditions. Such work also centered the importance of what I shall call the 'phenomenology' of classroom experiences. But—as the feminist and anti-racist movements were to demonstrate beyond a shadow of a doubt—this work did not take the differentiation work of school seriously. Either they could not understand the *productivity* of schooling or, in the terms we have come to associate with Foucault (1981, 1982), they did not attend to the *positivity* of schooling.

Speaking crudely, it seems that the 'old' sociology of education may have regarded the school (and schooling) as a 'black box' but at least they centered schooling (which they misrecognized as 'education') as part of the *media of modernity* (Corrigan and Sayer, 1987). But they, as with the 'new' sociology, also made a gigantic blunder, one which the very social organization of educational reality (Smith, in press) tends to make common and obvious, that is, to work within the disciplinary constraints of the (academic) social division of labour.[2] They ignored the *exactly* contemporaneous historiographical work which would, for example, have shown how the so-called 'hidden' curriculum, was so very *explicit*. In England this is true for the 1830s through to the 1980s (Johnson, 1970). I have found no evidence that (since 1976) it is not true for the Canadas, for the USA, for France, for Tanzania and, alas, for the USSR and China (Corrigan, 1985).

What this work put on the agenda for me was two themes, patterns, and textures—to investigate, to find out about: first, *how* the social context becomes part of the content of state-provided and/or regulated schooling; second, *why* 'identity formation' has become handed over (more division of labour!) to the school psychologists?[3]

In more political words: why do we not take seriously what compulsory schooling does to whole generations? And, take as seriously, although a different matter, that this was the intention of those 'schooling promoters' who flourished in their different 'moments' in different capitalist societies from the 1780s onwards? One of the larger themes which Sayer and I argued in *The Great Arch* (Corrigan and Sayer, 1985) was that what we, sociologically, have come to study as 'the social' was a construction of some radical bourgeois *men*. In psychoanalytic terms, these radical bourgeois *men* encountered a Significant Other which they sought, in important terms, to *socialize* and to *civilize*; to model (in Marx's famous phrase) after their own image. Does it still have to be said—this year—that *mass* schooling was oriented to (1) the youth, the children and the adolescents; (2) the *other classes* (other than the bourgeoisie and the aristocracy, where the latter still persisted as a socially significant grouping); and (3) *differentiation*, especially gender differentiation?

It is not experience which organizes expressions, but the regulated social grammar which organizes expressions (Bakhtin/Voloshinov, 1973)

I have recently been very impressed by the confluence of a number of very different studies, and I find them all relevant to a study of what I want to call the 'social curriculum' — the ways (contents and forms) through which the social ('The Social') context becomes the content of schooling experiences. Permeating any *system* of education is a simultaneous organization at once as general ('universal', 'natural', 'neutral') as can be thought or imagined, and yet as intimate and 'personal' as can be felt and lived. Bernstein (1971-1977) has called this 'the educational code' and has been exploring this for over a quarter-of-a-century. More recently, Bourdieu has examined, in a far from satisfactory metaphor, 'Human Capital' (see also Anderson, 1983; Colls and Dodd, 1986; Hobsbawm and Ranger, 1983; Morgan, 1987; Wilden, 1981). But one particular work, at least potentially, centers and focuses this investigation: Inglis' *The Management of Ignorance* (1985). But he does not sufficiently generalize toward the social curriculum, nor does he concretize in the direction of what pain, which violations, this persisting declaration of what most people know as ignorance, might mean. The regulated social construction of differential silencing and of categorized stupidity, within the vortices of sexuality, race, gender, class, language and regionality, seem to me to be, now as then, as central to capitalism as a mode of 'life'. (I am hesitant here since for so many millions, capitalism has been a slow lingering 'death'.) At least Inglis — as did Abrams (1963) — raises the centrality of *the functionality of ignorance*; the importance of declaring most people most of the time as unworthy, stupid, in a singular and exact guillotining and classifying word: *bad*.[4] And making them 'take-on' (i.e., wear as clothing) this identification as if it were their only usable, exchangeable 'ID'.

Opening Our Eyes

Following Poulantzas (1978), I have brought these arguments together as a slogan: *Schooling is more than Reproduction and Resistance* (Corrigan, 1986). To comprehend that we have to rescue and revive a different level of analysis, at once experiential (using a notion of pragmatics) *and* structural (using notions from both Marx and the wider psychoanalytics), but more important than both, we have to recognize, quite centrally, that all of this—curriculum, schooling—is *done to* bodies, growing bodies, different bodies. As soon as we acknowledge the multiple (and fragmentary) forms of subjectivity we can be freed from any way of seeing which fixates the analysands, through misrecognizing role compliance, as if it meant internalization of roles-as-rules, i.e., belief. Compliance is not commitment. Equally, from the other side as it were, role resistance is not to be misrecognized as rejecting what was desired but the forms and contents of what is being provided, here schooling, and central to that schooling *is* the social curriculum. To the standard abbreviation of the three Rs we need to add two further ones: first, Regulation (as in Moral Regulation) which was 'found again' (born again?) as the 'hidden curriculum' in the 1970s; and Religion (as in regulated belief of an axiomatic character) which is only now being refound after Althusser's (1971) notorious *stupidity* in relegating religion to a Feudal Ideological State Apparatus.

But these five Rs—registrations and representations of 'The Social' within schooling—act to structure the approved forms of expression; they are the social grammar of schooling, oriented to evaluative behaviours—to *how* teaching is taught, and learning is evaluated and approved. They are the primary differentiation device because I would argue more strongly now[5], and to even-up my critical swipes, that the grossest of all gross distortions accomplished by Parsonian structural-functionalism was its 'theory' of modernization or development, its central argument (way back to Parsons' earliest meta-theoretical papers) that modernity is to be found in achievement behaviors and value consensus, whereas other (backward?) social formations have ascription-fixation and particularistic-values. Schooling works, and has always worked, through ascription: achievement is measured and evaluated ascriptively and centrally around expressive forms—including the forms of embodiment, bodily expression and forms of dress and address. It is often asked why so much 'trouble' is taken, and caused, in schools around the seemingly minor and trivial infractions (dress forms and styles, chewing gum, talking out of turn, elective mutism, apathetic listlessness, hyperactivity, even gender confusion). These are, in fact, all measurable signs of expressivity, part of that rich texture of transformed power which we collect under the name of *the symbolic*, whether ritualized or routine, and central to the moral regulation project of the school.

One last clarification is in order. If we comprehend approved social identities as constructed in (a) subordination, and (b) contradiction, then we have no warrant for claiming the resulting behaviors (whether called positive or negative) to be constitutive of the *whole* subjectivity. They are part of the language-game (which is not a trivial matter) and all we

State Formation and Classroom Practice

can say, at a glance — and the sociological glance is often one of the briefest and bleakest of all our social ways of seeing — is that is *how* people are expressing themselves in *that* context at *that* time. In England there is a catch-phrase which sums up this grudging acknowledgment of the way-the-world-is: 'Seems so!' (see Yeo, 1979, 1986). But alongside, and interwoven with, this tactical seriousness is a sustained strategy of contempt, a distancing from precisely those core 'universal' values that are held to cement society-as-we-know-it together in an orgy of consensual bliss. (I am thinking of certain recent royal and religious events around the world.) These strategies of contempt are founded upon different kinds of knowing, belief and — yes — hopefulness, demonstrated in different forms of love and solidarity (see Bloch, 1986).

All of these entail historical investigation. By the 1970s not to 'do well' at school became understood, at least in part, as there being 'something wrong' with the child, the gender, the family, the group, the race/ethnicity, the class, and so on. Hence the world-wide phenomenon (in advanced capitalist formations) of compensatory or supplementary education for the 'disadvantaged' which Bernstein so admirably criticized in the slogan 'Schools cannot compensate for Society'. Of course, that moment, too, has now gone, although education is still highly centered as a political matter, but in a context of simultaneously withdrawing funds and urging a 'back-to-basics' approach. Whose basics? Basics for whom? Let us see from one viewpoint, a singular vision, where an unarguable 'technological rationality' informs our proper, approved *subjectivities*, our 'good' *social identities*.

Social Grammar in Ontario: 'Towards the Year 2000'[6]

Let me set the scene for the *governance* (a keyword for the Strategic Planning Task Group) entailed in this text of our times. Governance entails not only what is 'obligatory' but what is 'desirable and desired' (Durkheim, 1974, p. 45), it also entails the ideal expression of the existing flexible forms of rule (hence subordination):

> 'Vocation, destiny, task, ideal' are . . . the conditions of existence of the ruling class . . . which are ideally expressed in law, morality, etc., are more or less consciously transformed by the ideologists of that class into something that in history exists independently, and which can be conceived in the consciousness of the separate individuals of the class as vocation, etc.; and which are set up as a standard of life in opposition to the individuals of the

Re-Interpreting Curriculum Research

> oppressed class, partly as embellishment or realization of domination, partly as moral means for this domination. It is to be noted here, as in general with ideologists, that they inevitably put the thing upside down and regard their ideology both as the creative force and as the aim of all social relations, whereas it is only an expression and symptom of those relations. (Marx and Engels, 1846, pp. 472–473)

(There is an encyclopedia to be written around the last six words!) Within, not separable from, the spinning out of these webs and tissues of more or less comprehensive untruths, there are relations of rule, expressions of authority (legalized power, successful claims to monopoly). Hearken to a Chief Inspector from the Toronto Board of Education in 1915:

> The Provincial Government is therefore responsible, directly and actually, for the general nature and efficiency of the school system in every part of the Province. The members of the school boards exercise administrative and not constructive powers. They are trustees to whom is committed the duty of carrying out an important trust clearly defined by the school law. Thus the criterion of efficiency is not locally determined as in many places in the United States. It is Provincially prescribed. The criterion is virtually the expert judgement of the supervising authorities. There can be no local modification of this standard or substitution for it. (Toronto Board of Education, 1915, p. 42)[7]

(Is that clear enough? Expertise *and* efficiency!)

So, to the object itself: the text (Ontario Ministry of Education, 1984 b). Totalling ninety pages, the last four of which are a Bibliography, the text is broken into two major parts, preceded by a four-page 'Introduction and Basic Assumptions'. 'Part I — Conditions' extends for *eighteen* pages (Global conditions and implications for Education; Ontario conditions and implications for Education; beliefs and attitudes affecting education in Ontario). 'Part II — Strategic Options and Policy Considerations' extends for some *sixty* pages (including the one page 'Postscript'): 'Learners and Learning', *six* pages; 'Curriculum and Teaching', *sixteen* pages, and 'Service Delivery and Governance', *thirty-four* pages. This is not a mild case of bibliomania on my part; the proportions here are themselves significant, not least because of 'off-stage' references to previous SPTG documentation, some of which is very difficult to obtain.

Like all such discourses, this text has its rules. In setting the 'Agenda' it rules into emphasis and seriousness some understandings of the past, present and future, and rules the rest out-of-court, as system-disturbances.

State Formation and Classroom Practice

This is very clear in Part I which adopts what I have called 'the whole-in-the-middle' grammar. Early parts of the presentation talk emphatically of what 'will' or 'shall' be, and then, quite quickly, the discourse moves to a 'since' and 'it has been shown that' style. These early statements move from the intensely revealing to the deliberately anodyne. Three examples:

> In these terms it might be said that the education system is for civil society what the parliamentary system is for the state — the place where the individual and the society can express themselves to each other. (Ontario Ministry of Education, 1984 b, p. 3)

> In effect, we are becoming a culture of minorities. (p. 15)
> Over the next ten or fifteen years, no new family form will emerge in any strength, but the distribution of forms will change. (p. 15)

The text more generally also roots/routes our general and potential vision in the past, thereby celebrating an old friend as a hero; Egerton Ryerson as a Founding Father, Master-Disseminator!

> From its inception to the present, the public education system in Ontario has been sustained because of a general belief that it is a public good. Its founder, Egerton Ryerson, like other nineteenth-century social ameliorators, felt this to be true for several reasons. It would help preserve good government and constitutional liberty, since an educated populace could make informed and rational political choices. It would ensure a degree of social cohesion by virtue of being compulsory, universal and free. By being practical, it would prepare its graduates for lives that would be useful both to themselves and to society, and by dispelling ignorance, it would help reduce the individual and social ills of poverty and crime... While we might not justify the system in precisely these terms today, still a core of belief in the public utility of publicly supported education is a constant that has survived since the 1840s. Another belief which has not diminished in strength since Ryerson's day is that the Ontario system of publicly funded education should draw on the best practice from other jurisdictions around the world to achieve its own unique excellence. For Ryerson, who was given the job of creating an education system virtually out of nothing, this meant that his first task was to set out on a fourteen month tour to examine educational systems in other countries. In effect he learned what was best from a variety of sources, and these best practices, adapted to the special conditions of Ontario society of

> the day, became the basis of the Ontario system. As the system has grown, this openness to ideas from other jurisdictions, or lack of provincialism, has been a characteristic of education in Ontario. At the same time, other jurisdictions have found much to admire in the Ontario system, which suggests that we have not merely been copyists but originators in our own right. One of the reasons that publicly supported education has in general continued to be accepted as a public good is that it has been seen to exercise a certain kind of public or social responsibility. Broadly speaking, education—both formal and informal—is the means by which a society recreates itself; that is, recreates the knowledge, skills, habits and customs which are the characteristic components of its group or social life... Thus public education, by ensuring the transmission of these cultural artefacts from generation to generation, helps give the society shape and integrity, and assures that all members of that society become participants. For the individual, to learn is thus to participate in society's learning about, and re-creation of, itself. (Ontario Ministry of Education, 1984 b, pp. 19–20)

This is further elaborated:

> Interestingly enough, however, there is nothing new about our ability in Ontario to take advantage of appropriate technology. Essential to Ryerson's success in creating the Ontario education system was his mastery of the technology of the day. A common form of information access and dissemination was travel: Ryerson travelled first to America and Europe to gain the information he needed about other systems, and then five times throughout the province to hold public meetings and conferences with trustees, inspectors and teachers. In this way he was able to effect changes in public opinion so as to ensure, for example, that when his principle of free schools was made compulsory in 1871 there was little opposition. He made use of the postal system: he published a monthly *Journal of Education* which was sent to school boards throughout the province, and his office correspondence averaged six hundred letters a month. And he put in place a technology of standardization and accountability: he acquired the rights to republish a set of graded, patriotic, non-denominational, inexpensive textbooks, and he established a system of supervision and inspection.... Ontario's belief in its ability to use appropriate technology with respect to education has not altered. (*Ibid.* pp. 22–3)

And, later—in a crucial subsection ('Support for Communities of Interest') in the key section 'Service Delivery and Governance'—Ryerson's 'taking advantage of appropriate technology' is further celebrated as *the* way of solving key questions about 'pluralism and diversity' (Ontario Ministry of Education, 1984 b, p. 69).

> If we wish to be able to respond more flexibly to the increasing pressures of individuals and groups with special learning needs, and at the same time accommodate them within the framework of the public board system, the question of degree arises. Too great responsiveness could lead to fragmentation of the publicly sanctioned system and the rending of the social fabric in the province; too little could lead to the public system being seen as irrelevant or as indifferent to the legitimate needs of the people. Ryerson's answer to this question was decentralization of responsibility. He made provision for a central authority to distribute funds voted by the Legislature, to prepare regulations and curricula, to authorize textbooks, and to improve the quality of teaching through certification, inspection, and the establishment of a normal school; at the same time, local school boards were empowered to raise funds required apart from the grants, to hire and fire teachers, to implement curricula, to select texts, and to maintain school facilities. . . . We believe that the flexibility and adaptability of the public system may be further improved by following this tradition. Our aim is to establish a publicly sanctioned system for service delivery and governance which will be able, on the one hand, to respond to the needs of individuals and groups in the province, and on the other, to effectively address itself to the question of needed balance between the well-being of the individual and that of the province as a whole. (Ontario Ministry of Education, 1984 b, pp. 70–1)

Here we have the typical reduction of features and relations of politics to problems of administration. As Mannheim (1936) first clearly identified, ends disappear in a withering focus on means.

If Ryerson features as hero, the theme is resolutely set in the future tense: that crucial catch-all phrase or slogan, that keyword for the 1980s, 'Information'—notably 'information handling' (p. 18). It is becoming administrative commonsense that we live *in* the 'Information Age' and not *as* a 'Learning Society'. But here, precisely here, one major contradiction erupts from the smooth rhythm of the discourse: this 'information' does not allow either accurate labor market prediction (p. 30) or linkages forward from schooling (pp. 16 f, 38, etc.). Another contradiction—one already firmly centered in the social grammar of Ontario schooling—is a homogenous *individualization* (pp. 20, 35 f, 53 f), sometimes phrased, through quotations, as 'identity strength' (p. 34) or 'personal identity' (p. 46). This is further emphasized in the celebration of the values-emphasis in existing policies and programs—notably the 'correctness' and 'appropriateness' (pp. 45, 49) of *Ontario Schools: Intermediate and Senior Divisions (OSIS)* (1984 a), one of the most explicitly divisive, in terms of tracking or streaming, documents I have read.

Finally, all of this is set in a context of 'danger'. The social signs of danger vary from the links between the facts of a general non-guarantee of social mobility-through-education plus manifest unemployment amongst graduates, *and* the shifting qualities of the 'climate of opinion', to 'the possible threat of increasing cultural diversity' (Ontario Ministry of Education, 1984 b, p. 62)[8]. Over and again schooling—and centrally, as I shall immediately now discuss, the curriculum—is seen as the primary means (politics thus entering back in again!) of properly, correctly, firmly yet flexibly, relating 'the individual and society' (e.g., p. 57, para. 3).

Although the document does this pervasively, the section 'Curriculum and Teaching' (pp. 33–49), especially the subsection '5.2: Curriculum Development and Social Renewal' (pp. 35–40) is the most explicit about what I mean by 'social curriculum'.[9] Notice first the centering of *existing procedures* of governance to ensure 'service delivery'.[10]

> In its 1982 discussion paper, *Curriculum Policy: Review—Development—Implementation* (CRDI), the Ministry of Education set out its ideas about the processes of curriculum review, development and implementation, and outlined an operational model by which these processes could be carried out. For our purposes, a notable feature of this process is the review phase, the purpose of which is 'to gather information that can be used in making decisions to facilitate progress towards the achievement of educational goals'. Among the kinds of information to be sought is that concerning 'the educational, social and political trends in the province'. The assumption seems to be here at any rate, that a curriculum which best serves the interests of students is one which accurately reflects the conditions of the society in which they live. This is not a new idea, but it is a very important one. It is, moreover, congenial to the purposes of this paper, which are to bring certain informed speculations about future trends along with a review of the beliefs and attitudes that have shaped Ontario education in the past into a relationship that will be useful in planning for the future. Clearly the review, development and

State Formation and Classroom Practice

implementation of curriculum must be at the heart of such planning. The *CRDI* document deals, of course, with curriculum renewal in the elementary and secondary schools of the province. It is at least arguable that some of its general principles, such as the one noted above, apply equally to post-secondary and continuing education, and that government has a policy role to play in the process of curriculum development in these areas as well. (Ontario Ministry of Education, 1984 b, p. 33)

There is then a key paragraph — a bridge in the discourse — which facilitates the stabilizing, as 'what *is* going to happen', of the brief speculative material presented earlier:

In what follows, we will argue for more explicit linkages between curriculum development and social renewal, for a rethinking of the balance among curriculum objectives and for the development of new forms of support for teachers and the teaching process. Our arguments are based on the needs that are being created by the conditions outlined in Part I of this report. Throughout the report, but especially in this chapter, we are guided by the principle that, in an era of rapid and incessant change, the form in which a society negotiates its vision of the future is the starting point for educational decisions. (p. 34)

The section headed 'Curriculum Development and Social Renewal' announces:

In the previous chapter, we suggested that learning is basically an adaptive process, the achievement of a kind of mastery of the environment by assimilating and ordering information about it, the making of meaning. To this, the idea of curriculum is a natural complement. Essentially it is a vehicle by which key elements of a learner's culture or environment may be distilled and structured so that the learner's natural tendency to learn may be optimized. In this broad sense, curriculum moderates the precariousness of unguided learning, and by doing so helps ensure both the individual's and society's survival. In these terms, then, curriculum development must be at the very heart of any attempt to promote a dynamic and viable relation between individual and social well-being. (p. 35)

There is then a contrast offered between 'curriculum development and renewal' in stable times and 'during periods of rapid change like the present', and between subject-centered, traditional ways of thinking about and organizing curriculum versus 'a process-oriented conception of curriculum'. Favouring the latter (*OSIS*, you will be surprised to learn, is praised for its 'program individualization' and 'quickening in the rate at which material is learned', p. 45), the text centers the social curriculum before our eyes, blending past, present and future and raises a 'major (social) problem'.

> Though the comparison may be somewhat overstated, it is clear that the process-centered curriculum, while not denying the past, is more oriented to the future. Excellence can be measured in the same tangible ways as in the subject-centered curriculum, but also by less tangible ways, such as, for example, by evidence of growing maturity, independence and the ability of students to direct their learning. These two perspectives are more easily reconciled than the terms of their comparison might suggest, and the trend is toward doing so. To the extent that this is so, the possibilities for change in the curriculum would seem to be enhanced. For one thing, the 'hidden' curriculum—the diverse social or affective goals and expectations for education—begins to emerge, and therefore to become available for public discussion. Consequently, discussion about educational aims and objectives has the opportunity of shifting from sterile debate about particularities of subject content to engage broader issues of individual and social well-being. For another, the need to devise curricula which are more truly strategic, in that they are adapted to the rapidly changing conditions of our lives and therefore able to help learners themselves become adaptable, seems more likely to be met. One of the reasons that the subject-centered curriculum has had so long a life, and that the hidden curriculum has been able to stay hidden, is that there has been a fairly wide consensus in Ontario about the nature of education and the direction it should pursue. In effect, education was to conserve the culture and heritage (about which there was relatively little debate), socialize the young, advance individuals in the social structure, protect children from dangerous influences, select elites, support the economy through manpower training (and political life through patriotic teaching), and to do all this while teaching basic reading, writing and arithmetic skills, and the common knowledge and values of a reasonably cohesive society.... Although, in very general terms, there may be agreement about the validity of these purposes, we do not now live in an era in which most people would understand each of them in the same way, or agree to their specifics. Our society has become pluralistic to a degree

> which, even a generation ago, few would have thought possible. This pluralism has rendered the social mandate of the education system ambiguous, and its goals amorphous. Each sub-element within the pluralistic whole does, however, have particular goals which it seeks to promote in competition with other interest groups. The failure of education to respond clearly to the particular agenda of any one of these groups means that all are disillusioned and therefore critical — to the point, perhaps, of concluding that the public education system is not able to bear all the hopes and expectations of a modern society. (Ontario Ministry of Education, 1984 b, pp. 37–8)

What is, and I use the word deliberately, *scandalous* about this, is the total redefining of what the 'hidden curriculum' is! It is not the pervasive moral regulation and normalization which has been discussed by historians and sociologists, by anti-sexist and anti-racist groups for decades, but *diversity* which is the problem! Hence the need to manage, or, if you prefer, inform, 'public opinion' (through such controlling and agenda-setting procedures as curriculum renewal).

> To a large extent (perhaps ultimately), the problem of public opinion is a problem of curriculum (p. 38).

> Perhaps because of the past consensus about the purposes of education referred to earlier, there has not developed in Ontario a strong tradition of public debate about curricular goals and objectives. This is not to say that the education system has been insensitive to public needs, only that no formal means have been developed by which goals for the curriculum that are meaningful to all groups might be articulated. To do so would have significant advantages (and some risks, of course), yet it is an option we recommend, for by moving curricular issues more fully into the public domain, the public's educational consciousness would be raised. The various social, affective, and values concerns of the 'hidden curriculum' would become explicit and therefore susceptible to public negotiation. (p. 39)

That is why the largest part of this text focuses upon Service Delivery and Governance, within which, as I noted, there is an explicit procedure for how to recognize a genuine 'community' and thus facilitate the representation of 'communities of interest' in 'public' debate. What is being argued here is the detachment of the statutory authority (the Provincial State) from the *actual* supply of 'education' (service delivery) but the extension, in a manner directly recognizable from Taylorism, Fordism and more modern modes of managing societies/corporations, of *the span of control* (governance).

Explicitly dismissing both system-reduction and 'going on as we are' (the restoration of, or increases in, sufficient funding is of course not even mentioned!) the Report argues for a 'third option' for 'government':

> to devise new roles for itself and new ways of using structures, techniques and technologies that will be appropriate for mediating the complex needs that will arise. (p. 50)

> The third option is the one explored in this chapter. It demands, but also, reciprocally, guarantees the maximum in flexibility and adaptability. It proposes that not only individual learners and groups but also government should devise new roles for themselves in which their respective responsibilities would be less rigidly defined than at present so that both would become more able to learn and adapt. Thus two major themes will be developed in the chapter: the need for support of the learning of individuals and groups, and the need for learning by government, in order that both may be able to better encounter change in the future. (p. 51)

> Government will be better able to provide these forms of support only if it equips itself with better means for listening, learning, leading and governing — the primary business of government. This leads to the second major theme. We believe that government must be increasingly involved in the business of governance, and in relative terms, less involved in service delivery. (p. 52)[11]

This has consequences for who can teach:

> Redefining the teaching profession by recognizing the broader range of potential contributions of other professionals, both within and outside the formally constituted field of education. The needs of a complex information and learning society require that professionals with special training in learning and education processes contribute to the setting of the public agenda, as well as deal with the challenge, which emerge. (p. 59)[12]

> Strengthening the governance structure of the profession to better service the province in a period of greater sophistication and diversity in education. To what degree should teacher certification be removed from the direct initiative of government, the consequence perhaps being the separation of the unique self-interest of teachers from the broader public interest? Would the

State Formation and Classroom Practice

latter be better handled through the establishment of an independent body for the profession, which would resemble those responsible for the governance of other professions in the province? (p. 60)

Plus, drawing in 'Independent Extra-Government Agencies':

While considerable public resources for the support of education exist in Ontario, an equally considerable, and as yet largely untapped, storehouse of extra-governmental resources also exists. These independent agencies, ranging from commercial firms, to self-help groups, to voluntary or not-for-profit organizations, are often involved in some kind of learning enterprize, and have consequently built up a store of educational experience and interest which could — and should — be of use to the public boards in helping to meet learning needs within their jurisdictions. (p. 67)

Independent agencies have the potential for providing the increased diversity of services required since they are more highly customized to individual and group needs. They are likely to be seen as more responsive and less alienating. Independent agencies might provide some services at lower costs, with the possibility of sharing certain cost components with government. (p. 68)

There is ample evidence to suggest that independent extra-government agencies do have objectives which are shared in common with those of the publicly sanctioned system. Policies have been developed to variously recognize, certify, inspect, ensure accountability and, in some instances, actively promote the contribution of independent agencies as partners with government in education and training. Based on this experience and in order to meet the challenges ahead, government must develop an enabling policy framework which will encourage school, college and university boards to explore new possibilities and facilitate the active involvement of independent extra-government agencies. (p. 69)

We do not have to wonder too much, nor too long, about which sorts, and with which hidden curriculums, such agencies will be.

Conclusion

I can do no better than quote (with I hope, by now, the means to 'irritate the obvious' embedded in this social grammar) the last two questions from the 'Postscript' of *Towards the Year 2000*:

> What image of learning and education in Ontario should be realized five to ten years ahead?
>
> What must be done in the next one to five years to prepare for the period five to ten years ahead? (p. 85)

Who, Whom?

Postscript

All I have tried to do here, hence the full quotations I have provided, is to alert readers (principally citizens of Ontario, but the argument is somewhat wider than that) to the ways in which *one* (albeit strategic) text exemplifies the qualities Schecter (1987) outlined in my opening quotation. With this text—*Towards the Year 2000*—moreover, we are dealing with a published, but scarcely publicized, discourse which functions as a dictionary or, better, image-repertoire, from which combinations of the meretricious, anodyne, tendentious and the forceful can be drawn and assembled. Behind the *vade mecum* is the complex history of the Strategic Planning initiative (of whom? for whom?) that dates from 1975, and a recently reorganized Ministry of Education (plus the complementary extension of the Ministry of Colleges and Universities to comprehend Skills Development—with a promised Ontario Institute of Skills Development on its way). This text is, however, singular to the degree that it *is*, importantly, what its sub-title claims it to be—if we qualify (as Schecter does) the notion of 'options'. Here we have one of the most significant political documents (for citizens of Ontario—my use of 'citizens' is both deliberately republican and comprehends persons of all ages) in recent years which is issued administratively—in nothing less (and nothing more . . . contrast the media attention and participation-possibilities that attended the Shapiro Report (1985) on private schools or the Fullan and Connelly Report (1987) on teacher training) than a *Review and Evaluation Bulletin*—that daily reading of everyone! None of the fiscal initiatives of the Liberal Government, nor their promissory notes for their predicted victory after September 10, 1987, alter the contours of this logic. The social grammar stays in place, the lexical variation may differ: about a third will leave school without any certification of having been (properly) schooled; about a (generous) third will have some school-based certification; and, a (rather lean) third will gain access to colleges and universities (from whom, that is, some 10 per cent of the total cohort, *maximum*, will obtain a university degree). This is not *our* future, it is *theirs*. Who, whom—indeed![13]

Notes

1 This chapter is dedicated, *in memoriam* to Raymond williams (1921-1988). It is a considerably reduced and revised (October, 1987) version of the chapter which I presented on 2-3 October, 1986. In particular, the theoretical context for my analysis of the key policy document (Ontario Ministry of Education, 1984 b) has been reduced to a few key indications. It is thus important to stress the linkage between this chapter and my other writings on these themes, together with the particular historical-sociological context provided by the work of Bruce Curtis, my work with him, and our joint work with Robert Lanning (e.g., Corrigan and Curtis, 1985; Corrigan, Curtis and Lanning, 1987; Curtis, in press). Finally, I would like to acknowledge the important insights provided for me by graduate students at The Ontario Institute for Studies in Education (OISE) in Toronto.
2 Here I am punning upon the concept of 'discipline(s)' drawn from Foucault, and our more normalized idea of 'The Disciplines' within the academy.
3 Why is it — and should we not be investigating — that at three major centers concerning education (OISE, the Institute of Education of London University, England, and Teachers' College, Columbia University, New York) psychology dominates in the way that it does?
4 In their cognitive, rationalistic critique, much radicalism has simply ignored the affective, symbolic, ritualized and routinized *authority* of the categorization of most people as *bad*, and—'equally'—a few people, as *good*.
5 'More strongly' than in Corrigan (1977 b).
6 I chose this text not only for its extraordinary clarity of assumptions and methods/projects, but because for such an important document — subtitled, *Future Conditions and Strategic Options for the Support of Learning in Ontario* — it has received almost no publicity or public discussion. For a comprehensive analysis of strategic planning see Gorman, 1987, and Kodikara, 1986.
7 Kari Delhi provided this quotation from her forthcoming doctoral dissertation at OISE on the Toronto Home and School Association.
8 The savagely and institutionally racist features of Canadian society continue to shock me — even though I come from England (and being ethnically Irish *know* what that means!). See any issue—yes, *any issue*—of Canadian newspapers for the pervasiveness of *this* social grammar. Thus, for example, it 'turns out' to have been the *routine* practice of 'immigration investigators' to scan court-dockets and then investigate the 'status' of all *foreign-sounding names* (Poirier, 1986; Corrigan, in press-b).
9 This centering of 'the curriculum' (along with 'teacher quality') is another feature of the world-wide re-politicization of schooling, not least in England and Wales where the trinity of public examinations, teacher certification, and inspection had been thought sufficient (previously) to morally regulate curricular content.
10 Significantly, in my experience, this term first occurs in 'Hospital

Management' with dire consequences we are now witnessing around the world.

11 This jocular, avuncular imagery of state forms and procedures is such a friendly figure, but notice the *glissade* from the 'listening and learning' to the 'leading and governing', and notice the last sentence (at least announced as 'belief' and not as fact!). For some years now I have argued to qualify the Benthamite-Foucaultian *Panopticon* views of 'The State'—yes, and it *is* important—that state formation implies a monocular-monopoly of viewing and hearing, but this same set of forms and agencies can be blind and deaf! One has to be 'dressed' (and speak/write) properly to be recognized—just as Mr Speaker recognizes a Member of a Legislature—to be attended to, to be heard. As for learning, yes there is much of this, rarely though from the subordinated populations, much more from 'successes', abroad or in comparable institutions. The *daily* experience of those whose sexuality, colour/ethnicity, language, cultures, styles, manners, beliefs, customs, (i.e., *subjectivities*), differ from the acceptable norm demonstrates the violence within the consensual cosiness which marks out the surface of social democratic nation-states which are, after all, *jurisdictions*, that is, speaking machines for the Law. Fascism begins with categories of pervasive, comfortable normality—above all with 'little men' who can be mesmerized (as Reich called it) into the promise of a larger future. I am not alone in being horrified by the pervasive mesmerization of the verities offered by monetarism; their promised land holds promise for a few (however many statistically) in terms only of a denial of the many, of the Other—whether a distant 'Empire of Evil', or closer, 'dark, shadowy, aliens within'. What if there had been 155 English or French people in the lifeboats off the coast of Newfoundland in 1986? *Or* 155 Irish Catholics from the northern part of Ireland?

12 The significance of work done on 'discursive regimes' becomes clear when we begin to 'read across' texts of the type. Thus, on September 2, 1986, the US Secretary of Education, William J. Bennett, issued an eighty-three page report which outlines the 'social curriculum' for US Elementary Schools. It also argues, like *Towards The Year 2000*, as follows:

> A businessperson who has spent twenty years running a successful firm, a retired Army officer, the head of a government, the publisher of a journal, the director of an art school—all of these should be able to join the pool of prospective elementary school principals, provided they possess requisite personal qualities. (Fiske, 1986, p. A1)

Even in my most satirical (or terrified) I do not think I would be able to provide a script which would create a school principalship for . . . Ronald Reagan, Conrad Black, Paul Godfrey . . . if, that is, we presume them to have the 'requisite personal qualities'.

13 The first secular Inspector of Schools in England and Wales, H.S. Tremenheere, one of the gang of four studied in my PhD. thesis (Corrigan, 1977 a), wrote various versions of a book first entitled, *The Political Experience of the Ancients and its bearing upon Modern Times (1852)*, then *The Franchise: A Privilege and not a Right, Proved by the Political Experience of the Ancients* (1865), and then *A Manual of the Principles of Government as set forth by the Authorities*

of Ancient and Modern Times (1882), and, finally as a pamphlet: *How Good Government Grew Up, and How to Preserve It* (1893). Some of the 'new' discourse is very very old, as old as the social relations of which it is 'both symptom and expression'. As well as *First Lessons* (US Office of Education, 1986 a) and *What Works* (US Office of Education, 1986 b), with a preface by R. Reagan, see here *Education for Democracy* (American Federation of Teachers, 1987 a) and *Democracy's Untold Story* (American Federation of Teachers, 1987 b), *plus* two publications of the Ontario Ministry of Education (1986 a, 1986 b), and for 'internationalization', the October issue of *The Plain Truth* ('Education', 1987).

Methodological Alternatives in Curriculum Research

Feminism and the Phenomenology of the Familiar

Madeleine R. Grumet

In the introduction to their text, *Teachers' Lives and Careers*, Ball and Goodson (1985 a) describe the teachers who appear in research studies generated prior to 1960 as 'shadowy figures on the educational landscape' (pp. 6–7). Their shadow metaphor falls as well on the case studies and marxist analyses that focus our attention on teachers' experiences of work in classrooms and schools (Anyon, 1980; Apple, 1982 b; Lortie, 1975; Macdonald, 1980). For the source of light, like human knowledge, is always situated, here or there, rising or setting, or just breaking through as the clouds pass. The figure is never fully illuminated. Light moves through time as well as space, and so clear seeing is burdened with all the limitations of human consciousness, always situated in spatial perspectives and temporal phases. Furthermore, our work, no matter what its form, is not the seeing itself but a picture of the seeing. Some of us become fascinated with our own light equipment, checking our meters, our spots, our kleigs and gels, and we stumble into the diffuse light of our own life worlds like Sartre's actor Kean, who, leaving the deep shadows and brilliant lights of the theatre, is dismayed to find how flat real light is (Sartre, 1954).

So it is the shadow of the experience of teaching that this chapter pursues, hoping that as we catch a glimpse of its distortions and of the ground on which it falls, mingling the human figure with roots, rocks, curbs and stairwells, we will address the relation between what appears and what is hidden in accounts of teaching. I will talk about my ways of reading and interpreting autobiographical accounts of educational experience written by teachers. I worry about the narrative form and interpretive method I use and I tinker with them like a technician.[1] I look through the lens of feminist theory to find shadows flitting across the face of what, given our current ideologies, is visible and thus persuasive. And because so many teachers are women working in the shadows cast by the institutions of the public world and the disciplines of knowledge, I read to draw our life-worlds out of obscurity so we may bring our experience to the patriarchal descriptions that constitute our sense of what it means to know, to nurture, to think, to succeed. Finally, I look through phenomenology to read the intentionality in these texts, seeking meaning not only in story but also in the dance of the body-subject through the pre-reflective landscape nestled in the shadows of the text.

You may have noticed that people wince when a colleague announces an interest in phenomenology. Sometimes they wince because they do not know what the word means and, confusing it with phrenology, they fear a laying-on of hands. Sometimes they wince at the effort of not losing one of its many middle syllables along the way of utterance. But when our colleagues know what the word is they never wince. For a wince is an involuntary expression of pain, a crinkle of vulnerability around the eyes, a fleeting impulse to fold up your face like an accordion. Those in the know rarely wince. Forewarned and defended, they act as if they have nothing to fear and open their eyes and raise their eyebrows as if phenomenology were merely an amusing, if oddly irrelevant, distraction. But they can't fool us. They are terrified, for what phenomenologists do is not only an assault on the methodology of the social sciences; phenomenology displaces the very world that social science addresses. After all, if I designate the ground of my inquiry as the life-world, you can imagine what you're left to work with.

If we are strict constructionists in the tradition of Husserl, we sweep away the work of traditional social science as if it were a heap of leftover assumptions. If we are loose constructionists following Heidegger, we are contemptuous of our colleagues' positivism and display our engaged inquiries as evidence of our superior sensibilities and humanity. No wonder we are not popular.

Lest it sound as if I am describing pretensions that I do not share, let me be clear that this is my story too. When I was in graduate school, social science was the ground against which I located and established my own position. Then I was a strict constructionist, taking delight whenever I could detect one of their assumptions dipping below the hemline of their chi squares. When I tired of playing coroner to their corpses, I too turned to the life-world, quickly loosening my interpretation of the *epoche* so that I could do something with it. So I am arguing that phenomenology originates in acts of negation as we repudiate the methods of social science and of institutional knowledge.

The word *institution* comes from the Latin verb, *instituere*, which means to set up. The root of that verb is the same as the root of stature and state. It is *stare*, meaning to stand. And it is our upright posture, argues Straus (1966), that privileges sight instead of touch, an imposture of rationality that ranks structural abstraction above textured detail as the highest achievement of human cognition. Now as a partial response to the Sphinx who asks: what walks on four legs in the morning, two legs in the afternoon and three legs in the evening, we can, with Oedipus reply that the child is the four-legged creature, close to 'Mother Earth' and to the sensuality of pronecreation.[2] Children, and the women who bear them have never had the status of men, excluded from the institutions, the standards and the state that ensure patriarchal privilege. And as O'Brien (1981) has shown in her critique of political thought, women do not even appear in the theories constructed to deconstruct the institutions, the standards and the state. Only men, according to Hegel and Marx, can attain second nature, the rational culture of the upstanding citizen. That consciousness is achieved through labor, and neither theorist is willing to recognize the work that women contribute to child rearing as real, honest to goodness, social, material labor. This exclusion is supported by Freud, as well, in his assumption that women, less scarred by the desire, castration fear and ultimate identification with power that emerges from the male oedipal crisis, would identify with society only provisionally, failing to develop the collective super ego that brands male consciousness with a 'c' for citizen.

While classic idealism, the Enlightenment, monotheistic traditions of Judeo-Christian thought and Victorian sublimations can all be invoked to explain the limits of these theorists' imagination of female consciousness, it is interesting to note a similar theme in contemporary curriculum theory. Fascinated by the factory and the corporation, the so-called left in curriculum theory faithfully repeated Marx's phallocentrism, identifying the forms and conventions of the public world and of its laboring men as the only significant influences on the development and education of the next generation. Their reproduction story was a story about how factories and corporations and schools come together to make people, a correspondence version of the immaculate conception.[3] Ultimately embarrassed by this masochistic story, the only gesture of resistance they could find to interrupt it was lying down on the job.

Entering the field in the mid-1970s, a grown-up woman filled with the sights and sounds and needs of my three children, I was struck with the absence in theory, research and practice, of the commitments, logic and contradictions that plague female consciousness. It was still the

Sphinx's world of four-legged and two-legged creatures; babies and animals cavorted in it in the morning, men took over in the afternoon. What of the women who cared for the babies, but were neither as up nor as right as their upright men? Like the child, like the wild, women, we are told, are supposed to be context dependent, hugging the horizontal. At what cost did we uphold the curriculum as teachers? Through what repressions did we subordinate our own experience of reproduction of labor, of value, of relation to the institutions, the standards, the state? Accordingly, I was drawn to phenomenology's texture and presence, too short, or bent to appreciate systems theories, the structure of the disciplines, behavioral objectives, or other tall tales that towered over curriculum theory in the 1970s.

Phenomenology took me home and extended the horizons of educational theory to embrace the passion, politics and labor of reproduction. I was not the only one of us to turn to the life-world of the family to understand the child and our own understandings of education. For many of us the family is the place of feeling. There sound and touch compete with sight. Sensual, engaged, caring, it appears to offer us a first nature much richer than the culture of the public world, and we fall to the task of describing it with earnest effort.[4] Because the family is the first nature for all of us, because its politics are threaded through our bodies, separating ourselves from our assumptions about our mothers, our fathers, our own children, our mates is like separating ourselves from breath, from hunger and from sleep. The very act of description is a naming that splits the fusion of intimacy into words for the stranger. And the memory of that primal intimacy is under language, burdened with the weight of loss and the disguises of repression. Douglas (1977) calls this glorification of our lost world 'sentimentalism':

> Sentimentalism is a complex phenomenon. It asserts that the values a society's activity denies are precisely the ones it cherishes; it attempts to deal with the phenomenon of cultural bifurcation of this manipulation of nostalgia. Sentimentalism provides a way to protest a power to which one has already in part capitulated. It is a form of dragging one's heels. (pp. 11–12)

Here is the methodological dilemma this chapter addresses. How do we grasp the life-world of family relations and of reproduction without falling into the sentimentality of the immigrants who can only remember how wonderful everything was in the old country? Tied to the constraints of the phenomena, that which appears to consciousness, how could the phenomenologist cope with false consciousness, specifically with the sentimentalism that so sweetens our sense of reproduction that we can neither discern its ingredients nor metabolize it in our theory?

Now it is reasonable to assume that feminists and phenomenologists share a common project to describe subject-object relations with a clarity that dispells ideology. The phenomenologist is committed to showing how subjectivity and objectivity are reciprocal, constituting both person and world. Phenomenology's search for the ground of knowledge and meaning always leads to reflection on the relation of the knowing subject to the object of consciousness. Feminism's hospitality to object-relations theory is drawn from the understanding that the development of gender is not an isolated process but intrinsically related to and contingent upon the processes of becoming a knowing subject in a particular set of relations filled with desire, need and love. The family should be the obvious place for such studies and we would expect to find phenomenologists and feminists huddled around the kitchen table, but in the last few years we have seen feminists rushing from the family just as phenomenologists were rushing toward it. We have avoided crashing into each other because we have defined our discourses as mutually exclusive. Feminists see phenomenology as naively apolitical and its exclusion of psychoanalytic theory as a refusal to acknowledge desire in the constitution of knowledge, communication and gender. Phenomenologists see feminists as ideological, imposing a political or psychoanalytic determinism on their accounts of 'the things themselves'. We have much to learn from each other. Phenomenology can correct a feminist's temptation to lie to herself about feeling and affiliation in order to deny the constraints of attachment. The feminist can correct the phenomenologist's refusal to remove the veils of repression that psychoanalytic theory have revealed.

For the family, the child, are, finally, like the institution, set ups. The phenomenologist cannot crawl back there on four legs, for it is a romantic fantasy that desires such a recapitulation of wordless intimacy. Nor can we stand on two legs, like an upright anthropologist in the midst of the kitchen, dividing the contents of the refrigerator into the raw and the cooked. The riddle of the Sphinx leaves one more option. What walks on four legs in the morning, two legs in the afternoon and three legs at night? The third leg, like the old man's cane, must mediate the dichotomies that have divided us from our theory and from our experience. It is the old man, softer, wiser, not so upright, who knows like a woman. Women are three-legged creatures, neither baby nor man, we need a dialectical phenomenology that moves back and forth between the world as it appears to us and the world we refuse to see. We need a mediating method that stretches between lived phenomenon and ideology of family life to help us diminish the distance between the private and public poles of our experience. For the world we feel, the world

Re-Interpreting Curriculum Research

we remember, is also the world we make up. The place that is familiar can be the place where we are most lost. That is what Emily Dickinson understood in this letter written in the spring of 1883 soon after the death of her mother:

> Dear Friend,
> ... All is faint indeed without our vanished mother, who achieved in sweetness what she lost in strength, though grief of wonder at her fate makes the winter short, and each night I reach finds my lungs more breathless, seeking what it means...
>
> Fashioning what she is,
> Fathoming what she was,
> We deem we dream —
> And that dissolves the days
> Through which existence strays
> Homeless at home.
>
> (Dickinson, 1883, cited in Olson, 1984, p.231)

The text

Existence strays through three autobiographical accounts written by this teacher, Jane McCabe.[5] She has been asked to provide three narratives of events of moments in her life that she associates with the phrase educational experience. We have read Didion's essay, 'On Keeping a Notebook', (1961) together and have taken her distinction between *what happened* and *what it means to me* as the space that these stories will fill. Fidelity rather than truth is the measure of these tales. But fidelity does not imply being faithful to a continuous and consistent ego identity. Earle (1972) urges us to think of the composing ego as an index rather than an identity. The I of autobiographical consciousness, he tells us, is an index to a subjectivity that is always open to new possibilities of expression and realization . The I is the location of a stream of possibilities. So there is no search for the hypostasizing and romantic ego themes of the 1960s, no genuine, authentic, real, deep-down selves we seek in these texts. Altieri (1981) celebrates this repudiation of idealism in Nietzsche who pursues it through autobiographical narratives constructed to repudiate idealizations that excuse us from responsibility for the sense we make of ourselves, our work, our world:

> Thus traditional philosophy can be seen as a willful attempt to posit a principle of authority which one then appears to discover as an objective principle for controlling the will. If this situation is to be even partially changed, the philosopher must turn from

> truth to truthfulness. Truthfulness provides an immediate state of personal expression. Thus it affords a measure of the relation between thinking and existential conditions because it tests the powers ideas confer for living a certain kind of life. Philosophy, and autobiography, must prove their worth as forms of power. And one basic index of power is how fully one can consciously 'become what one is' — Nietszche's subtitle — precisely by avoiding the delusions of ideal truths and noble rational selves in pursuit of those truths. To the extent that fantasies of power go unacknowledged or get denied on unspecified methodological grounds, ideas of reason are the most pernicious enemy to true thinking and to the possibility of people taking responsibility for themselves. By pursuing ideals one stages oneself as what one is not. (p. 394)

If subjectivity is invited to be both multiple, varied and still coherent, objectivity as well, that which is related to, yet other than, consciousness, is also fluid. Categorical meanings are suspended wherever possible in the composing process, for we are not seeking an illustration of our categories but the dialectical interplay of our experience in the world and our ways of thinking about it. In this way the literary narrative that is autobiography resembles the social event that is curriculum: both function as mediating forms that gather the categorical and the accidental, the anticipated and the unexpected, the individual and the collective. The gap, or error, or surprise that erupts in the midst of the well-made text is what deconstructionists seek, not to embarrass the author of the *erratum*, but to demonstrate that the power of the person, the text, the meaning is spurious when we impute to it an utterly consistent, exclusive, bounded and delineated logic.

Separated from the world, from other people and other texts, such meanings whether they emerge as persons or texts can be easily objectified, bound, named, possessed, bought and sold. Their separateness is necessary to their commodification. These days 'teacher thinking' is a hot number. But if the text is to display teacher thinking for the thought of the teacher, for her reflection and interpretation, rather than for someone else's utilization and marketing, then the gaps, the contradictions, the leaks and explosions in the text are invitations to her own self-interpreting and self-determining reading.

It is the ambiguity of self-determination that initiates Jane's first story.

> July, 1980, Sunapee, New Hampshire
>
> Free, white and twenty one! I remember those words my grandfather used implying the world was his oyster. I remember

him as not a very free spirit, but rather a seeker of independence in thought as well as deed. He used to paint lovely free-form birds on the walls of the back room of his farmhouse — always blue and never attached to anything. I invariably glanced at them on my way through the room, taken with their fluidity and the fact that my own grandpa could, would, do such a thing. And, he used to smell of the molasses he sheeted by the panful on the hay in the barn. He sat for hours on the front porch, cool and still.

These reflections were a part of that July day as I sat on the steps of the timeworn cabin by the lake. My youngest son was napping contentedly in the crib which I considered musty and not as clean as I would have wished. I rationalized that clean sheets from home would protect him. My older sons were boating and fishing with their father. Alone at last. Time for me to do just what I pleased. I'd waited for months, expectantly, for this time-warp as I'd plowed through reading groups, P.T.O. meetings, piles of laundry, oil changes, and diaper changes.

The steps smelled of creosote. I wondered if the oily residue would stain my jeans. They were incredibly comfortable and I hoped so. A little stain might allow me to hold fast to this moment in time. Blue jays chattered in the evergreens. I wondered what kind of trees they were. They made a dancing filigree against the warm blue of the sky. I've been told that blue is a cool colour — I felt it to be warm and comfortable. Something rustled in the grasses at my feet. Out of the clear sky came a light plane to land without a bounce. As it motored the length of the lake I remembered another plane years ago in my childhood — a different place and a different time but one with evergreens, water, and quiet.

The undulating waves created by the plane lapped at the stones and caused the old dock to creak and groan. The water was crystalline. The light, disturbed by the movement of the water, was hypnotic dappling the lake bottom brown and gold. The tranquil surface was dimpled by a dandelion parachute as it landed in the water. It soon looked like seaweed swaying to the cadence of the waves. Gradually it rode ripple to the shore. I wondered if that puff of fluff carrying a hope of life would fulfill its destiny or merely rot away. I looked at the pinecones at my feet. What would be their fate? And the spider at my side? And how about the worms hidden in the black dirt in the can on the bottom step? White snow-flakey blotches spread on the top of the dirt — milk my son said the worms needed. They couldn't possibly know their purpose in life unless they were male and female and that was their immediate interest. The confines of a can wouldn't necessarily interfere with that, or are worms hermaphroditic? The quiet was numbing.

I have no idea how long I sat there, quite some time I'm sure, but suddenly a restlessness came about me. I felt compelled to check my somnolent son and scan the horizon for a familiar face. I paced through the cabin, baked gingerbread in a battered and rusted pan, put buttercups on the table in a red and black rimmed glass.

I found myself provoked with myself. I'd been waiting for time for me. Time to sit cool and calm and think out some of the dilemmas of life. I thought nothing through and sought refuge in activity. There I was in perfect contradiction.

Jane chooses the suspended moment to catch her own intentionality at work. The horizons of the narrative stretch into history and zoology as culture and nature are invoked to frame a few moments of thought. The story is framed by labor, her grandfather's and her own. Trying to find her own freedom, the writer recovers the path of her own gaze as she looks from trees to sky, to seaplane, from waves to light to dandelion destiny. The meditation on purpose offers pinecones posterity, spiders serendipity and worms will, a teleological version of nature that abandons her to a question somewhat like Freud's 'what does woman want?' The sensual mapping of the narrative could be read to confirm the first nature of the female. We move from sight, the remembered images of the grandfather's birds, 'free-form', 'never attached to anything', to touch, as detachment surrenders to the wish that the oily residue of the steps will stain her jeans and as the meditations on the telic character of life are displaced by baking gingerbread. 'Earth's the right place for love', Frost (1950) tells us, and she too, it would seem, confirms this position as she moves her eyes from the horizon and returns to care, to making things, to domestic labor, immediate, context specific, perishable. The phenomenological display of the scene as it appears to consciousness invites the collusion of this story with the attribution of field dependence to female consciousness. But this reading of the text is undermined by the idealism of its icon. The bluebird image is shown to be apocryphal by its containment on the farmhouse wall. Oysters are, after all, closed and contained, neatly hinged and locked up tight as a farmhouse on a winter night. And whatever their internal visions of detachment they, like the worms in the can, are somewhat internally attached, for they too are hermaphrodites, changing their sex to provide sperms and eggs in an orgy of self-sufficiency that sustains their isolation. Even free, white

Re-Interpreting Curriculum Research

and twenty-one are all freedoms that rely on a history of exclusion to be perceived. They imply a recent, if not chimerical, evasion of racism, agism and, probably, sexism.

The conclusion of the story portrays her desire for the other. First she checks the sleeping child (for her benefit or his?) and then scans the horizon, she tells us, for a familiar face—husband, children. Sexuality is connection and rather than being a form of dependence and containment it is a form of freedom. The desire for the other is a restlessness that liberates its subject from the oyster shell, the can of worms, the claustrophobic farmhouse and the isolation of idealism's detached meditations. This disassociation of thought and activity, association and independence, desire and strength are the themes in the heterosexual division of gender, themes that are lived by this writer but can be obscured if the reading she receives rushes to the world as it appears.

The second story is a story of teaching. It takes place six years earlier than the first. The order of the stories is established by their writers. I read them accordingly.

Fall, 1974 Colebrook Consolidated School, Colebrook, CT.

> I had substituted in Colebrook School often enjoying this classroom. Two walls of windows, one facing south. The room felt warm. I recall feeling cold in the gym, the hall, or other rooms, but this one always was warm. The bulletin boards were all the same—blue background with children's papers mounted neatly on red. The desks tidily in rows, the room shipshape. It smelled of paste and crayons. I could hear the clock tick away the seconds and the heat bang in the pipes.
>
> This day is different. I am no longer a substitute. Now this is my classroom to share with twenty-one expectant little faces. Last year was my first year of teaching and I survived sixth graders. Now I'm teaching my dream, first grade. Today is my first formal observation. Mrs Burnham will come, impeccably dressed, yellow pad in hand, to sit, observe and write for an hour. Will I measure up? Will the children show growth? Will they be at ease? Will I?
>
> My place will be behind the new half-round table. The table came at my request to provide what I hoped would be face-to-face teaching. Plans in duplicate. Interest centers set—a short vowel tape, beads and pattern cards, Indian vests to make from paper bags, leaf rubbings and boardwork neatly written. If there was more I cannot remember.
>
> The room looks different. The bulletin boards are all different

colors. One has stories, one has artwork, another, an arithmetic project, the last is for the children to decorate for fall. It is a hodgepodge of leaves and seeds and milkweed fluff that drifts around the room. The desks are in groups basically arranged by the children. Would this be acceptable? Too much disorder?

The lessons were going well. The children were busy. Steven turned his chair over which was par for the course. He interrupted to tell me his father was like a teddy bear — all furry, but he had freckles even on his tummy. I caught Mrs Burnham's eye and we smiled. The children went to her to show their work. As I glanced around the room I felt passable.

Paul came to me. He opened his mouth to speak and threw up — all over the half-round table, books, papers, and me. He turned to repeat his illness and there on the floor in the middle of the vomitus were his false teeth. Paul was a very special child. Before I could reach him he had picked up his teeth and fled to the bathroom. I wiped off his shoes. He was cleaner than I. We went to the nurse's office as I bid the others to 'sit tight'. Thank God the nurse was there. I hailed a janitor with a can of sweetly malodorous stuff to throw on the mess. I returned to the moans and groans of twenty youngsters threatening to be sick. I surveyed the room, Mrs Burnham waiting expectantly, and twenty miserable children. I ordered everyone in line. What we all needed was fresh air and exercise, recess.

My evaluator ended up staying all morning. As she started to leave several of the crew felt compelled to gather around her, hugging and begging her to stay. She told them she would count to three and they must let go because she had work to do. In her eyes was unmistakable hope. I was struck with the thought that she didn't know all the answers. She counted. It worked. Her exit was graceful.

I can remember little of what transpired from that recess till noon when I sat at my desk, the class gone to lunch. I still reeked of sickness, my slacks were damp. The art project we had after reading was incomplete — shreds of paper littered the floor. The geraniums bloomed on the windowsill. I was conscious of the clock ticking and the pipes banging. For the first time that I can recall I felt comfortable with teaching. Whatever that morning had been was what teaching was for me — at the point in time.

This narrative celebrates the constructed world. The power to shape, to be the source is announced in every detail of order and design. Coming after the first story where order is suspect and drifting intolerable, this story asserts the second birth that is curriculum. If second nature is designed to provide a collective consensus, the rule, the rationale, the form, then this room is its icon. And so we see our writer turn to it from making gingerbread, from waiting for the men to return from sea. She is the captain of this 'shipshape' room—until Paul vomits. All the divisions so carefully marked and ordered in the classroom as it appears, collapse into this eruption of body, of intimacy into the public space. The half-round table to permit just so much contact disappears as she cleans Paul's shoes. This illusion of the children's separateness, confirmed in the spatial presentation of their expectant faces, sans bodies, sans belches, sans sound, sans everything, collapses as Paul's teeth, his power to bite, to eat, to speak, land at her feet. She finds shelter in the euphemism, 'special child'. It is a convenience that permits her to subordinate her revulsion, her desire to name him, to keep him other. The evaluator can leave. She escapes with a number game. Order regulates her comings and goings. But our writer remains, reeking, damp, and her closing lines repudiate the idealism of her opening scene and the futility of construction in a world that denies intimacy. What teaching was for me becomes a practice mediating first and second nature, a three-legged walk through women's work.

The third story brings us back to 1962 where the body question is her own.

> Spring, 1962 Chardon High School, Chardon, Ohio
>
> I was a high school freshman then, acutely aware of myself, in some ways perhaps as ego centered as a two-year-old and conversely painfully aware of those around me.
>
> That day as I hurried from gym to Latin class I was aware of my hot sweaty body and the fact that I was required to wear my winter coat between the buildings which encompassed the two events. The former was the high school, a yellow brick edifice with brown-red heavy metal double doors. The latter was the same yellow brick double-doored affair but an elementary school into which classes, swelled by the baby boom, necessarily spilled. I was ambivalent about going to the elementary school. My mother taught there and was both a comfort and a vexation. It was a step down but I did enjoy the Latin classes there. They were taught by a young man whom I held in the highest regard. He was learned, demanding and he liked my green tweed, raccoon-collared winter coat. He always wore loafers, white shirts and a tie and preferred browns and greens. I'm sure he was my first love. We were reading Caesar. When I was to return to

rework part of Caesar in a college class I could never see what I had even found palatable about the works.

As I entered the classroom that day perspiration rolled down my back. The collar of my yellow blouse was stuck to my neck. My clothes felt twisted and tight. I resented the fact that gym class ran late and I was the only one who had to change buildings. As a genetic endowment my face has always had the propensity to be very red when I am overheated or embarrassed. That day I could feel my face beaming like Rudolph's nose. The fact that class had begun didn't help. The atmosphere was hushed, books open, heads bent to task. When questioned about my tardiness my excuse was mumbled as I slipped amoeba-like into my chair. I struggled to find my place in the frayed blue Caesar pushing damp hair off my face and searching for a writing utensil. When I was told by the instructor that my face resembled a shiny red Christmas ornament disarray dissolved into total confusion and I was sure red had given way to purple. What was to come next didn't serve to reinforce self-confidence.

As I translated at the board I simply could not remember how to spell January. Did it have an 'r' in it as did February? The chalk dust felt abrasive, the green board, unbounded. Confusion melted into panic. I felt tears smart in my eyes as I retreated to my place. Glenn, seated next to me, whispered that January did not have an 'r' in it and I returned to correct my error. My translated passage stood correct, a breeze drifted through the open side door and the remainder of that class has drifted somewhere into the oblivion of the past.

After class the day seemed balmy as we walked back to the high school. Glenn and I chatted. He conjectured as to why I had put an 'r' in January. We reminisced about a third grade in a red-brick building and a teacher as straight and grey as an elm. She always dressed in grey, always with a white collar or blouse and always smiling. We remembered her reading *Cinnabar the One O'Clock Fox* to us and telling us about a 'rat' in separate and how we would rue the day we misspelled February in January. It was comforting to share those memories and to recall that teacher and to have some possible logical reason for my idiocy at the board.

Ego and body are conflated here, as the writer presents herself as a four-legged creature overwhelmed with sensuality and the shame that accompanies it in the place called school. Her mother's presence in the school is described as a vexation and a comfort. She steps down to the classes taught by the upright man, torn between the past and her desire to repudiate her own body, the body of her mother, the world of her mother for the ghost of this Roman Emperor and his autumnal deputy. Body strains against clothes and finally encompasses all constraints and slips, amoeba-like into her chair. Regression plunges back through the phylum into the shapelessness of primordial life rather than acknowledge the infantile identity of daughter, baby daughter to this mother who teaches in this school. Redness associated with Christmas intensifies the association with infancy as the Christ child, the link between woman, sexuality and the spirituality that subsumes them both is established. Chaos erupts when she cannot spell January. Janus, the first month of the year, marks the beginning and the ending. He is liminal deity, this Janus, two-headed, looking backwards and forwards. Accordingly, Janus is the presiding spirit of gates of doors and we remember that both the high school and the elementary school are double-doored affairs. The phenomenal reading of the story gives us a text of adolescent self-consciousness, infatuation, shame over sexuality. It is enunciated in the taken-for-granted drama of heterosexual attraction, as she is drawn to the young male Latin teacher and comforted by a boy her own age. The relations of women to each other, of girls to their mother to their female teachers is obscured by this reading as it is obscured by our culture and it is feminist theory which returns those relations to this text, to our understanding of the process of engenderization and the differentiation, betrayals, and denials with which it is accomplished.

Does the 'r' in February belong in January? In Latin, *februarius* stands for the feast of purification held on the fifteenth of the month, entailing a ritual involving fire and smoke. Her confusion is accomapnied by redness, by heat. A breeze enters the room once she has corrected the error and February's 'r' is removed from January on Glenn's counsel. Only as they leave the elementary school setting of the Latin lesson and walk back to the high school does the day seem balmy. The cause of the confusion is then identified as another female teacher, 'always dressed in grey, always with a white collar or blouse and always smiling'. This standard bearer of the patriarchy delivers the logical reason by inverting maternal logic, displacing intimacy and the female identification. The feminist reading is not the one that phenomenology discovers. It is under cover. It must be dragged up through associations, etymology, through the denial of human history and human relationship. That is what Lacan and Freud mean when they say that coming to know and coming to be gendered is one and the same process. The differences that mark us as male and female and shape our consciousnesses are patterns extended through our perceptions of the phenomenal world and inscribed in the philosophies, ideologies and pedagogies that constitute our culture. The women who would teach to provide a path to a richer, fuller sense of human possibility and agency must read the shadows of their stories to recover their intentionality. In order to understand our own experiences of teaching we must truly stand under them in those places where the bluebirds never fly.

Notes

1 See, for example, Grumet (1987).
2 This reading of Oedipus is drawn from Griffin's interpretation (1981).
3 'Correspondence' theories were conspicuous in Bowles and Gintis (1976) and Carnoy (1972). Some of the essays in Apple (1982 b) acknowledge the determinism of the 'correspondence' theories and call for less reductive work that grants the complexity of schools and the agency of students and teachers.
4 See Noddings (1984), and the journal, *Phenomenology and Pedagogy,* published by the University of Alberta.
5 I am grateful to Jane McCabe, first for writing these wonderful stories and then for permitting me to translate their wonderful images and cadences into curriculum theory in this reading.

The Persistence of Technical Rationality

John Olson

Technical rationality

The doctrine of technical rationality, as described and critiqued by Schon (1983), suggests that improvement in professional practices is to be based on applied research from which efficient methods can be derived. In particular, the doctrine ignores conflict by assuming consensus about ends and by attending exclusively to means. Examples of the influence of technical rationality are not difficult to document.

The doctrine of technical rationality may be found at work in, for example, the innovative 'packages' schools adopt in order to reform the curriculum. These packages are based on behavioral objectives, teaching styles, mastery learning, thinking skills, or consensus-based adoption. They are the result of social-science research done at educational research institutes. According to the doctrine of technical rationality, these packages are warranted by the research on which they are based. The warranty not only guarantees their efficiency but their worth.

The doctrine is also pervasive in curriculum change, which is often construed as a technical-rational process whereby a central administration decides that this or that way of doing things becomes standard system-wide. Frequently, these changes are stimulated by mandates from government. The work of social scientists, using policy ideas based on what they know about human behavior, is to engineer compliance with policy directives from the system. A classical example of an engineering view of change is the techniques developed in Texas (Hall and Loucks, 1977), which make use of research on the concerns of teachers—especially concerns about one's adequacy as a teacher—to engineer 'high fidelity adoption and implementation of innovation' and measure 'level of use'.

The Persistence of Technical Rationality

Elsewhere (J. Olson, 1984), I have described and critiqued these techniques.

Others have been critical of social-science techniques used to manipulate human action. Schon (1983), for example, notes that contradictory value positions find no expression in these models. In education we can detect this avoidance of important questions in the way that curriculum systematists assign value conflicts to such 'junk' categories as 'needs assessment'. Fay (1975) argues that the real needs of people are ignored because their behavior is treated as determined by environmental or policy factors — the folk are not consulted in the process of making sense of their actions. Contradictions in practice which bedevil teachers are ignored in the policy directives that come from above, especially those that require teachers to change the way they relate to those they teach.

We can say, in short, that the technical-rational view of change takes practice as rational only if it follows procedures which are themselves licenced by scientific knowledge — knowledge of human action construed as a natural science. Only by using scientific knowledge of this kind, it is asserted, can rational action be taken.

Although Schon (1983) offers reasons why reflective practice, which he contrasts with technical rationality, is difficult to accomplish in systems such as schools, he does not deal with the question of why the doctrine of technical rationality itself persists in such systems. The doctrine persists, I will argue, because of the expressive needs of those who espouse it — school administrators most importantly, but teachers as well.

Technical rationality — the belief in science-based professional action — persists in education in spite of its critics. Why is this so? I maintain that taking professional action within the institutions of education is especially hazardous in Goffman's (1962) sense of the term. Hazards are occasions, he says, when reputation is risked.

Take the example of school examinations. As Harré (1979) notes, an examination is a hazard for the student. It is a social event 'the results of which are publically promulgated and which a candidate could fail. He [she] gains respect by passing and risks contempt in failing' (p. 312). Thus hazards have to do with the pursuit of reputation — they are part of the expressive dimension of professional life. Think of the hazards to reputation teachers and administrators face each day; making decisions concerning discipline and dealing with angry parents, for example, are occasions of hazard — they are public, social events where reputation is risked. They are events that matter.

My suggestion is that because the education profession is hazardous in Goffman's expressive sense, teachers find it difficult to pursue a career. But what has technical rationality to do with one's career?

Given the public nature of a career in education and the high risk of challenge to decisions and thus to reputations, it is not surprising that school people persist in their faith in technical rationality. The appeal to technical rationality as a basis of decision making makes action less hazardous. One risks less because if failure occurs the blame can be shared with science itself. 'Look', says the educator, 'I acted on the basis of the best science available. You cannot blame me if things did not come out well; blame the science-based procedures that guided me. On the contrary, I should be applauded for basing my decisions on science — even though those very procedures have led me astray'. It is more important that the procedures be based on science than that they work. The appeal to science allows the professional to off-set the risks of action by evoking the mandate and the mantle of science — of technical rationality. Rather than the 'devil made me do it', 'science made me do it'.

The Question of Reputation

Why do schools persist in grounding the process of change in technical rationality? On the surface, it fits well with the bureaucratic organization of schools in which teachers are reduced to implementers of system plans managed by staff (superintendents, consultants or principals) according to social-scientific methodology. Educational research institutes use knowledge from the social sciences to develop policy positions for government. The teacher is a target of 'top-down' management processes of which the curriculum document from above forms a part.

Such a process is appealing to school systems because of their bureaucratic structure and because of the demands of the public they serve. It is reassuring to say publicly that 'our practices are reliable because they are based on social-science knowledge and created according to scientifically warranted procedures'.

Systems theory, in addition, provides a form of accountability that appeals to budget-conscious politicians. Senior school administrators find that research-based management strategies are similar to the corporate values of important members of the public they serve. The management of apparently uncontroversial, warranted practices through a hierarchical school system gives administrators credibility through association with such practices. It allows them to operate smoothly. Managers are given what appears to be a scientific basis for their work. In a climate of suspicion, managers can claim to possess the necessary skills for improving the system and thus be well-placed when called to account.

The Persistence of Technical Rationality

This argument from efficiency and accountability for the persistence of technical rationality seems on the face of it to be valid. But considering the problems schools have when systems-based packages are installed, it is difficult to understand why they continue to adopt them. Harré (1979) makes much the same point in reference to hospitals:

> Goffman has pointed out the equivocal character of many institutions which at first sight we would describe in an instrumental or practical rhetoric, that is we would describe activities that occur in them as means towards practical ends. For example, a hospital would be described as an institution in which the activities undertaken by the staff and inmates are directed towards the instrumental end: the cure of sickness. But a close examination of such institutions suggests that this rhetoric would be quite insufficient to provide a conceptual system for understanding everything that goes on. (pp. 313-314).

The rhetoric of means and ends is likewise inadequate to understand the persistence of technical rationality in school systems.

Thus, the fundamental question remains—why does technical rationality persist as a basis for change in school systems? To answer this question, we have to look at the expressive dimension of the practice of the administrator. What is the administrator saying about the kind of person he or she is in the role he or she occupies? What risks can be avoided by accepting the doctrine of technical rationality? How does this help pursue a reputation?

By using language which gives his or her position an aura of specialism and of expertise, the administrator is able to convey to others that he or she is now part of the group which manages rather than is managed. It would be quite odd if the administrator did not participate in the culture grounded in technical rationality, given the difficult transition, in a field such as education, from being managed to managing. Whether or not the administrator understands the practical implications of the doctrine, or the science upon which it is based, or whether any of it has any bearing on the tasks that confront him or her, are not the immediate issues—making the transition is.

But beyond that, being able to invoke science in support of one's decision off-sets some of the risks of failure since science has to carry some of the blame if things do not go well.

That the doctrine persists is also evidence of the positive regard in which it is held by all in education. Although teachers are aware that technical-rational policies of their school systems make their life difficult, they think that they themselves are the cause for those difficulties. After all, does not the doctrine guarantee a rational way of doing things? Even sceptical teachers think twice about criticizing the policies and their technical-rational base. The doctrine persists not because it is thrust upon unwilling teachers by school administrators, but because both believe that science-based policies are the only possible ones.

Why should we be concerned about this? The technical-rational doctrine excludes debate about questions of value. For example, what the state has a right to expect of the school system and what those whose task it is to educate have a right to claim, are not settled issues. Competing claims on the school ought to be discussed. But technical rationality does not address these important questions of value. This is the crux of the matter.

Why are these contradictions not more vigorously addressed in public forums? Given the contradictions that exist, perhaps no one wants to face up to them. Thus there is a tacit agreement to avoid them. This is especially likely in systems where state control is great. Yet as states mature their influence in educational matters ought to diminish. Such irony ought to concern school people. But reconstituting the school practice in other than technical-rational terms may not be something school people want to contemplate. That doctrine does not encourage the confrontation of conflicting value positions, given its stress on techniques and assumed consensus.

I do not want to say that those who espouse the doctrine have sinister motives. Those who work in complex systems look for guidance for their actions and for relief from the crippling ambiguity that attends to their work. Indeed, I think that the grounding of change in the doctrine of technical rationality is a well-intentioned effort to deal with the perplexing hazards of schooling.

In short, bureaucratic organization does not serve schools as a framework for confronting issues of conflict, and the doctrine of technical rationality which is well-adapted to this framework, ironically, preserves it by not encouraging the critical analysis of means and ends that schools so much need (MacIntyre, 1981). What can be done?

Going Beyond Technical Rationality

Given the contradictions that the doctrine ignores, how can we continue to rely on it as a basis for improving education and the professional practice the process depends on? Those whose expressive needs are served by it must confront the limitations of technical rationality, the practice that goes with it, and the organization that supports it. While teachers complain that their systems suffer from policies based on technical rationality, they also say that there is no other way of 'improving the system'. Even so, paradoxically, they like neither what they see as the incoherence of the policies, nor the disruption of their professional life that goes with 'improvement'. When I press them on this topic, they say that while they agree with the intent of the improvement being sought, it appears to them that the process is clumsy and dismissive of what they already know about the problems the policy is intended to deal with. In short, they see the 'system' doing things that they consider crude but worthy. They are not alone. The case-literature on change suggests that this is how teachers often perceive innovations — well-intentioned, but much less sophisticated than what they are already doing (Elliott, 1985; Lampert, 1984; Olson, 1982 a).

My own research has brought home to me the power of the expressive dimension of human activity as a way of understanding change in education (Olson, 1982 a; Olson and Russell, 1984; Olson and Eaton, 1986). As was noted earlier, Harré (1979) urges us to look at how we try to influence the way people perceive us — how we conduct ourselves so that people will think well of us.

It can help us to understand the appeal of the doctrine of technical rationality if we keep this part of professional life in mind. Our reputation matters to us. That which might undermine it is a source of great anxiety to us. Working in education is a difficult place to pursue a reputation. There are many hazards in the process of educating and so little faith in the knowledge of those who practice there. Efforts at innovation often increase the hazards.

There are many contradictory pressures to deal with. Wilson's (1962) analysis of the expressive aspects of teaching helps us see why it is so difficult in teaching to present oneself as expert and competent. It is not surprising, in the light of Wilson's analysis of the expressive dimensions of teaching, that teaching is an anxious business. He notes, for example, the diffuseness of the tasks of the educator, the lack of task delimitation, and the lack of assurance that anything is being achieved.

People in education are perplexed by the hazards of their profession, rather than downtrodden by an oppressive system. When people work out from their anxieties to the contradictions in which they find themselves, they leave behind such anxiety-reducing solutions as the doctrine of technical rationality. Schon's (1983) analysis of the 'fear of failure' as a barrier to reflective practice comes to the same conclusion: resistance is a critical issue.

Fay (1975) considers resistance as a major barrier to a critical social science. Wilson (1979), in his analysis of the fantasies of education, also notes the problem of resistance. He observes that people do not want to face up to certain realities about their condition. He says that we often hold competing positions to be true and that: 'men (and women) . . . make deals with various parts of themselves. For fear of going mad they do not always make the best deals' (p. 34). Similarly, Fay (1975) notes:

> A person's ideas about himself[herself] are never merely true or false . . . [nor is he or she] free to accept or simply reject on the basis of rational argument. The reason why this is the case is that these ideas are also ways of coping with the social and natural conditions of life . . . . they make it possible for him[her] to go on living as he[she] does in the situation he[she] lives (p. 89).

Philosophical analysis, as Wilson (1979) suggests, is one way of dealing with unpleasant facts about oneself. By being clear about how we think, we can act more intelligently, and become free of illusions. However, for Fay (1975), this is not enough. Unless conditions change, he argues, people will resist coming to terms with their anxieties and continue to suffer. The conditions themselves have to be dealt with. They have to become the object of a science which considers them as quasi-causes of the madness — analysis of oneself is not enough (Kemmis, 1987). The madness, he argues, is caused by objective external conditions that need to be seen as sources of constraint of which we are often only dimly aware. It is the task of social science, he says, to put an end to suffering by studying those conditions and using that knowledge to help people become well again. Fay's is a medical model — the scientist as healer.

However, I believe Fay moves too quickly away from the nature of the hazards as experienced by people, and away from how they cope both with the world as it is, and also with the anxieties that occur. The contradictions will not go away; people need appropriate ways of dealing with them. How can these contradictions be dealt with? Clearly, attention has to be given the nature of values and purposes and to structural problems — to practical problems of means and ends (MacIntyre, 1981). But besides these questions there is the difficulty of pursuing a career — the difficulty of being a teacher in a world that demands more than can be done.

Perhaps it seems odd to say that anxiety about a career is a problem for change in education, but people fail to do many things they might otherwise do were they not anxious about hazards to their reputation. It is out of such anxiety about reputation, I think, that people resist the insights that could free them from the fantasies they have about how they ought to conduct themselves and about the real nature of the difficulties that face them. These anxieties, I believe, are related to the hazards that threaten careers in education. Until those anxieties are confronted, the doctrine of technical rationality will continue to hold education in its thrall.

Action Research: A Practice in Need of Theory?

Catherine Beattie

A perennial complaint of educators — perhaps especially among those who teach in elementary and secondary schools — is that educational research and post-graduate courses in education are 'impractical'. Theories about the stages in children's cognitive development, or the logical structure of human knowledge, are seen as irrelevant to the pressing problems faced by classroom teachers. In recent years this complaint has been taken seriously by some of the academics who produce the research and create the courses; action research has been embraced by many of them as an attractive and appropriate response.

Action Research

In origin, action research is reasonably respectable. Dating back to the 1940s and developed initially by the social psychologist, Kurt Lewin (1946), it was first employed in the context of social programmes designed to improve conditions among deprived segments of society. At Teachers' College, Columbia, it was promoted by Stephen Corey (1953) as a means of improving the quality of school practice and our knowledge of how to promote learning. From the mid-1950s until the early-1970s action research rather faded from view. During that time it seems to have had exponents among a rather small number of Americans in the social sciences (Kemmis, 1984 a; Sanford, 1984) and in England among researchers involved in social programmes and investigations of human behaviour based at the Tavistock Institute (see, e.g., Rapoport, 1970). Perhaps the main appeal for those academics advocating action research was its

Action Research: A Practice in Need of Theory?

promise that social conditions could be improved at the same time as useful knowledge was generated.

Work carried out in the early-1970s by Lawrence Stenhouse in England, and his advocacy of the 'teacher as researcher', may be seen as the stimulus for a new phase in the life of action research. Developed by such co-workers as John Elliott, it was effectively disseminated through international conferences at the Cambridge Institute of Education. Today, action-research methods are taught in many graduate courses, and used in classrooms under the auspices of educational authorities (e.g., Nottinghamshire). Results are published in *The Action Research Network*, in funded project reports, and in the academic journals of virtually all English-speaking countries. Currently, in Canada, Australia and such European countries as Spain and Austria, action research is being used to improve school practice.

Given this success, as measured by range of 'adoption', one might expect to find an extensive theoretical literature on action research. Yet should one? The first response of action-research advocates might in fact be that the question posed in my chapter's title assumes something which they reject, namely that theory and practice are distinct. It is a primary tenet of action research that practice should be informed by, and be a test of, some idea generated by reflection on what one has observed in the classroom. The planned action may be considered an 'hypothesis embodied'. As the action is carried out, one observes the effects that it has and then reflects upon their significance for the initial hypothesis. In the light of one's results, one devises a new, related action. Thus practice and theory are seen as moments in the process of devising, carrying out, and reflecting upon, intentional actions. We can conceptually divide up the phases in the process. We can even assign responsibility for the phases to different individuals. In the case of education, curriculum developers may decide upon ends and means, and professional evaluators may assess the effects of using them. The teacher may be seen as simply carrying out someone else's intentions, at best modifying means to accommodate unforeseen constraints. Such a division is objectionable from the point of view of the action-research proponent. It is morally unacceptable, practically ineffective, and unlikely to produce genuine or practically useful knowledge at the end. For the teacher's autonomy should be respected; he or she must understand the grounds for a practice if it is to be effective; and the context in which a practice is used inevitably conditions learning outcomes.

Let us take as a definition of action research Rex Gibson's (1986) characterization, recognizing that it is not the only or best one available and certainly would not receive endorsement from *all* of those who style themselves action researchers.[1]

> It is research into their schools and classrooms by teachers who are committed to improving their practice through the process of self-reflection and collaborative action . . . they work out their own solutions to their own (not others') problems, and they employ their own language and concepts rather than those of 'experts'. Action research thus offers to participants the opportunity to gain greater control over their lives. (p. 162)

The significance of such an approach for those who engage in educational research is spelled out by Elliott (1983) when he says of the action-research model of social analysis that it is:

> a view of educational research as a science which aims to improve schooling by helping teachers to test and revise their practical theories. On this view of educational research there is no room for a rigid division of labour between teachers and theorists, and no body of social science theory which can be logically demarcated from the practical theories teachers use to guide their practice. (p. 29)

So it appears that a defining feature of action research is the denial that there is a split, or perhaps better that there should be a split, between practice and theory. But if the theories of concern to teachers are 'practical', does that not imply that there are other sorts of theory? If there are, then have we eliminated the theory-practice gap at one level only to have it re-appear at a higher or more abstract one?

It seems to me that a number of different senses of the word 'theory' are used by action researchers. The result is that everyone can be a theorist. What is obscured is the point that the generality of theory which one devises, the purposes it serves, and the social value it has for the author may be very different. So to respond to the question posed in the title of my chapter one must first specify the sense of theory being considered, and one's place in the knowledge producing-conveying complex.

To answer 'yes' at all is indeed to risk denying that action research has the unique feature which brought it converts—its unification of theory and practice. As Gibson (1986) notes, 'The conception of "theory" at the heart of the action research enterprise is . . . very different from that which has traditionally characterized educational studies . . . . Theory is *in* all practice, is grounded in it' (p. 162). Instead of applying theory from 'outside' to their practice, action research 'encourages teachers to study their own practice, and thus to derive their own theories (hypotheses) about teaching and learning' (p. 162).

What I want to do now is explore the senses of 'theory', the grounds upon which one might say that action research does not need a theory, and the grounds upon which one might say that it does need a theory. Here 'grounds' covers a lot of territory. In the process of this exploration, I hope to exemplify the sort of attitude which so-called critical theory urges us to adopt. Thus although a proponent of action research, far from defending it, I feel obliged to scrutinize it and to seek some awareness of the social and conceptual framework in which I am myself located. As a preview of my answer to the question in this chapter's title, let me say that I believe that action research can be more satisfying as a practice and ultimately more effective in improving education if the people who practice action research generate theories to explain and justify it as a research method and as a means to improve education. If academics are acknowledged to be the only legitimate purveyors of justificatory theories, then action research will likely become as isolated from the practitioner's world as the method and theory which it was designed to supplant (or perhaps less ambitiously, to supplement). On the other hand, one must worry that the production of diverse, possibly contradictory, theories to justify a loosely defined research practice may severely inhibit the development of a body of knowledge, as well as limit social support for action research. May not a promising critical and emancipatory movement then expire from self-inflicted wounds?

Theory

Let me distinguish the varieties of theory which action research might be said to 'need'. I shall set aside the most inclusive sense of theory, where it is in effect equated with reflection on experience. Such loose definitions are often used to confer academic status upon anything that goes beyond minimally interpretive description.

Certainly, some explicit statements to describe action research are needed if a coherent set of practices is to be included within its orbit. Does the definition count as theory? Let's say not, while conceding that the definition will have interpretive and normative aspects and so will embody theoretical commitments. Thus the senses of theory I want to consider fall under the conception of theory as a set of logically related propositions which provide an account of some phenomenon or phenomena. (I include accounts of what theory and theorizing should be like.)

Action research as the study by a teacher of a particular classroom practice and its effects may be said to generate a theory about their relations, or about the effects of a given context on their relations, or about the nature of a pupil's value system, and so on. This, following Glaser and Strauss (1968), could be described as a substantive, grounded theory. But when we move to a more general level, and attempt to relate a number of case studies, then it seems we are theorizing in a way that involves new concepts and generalizations of a different order. Again following Glaser and Strauss, one might call these grounded formal theories. Thus if someone puts together recurrent themes from a variety of case studies on enquiry learning and introduces new concepts and principles to link them in certain ways, then a formal theory results. At a yet more abstract level, one might try to link, say, school practices and those of hospitals and prisons. Ultimately, 'grand' theories about society may be formulated. For Glaser and Strauss, these embody views about how society should be organized and are, they charge, usually divorced from the theories grounded in the systematic study of phenomena. All these theories are explanatory and descriptive and, depending upon one's epistemology, may be held to possess some normative elements.

But there is another level of theorizing. What one says about the character and purpose of the theories takes us into a different level or category, to meta-theory, to a theory of knowledge and perhaps into more comprehensive 'grand theory'.

Now the theories and the meta-theory do and presumably should influence each other. The practice of studying classrooms may have some loose rules to it and some procedures. But how it is conceived and the nature of the results construed, will influence the practising researcher, for example in identifying something as a 'problem'. In saying this, I am of course speaking from a standpoint, basically that of the so-called critical theorist. If I took a positivist position as my meta-theory then the phenomena could be studied *per se*, my results uncontaminated by my values and context. The other alternative would be interpretive. On this meta-theory I would try to portray the phenomena as seen by the participants, acknowledging that some slant of my own was involved.

Thus meta-theories give an account of knowledge, of what it is and how it is acquired. This has implications for the methods of social science that are judged defensible. And, of course, the account of knowledge will determine what one can legitimately assert. In the case of positivists, for example, ostensibly only factual statements that can be verified through experience qualify.

In what sense or senses, if at all, does action research 'need' any of these sorts of theory?

Action Research: A Practice in Need of Theory?

Why Action Research Needs Theory

If we are concerned to build up an inter-subjectively meaningful body of knowledge about classrooms then it would seem that we need substantive theories and formal theories. Teachers, as they now tend to conceive of themselves and as they are viewed by others, are in need of substantive theory and can produce it on the action-research model. Indeed they have done so (see, e.g., Kemmis, 1984 a). Formal theory might be the result of a research project involving a group of teachers working upon related problems. Those academics who work with teachers engaged in such work may 'need' theories of this sort as tangible products of their research effort.

We can say that a meta-theory is 'needed' if a practice such as action research is to be understood and rationally assessed. There is, shall we say, a logical need for a meta-theory.

But there is also, I would contend, a very practical need for meta-theory, if one is an academic. To obtain funding for research one must satisfy a rather conservative group of fellow academics that one's research is academically respectable. As a class, academics have to justify their salaries and their status. They have a common interest in claiming special capacities and skills. Maintaining 'standards' and controlling admission is essential to survival. Theoretical reflection and theory construction are our special preserve. It seems to me that to a great extent the felt need for a theory of action research is a function of one's social location. However, to be consistent, the action-research proponent, and most especially one who embraces the basic tenets of critical theory, should require that the meta-theory be generated by teachers reflecting on their practice. This does not seem to have happened. What we have is academics producing meta-theories and formal theories while practitioners generally limit themselves to developing substantive theory at best.

This state of affairs is hardly surprising, given the division of labour within the educational structure. After all, classroom teachers are expected to direct lessons for most of the day and to perform many administrative tasks after the school day is over. Academics do have the time, and indeed are expected to produce theories. The irony in the case of action research is that in promoting it as the way to conduct educational research, academics may be implicitly or explicitly recommending that they be made redundant.

Nevertheless, the demands of logic and the course of events in the social world rarely coincide. The meta-theory which has been offered to action researchers comes from academics. And the theory has been attached to the practice in a rather *ad hoc* fashion. Kemmis describes critical theory as 'so abstract as to defy practical implementation in participatory educational research' (Kemmis, 1984 a, p. 20) and yet useful to 'underpin' the methods of action research. For whom is it 'useful'? Given that before he and Carr produced their book *Becoming Critical* (Carr and Kemmis, 1983) action research had been conducted for over thirty years, it seems clear that practitioners did not experience any compelling need for their meta-theory. Particular individuals with a philosophical bent may well have pushed the questions raised by action research to the point of asking how it could, as a method, be justified. But such reflections apparently never produced a systematic theory.

In justifying the effort to 'underpin' action research, Kemmis (1984 a) notes that Lewin's view of knowledge was an inadequate base, and that an antidote was needed to what Kemmis describes as 'technical rhetoric which permitted the retrogressive reinterpretation of action research' (p. 21). He acknowledges that critical theory is not necessary to *do* action research for he states that 'action research provides a simple, practicable guiding image for *doing* critical social science which theoretical accounts have so far failed to furnish' (p. 21). It seems then that action research as a method is an instance that vindicates and illuminates a meta-theory. Critical theory is to be seen as a theory in need of a practice and action research is one which fills the bill. This hardly seems the sort of basis for connecting theory and practice which a proponent of action research should endorse.

My own initial reaction to the book of Carr and Kemmis (1983) was very favourable. Here was a carefully worked out philosophical justification for a method that appealed greatly to my liberal democratic sentiments. On reflection, however, it seemed to me that many alternative defenses might be advanced. Further, Carr and Kemmis seemed very dogmatic about what action research should be, strangely so, given their exhortation to 'be critical'. This facet of their book was a central concern of one reviewer (Gibson, 1985). As he put it, 'Maybe the first principle of a critical approach should be "no gods"' (p. 63). Yet if we have no gods and push critical questions it seems that we get into an infinite regress. Such a regress can only be stopped by asserting that justificatory demands must cease at a given point — theorizing in a sense must be halted. In the case of action research we can ask for a justification of the particular results, of formal theory, and ultimately of the meta-theory that is supposed to explain and justify the method as such. Critical theory can be used as a meta-theory which itself is justified if it 'works'. This is the terminus. Loosely stated in Habermas' terms (1970, 1979), if people on a more or less equal footing can explore an issue and reach agreement about what constitutes appropriate and just action, then rationally defensible and morally acceptable decisions have been made and can be acted upon. For Carr and Kemmis, as well as for Gibson, critical theory can serve to emancipate teachers and improve educational research. Action research can be viewed as a method that is an instance of this theory in practice. Perhaps we can say that if action research is to realize its promise as a means of improving people's control over decisions which affect their lives, then it needs critical theory as its justification. Alternative meta-theories may direct attention to much more limited goals or to goals that do not challenge the instrumental bias of educational research as traditionally conceived.

Why Action Research Does Not Need Theory

The arguments I want to consider here are those which might be advanced against the view that action research needs to produce theories about educational phenomena and needs a meta-theory to legitimate the method and its results.

The claim that action research should produce educational theory rests upon the assumption that one wants to produce generalizations which can be applied in many contexts. This assumption can be challenged on at least two counts. First, it may be argued that each classroom situation is so different from every other that the goal of providing tight or even loose causal laws is unachievable. Secondly, it can be argued that a key factor in classroom decision-making is the judgment of a teacher about the nature of a given situation, and the weighting to be given to what are judged relevant considerations.

In view of these points the pursuit of personal practical knowledge as opposed to 'scientific' knowledge may be judged the distinctly educational knowledge which teachers need. Now it is just this knowledge which action research is supposed to provide. The goal is quite different from that of traditional research. Whether one wants to go so far as Carr and Kemmis, and in effect claim that only action research qualifies as educational research is another matter. More modestly, one can hold that action research promotes a heightened awareness and sensitivity on the part of the teacher. As a result of this a topic may emerge for study, and an improved understanding of the topic will be the consequence of observation and reflection. The final outcome of research will be an altered understanding and a decision on how to act — that is, informed practice.

Clearly such a process can be reported upon by the teacher and the report can be shared with others. But the whole process may be thwarted if an objectively testable theory is seen as the ultimate point of the practice.

Thus one might complain that the push for educational theory as an outcome of action research is based upon a misconception of the nature of social science and the proper function of educational research. To quote Kemmis (1984 a) on the results to date, 'action research projects . . . add up, not to systematic theory or uniform practice, but to the development of a critical perspective' (p. 6). Neither substantive nor formal theory *need* be the outcome of legitimate action research.

Why oppose the development of meta-theory to explain and justify action research? There is an obvious danger in appropriating a meta-theory developed quite independently of the practice it is supposed to 'underpin', and without the participation of those who are supposed to be the beneficiaries of it. Carr and Kemmis have tried to justify action research as an instance or example of a practice which embodies the critical theory of Habermas. Although not so fully worked out, Elliott (1983) has proposed Gadamer's (1975) conception of knowledge as a better underpinning. In each case, it seems that the political convictions and the preferred research styles of these academics may have drawn them to different meta-theories. The suspicion arises that an attempt is being made to steer the practice of action research. Yet is this not to violate its basic commitment to practitioner control over research questions, purposes and methods?

Meta-theory construction may be seen as representing a move that re-introduces the split between practice and theory, practitioner and academic researcher, practical knowledge and theoretical knowledge. It may not underpin but rather undermine the practice it is supposed to justify and legitimate.

Conclusion

So we return to the issue of what counts as educational research and the question of how to ensure that such research is 'practical'. Just as specific groups have tried to secure a place on the curriculum for 'their' subject (Goodson, 1983 a), so many academics who advocate the use of action research want respectability for their enterprise within the research community. That means that a 'properly' theoretical body of knowledge is needed as a product, and a respectable meta-theory wanted to justify the method and its results. Yet this means that the aims of action research will be removed from the practical concerns of teachers who wish to solve specific problems in their classrooms. Can the quite different needs of the two groups be reconciled without destroying their common central aspiration improvements in classroom practice?

At a recent conference which I attended on enquiry-based, award-bearing courses for teachers, a quite heated debate broke out over the apparent isolation of academics from classroom life and the hypocrisy of their claim to allow graduate students to formulate and pursue what *they* see as problems. At one point the issue was couched in terms of the 'ownership of knowledge', and it was suggested that academics were not prepared to surrender any territory. Carr and Kemmis (1983) project an image of emancipated teachers who go on to free other members of society from the thrall of false ideologies. Yet if they are to be consistent, they must argue that teachers themselves should decide just what their research projects should be and *what ends they should serve*. It must be open to teachers even to reject critical theory as the road to enlightenment and action research as the best means of improving schools and society.

To argue for theories to explain educational phenomena as the proper outcome of action research would be to shift the emphasis of such research from a process to enhance practitioner understanding and control, to a method for producing a questionable product, 'scientific' knowledge. Meta-theories proposed to date are academic products designed for other academics. Teacher researchers should produce their own.

Perhaps action research really *needs* only one theory from academics. That would be one which explains how an emancipatory practitioner-controlled research style can be sustained in hierarchical institutions in which power is lodged at the top.

Notes

1 Some alternative definitions are the following:

Action research aims to contribute *both* to the practical concerns of people in an immediate problematic situation and to the goals of social science by joint collaboration within a mutually acceptable ethical framework (Rapoport, 1970, p. 499).

The research reported in the following pages was initiated, conducted and disseminated *from the inside*. It represents a tradition of systematic enquiry, by means of which teachers are able to communicate to colleagues and other interested parties insights culled from their classrooms, and to use these insights in such a way as to improve their own teaching (Nixon, 1981, p. 5).

The (Ford Teaching) project is an excellent example of teachers adopting a research and development stance to their work and of the development of a researcher role which supports such a stance (Stenhouse, 1975, p. 163).

In my view what is now called *educational action research* constitutes the concrete expression of a reconstructed interpretive paradigm with respect to the study of schooling. The action-research model of educational enquiry was, to my knowledge, first articulated in the UK by Lawrence Stenhouse in connection with The Schools Council Humanities Project (Elliott, 1983, p. 22).

Re-Interpreting Curriculum Research

Action research is a form of self-reflective enquiry undertaken by participants in social (including educational) situations in order to improve the rationality and justice of (a) their own social or educational practices (b) their understanding of these practices, and (c) the situations in which these practices are carried out (Carr & Kemmis, 1983, p. 152).

Evaluation as Subversive Educational Activity

Joel Weiss

Introduction

The major purpose of this chapter is to examine how 'evaluation' as a form of enquiry can be educative, not only for the objects of enquiry and the stakeholders, but especially for the evaluators as well. By 'educative' I mean creating the conditions for questioning what is, or might be, taken for granted. To my mind that is synonymous with what it means to subvert, to turn from beneath. Perhaps by exposing some of the roots of evaluation, healthier stock may emerge.

Although the focus of this chapter is evaluation, 'research' is, at times, used interchangeably with 'evaluation'. Both are forms of disciplined enquiry (Cronbach and Suppes, 1969) — the differences lie in the distinctions between activity which is decision-oriented to determine worth (evaluation), and that which is conclusion-oriented to generate new knowledge (research). Research on policy matters is often used synonymously with evaluation, and is referred to as policy research or evaluation research. Since I mostly refer to program evaluation, it will be assumed that policy research and evaluation research are included.

The Field of Evaluation

The professionalization of the field of evaluation is virtually complete. Over the last decade-and-a-half there has been an explosion of writings on evaluation in education, and other social policy areas. A plethora of books, journals, handbooks, newsletters, encyclopedias and primers are readily available which offer a veritable smorgasbord of models, strategies, techniques and practical hints. The distillation of much of this material would lead a reader to believe that special languages have developed within the field, a criterion that some sociologists consider as necessary for the emergence of a profession. Another indicator of professionalism is the emergence of professional organizations, and evaluation can claim several in its behalf (e.g., Canadian Evaluation Research Society, American Evaluation Association). And perhaps the field is coming closer to meeting the necessary *and* sufficient criterion of controlling membership into the profession. A number of universities have developed programs in evaluation, although as yet no formal requirements exist as to what credentials are appropriate to 'ply the trade'. As to maintaining control of practising evaluators, several examples already exist of 'standards' for conducting evaluation studies (e.g., Evaluation Research Society, 1982; Joint Committee, 1981). Again, no legal mandate exists for implementation, but moral persuasion has been attached to these efforts.

Evaluators are found in just about every nook and cranny of social services agencies, government offices, university towers, and business establishments, as well as in consulting firms. In Ontario, most of the larger school boards have research officers who spend time in evaluation activities. Evaluation has become 'respectable', and researchers have become members of the 'establishment'. Nevertheless, despite an abundance of intellectual ferment and resources, evaluation has probably not appreciably improved the quality of our lives.

There are several possible explanations for this state of affairs. First, while we may believe that evaluation is an indispensable ingredient in policy-making, in fact it is but one of many ingredients. Other factors such as inertia, lack of viable alternatives, paucity of financial and human resources, change in political agendas may be more than equal as potential influences.

A second reason why evaluations may not be successful is the potential discrepancy between 'who calls the tune' and who is 'doing the dancing'– between program sponsor and program participant. How often do evaluators gain a perspective on the 'lived experiences' of those who are most involved in the program? Since the initial contact for the evaluator is with program sponsors or administrators, it is usually their agenda that dominates the evaluation. It would not be surprising if those who control the evaluation have a vested interest in preserving the *status quo* (e.g., program or organizational structure); thus, there is no guarantee that other voices will be heard. In addition, traditional evaluation reports seldom render those 'lived experiences' in a way that enables those who are most involved to gain access to these experiences, i.e., provide a context for individuals to reflect upon their circumstances, to question the 'taken-for-granted'. Such a process of interrogating experience may include an understanding of the way things are, why they have come to be that way, the limits for change, and what opportunities can be taken to make things otherwise.

A third reason for evaluation's questionable track record is that professional evaluators usually do not question what is 'taken-for-granted' about their own work. This is not surprising, since many evaluation reports are written without any 'persona', as if evaluation was a surreptitious activity. Often, the only information offered is a brief summary of the evaluator's credentials; what may be missing is more extensive information offered about the history of the evaluation, including details of how the evaluator may be involved in the institutional social relations of the commissioning agency. Part of that story might be understood if evaluators provide information about their own underlying ideological, epistemological and ethical concerns. Without such information, we may only guess at how the evaluation's apparatus for knowledge production, especially with a technical emphasis, may reify the existing social relations of that which is being evaluated.

Let me suggest a few possible situations (albeit hypothetical) that illustrate these relationships. How many evaluators employed by a government agency dare to question the power structure underlying the social relations of those who govern and those who are governed? What is the likelihood of a private consultant with fixed overhead costs trying to suggest that the outcomes of a firm's policy is to contribute to a pernicious form of social injustice? There are, no doubt, situations in which evaluators might raise such questions, especially those who have the luxury of working within the university setting. But to suggest that the 'academy' is not also meshed in institutional and societal relationships that may severely restrict such activity would be a misunderstanding of the history of universities.

It is not just a question of where the paycheck is coming from, but also a question of the personal histories of evaluators and the forms of evaluation available to them. Underlying method are ways of 'asking questions which assume an underlying set of assumptions, a structure of relevance, and a form of rationality' (Simon and Dippo, n.d., p. 1). The way that evaluators are trained (and by whom) is an important factor in understanding their actions. Most evaluators, for example, do not take courses in social philosophy.

Recent Changes

All may not be doom and gloom. There are several recent trends which have opened up our views on enquiry in general and evaluation in particular. These trends provide alternative scenarios for evaluation. First, there has been a movement away from the traditional positivist epistemology to other paradigms, especially those of the qualitative variety (Eisner, 1979; Guba and Lincoln, 1981; Lincoln and Guba, 1986; Stake, 1978; Willis, 1978). The extent of the shift may be seen in the diversity of metaphors for evaluation, such as evaluation as art criticism, law, journalism, folk singing, literary and film criticism and water-colour painting (Smith, 1981). In large measure, these approaches represent an epistemological change from scientific verification of a predictable world to understanding through personal interpretation.

A second trend in the questioning of our traditional views of educational enquiry has been a shift in responsibility for enquiry from experts (i.e., professional researchers and evaluators) to practitioners. The resuscitation of the action-research movement so prominent forty years ago, by Stenhouse (1975), Kemmis (1984 b), and others, and the distinctions between 'insider' evaluation and 'outsider' evaluation made by McCormick and James (1983), have given some legitimacy to the notion that practitioners have sufficient expertise to conduct enquiries in their own settings. In consequence, the question has shifted from 'what knowledge'? to 'whose knowledge'?

A third trend in the recent literature is to view enquiry as an educational process — a recognition that knowledge generation is a complex pedagogical process. The explicit delineation of the educator role is only a recent phenomenon. Wise (1980) argues that evaluators ought to be viewed as educators since they function educationally, 'first, in the extent to which the evaluator encourages in the client an openness to new understanding; secondly, by sharing the special knowledge that the evaluator comes to possess about the program being evaluated' (p. 12). Others have also pointed to this role for evaluators. Cronbach and Associates (1980) make this very explicit: 'The evaluator is an educator, his success is to be judged by what others learn' (p. 11). Guba and Lincoln (1981) suggest that one of the four purposes of case-study research is 'to teach, that is, to provide with knowledge, or to instruct' (p. 371). I will elaborate upon the curricular and instructional possibilities for evaluation in a later section.

A somewhat different orientation for viewing enquiry as educational activity comes from the body of thought that is known variously as the Frankfurt School or critical theory. Briefly, it numbers among its important features the notion that research should be viewed and conducted as emancipatory activity, emancipatory in allowing individuals to understand how particular features of their life are embedded within a system of social relations in which resources and power may be inequitably distributed. Within this perspective, research is seen as a way of questioning the 'taken-for-granted' in a way that not only looks at limitations, but also at the possibilities for change. Lather has addressed this as 'research as praxis' (1986 a), and provides useful insights in her suggestions for conducting 'openly ideological research' (1986 b). Research concerned with critiquing current practice and developing a more just society must be conducted by individuals engaged in a useful critique of their own research practices.

Is it reasonable to expect that the field of evaluation can extricate itself from the kinds of entanglements that I have described, that evaluators can change the circumstances in which they work? Evaluators, it must be stressed, are limited in making major changes to a system of social relations in which power is unevenly distributed. It would take great courage for them to jeopardize their economic, social, and even political positions to bring about such change. It is equally true that most evaluators see little reason for making those changes. In light of the gulf between my indictment of evaluation and my perception that most of the practitioners see the world differently, I do not expect ready converts.

However, some thought is being given to making evaluators aware of their pedagogical responsibilities toward themselves, their work, and those whose lives are affected by such work. The remainder of this chapter will briefly sketch some of this thought by beginning with a general framework for evaluation as an educational activity and then moving to more radical ideas about enquiry and emancipation. Concluding remarks will take the form of a suggested educational agenda for evaluators.

Evaluation as Education

Earlier I pointed to the trend toward viewing enquiry as an educational process. Here I would like to elaborate on looking at evaluation in curricular and pedagogical ways and some implications for evaluators and the field.

I find it helpful to view evaluation as education within a set of widely used curriculum commonplaces. A minimum set of terms for defining curriculum includes the 'learner', 'the teacher', the 'subject matter', and the 'milieu' within which these components function. For our purposes, the learner may be seen as the audience(s) for the evaluation—including participants in the evaluation as well as the recipients of reports. The evaluator may be viewed in the pedagogical role of the teacher, with all that the term implies when interacting with adult learners. Subject matter includes all the types of information made available, whether through personal interactions between teacher and learner or through more formally developed curricular materials in the form of reports, tables, graphs, tests and the like. The milieu represents the variety of conditions under which learner, teacher and subject matter interact. This includes those historical forces that helped to shape the context for the evaluation as well as the specific conditions under which the evaluation is conducted.

This set of commonplaces can be seen as a generative metaphor — what Schon (1979) defines as a pervasive, tacit image that influences our thinking about policy. Ideally, one may imagine policy being changed through educational means, with evaluators involved in pedagogy and curriculum-making. The conception of evaluator-as-teacher is one which sees her as a co-learner, one willing to learn as well as instruct — that is, participating in the learning process by being open to new experiences, and altering conditions for learning as a result of continuing appraisal and reappraisal of circumstances. A model of one view of the evaluator-as-educator might be found in either Stake's responsive evaluator (1976) or Parlett and Hamilton's illuminative evaluator (1976). These approaches are very clear about the importance of the stakeholder's agenda, and therefore the reality may not necessarily be marked change in policy.

Evaluation can be seen as curricular in a number of respects. First, both curriculum and evaluation are concerned with uncertain practical problems, i.e., those problems whose answers do not depend upon procedural solutions. Secondly, evaluation can also be seen as a practical field in its emphasis on complex means/end dialogue. Thirdly, each field involves processes of valuing — judgments are made about what to pay attention to and why. Fourthly, both fields are engaged in curriculum development — curriculum workers with materials, modules, texts, lessons, and evaluators with reports, mostly written for particular audiences. Finally, such curricular products represent a paper curriculum (i.e., intended curriculum) for learners to interact with. Unlike curriculum materials, the production of final reports typically signify the end of an evaluation. But in both cases it is difficult to know how such curriculum materials are used. Just as teachers use materials in ways different from developers' intentions, so do readers have different ways of using evaluation reports.

Reporting on evaluation endeavours as an occasion for educating poses difficulties in communication similar to problems arising in teaching any form of knowledge. Buchmann (n.d.) has concerned herself with some of these issues in focusing on research reporting as an occasion for teaching. She identifies three conditions that research communication has to meet: access, belief and impact. Access is perhaps the easiest to understand, since without it material remains 'closed territory' to readers. We are starting to pay attention to such matters as form, style of writing and language. But we need to learn from other fields (e.g., semiotics) and conduct research ourselves in order to understand why readers are attracted to certain formats.

All writers wish to engender 'belief' in our audience. However, an even greater problem than having something read without being believed is to have a work believed but not understood. The problem with credibility in evaluation is that often it is associated with a particular form of a report or the status of the evaluator, i.e., belief granted rather than earned. To the extent that evaluation reports which look scientific are perceived as having cultural capital, then understanding may have become secondary. Often, the best pedagogy is that which is unsettling; but how many people enjoy being unsettled by encountering the questioning of warranted claims, either their's or the evaluators'?

So far, the argument has focused upon professional evaluators, those who might be considered 'outsider' evaluators: but what about those practitioners who do evaluation precisely because they are educators attempting to do evaluation in their pedagogical settings. I refer to such individuals as educators-as-evaluators, although at times they may be seen by others as 'insider' evaluators. According to Grundy (1982) the minimal requirements for action research are: (a) the project takes as its subject-matter a social practice, regarding it as a strategic action susceptible for improvement; (b) the project proceeds through a spiral of circles of planning, acting, observing and reflecting, with each of these activities being systematically and self-critically implemented and interrelated; and (c) the project involves those responsible for the practice in each of the moments of the activity, widening participation in the project gradually to include others affected by the practice and maintaining collaborative control of the process (p. 23).

Within these necessary and sufficient conditions for such enquiry lies the possibility of pedagogical moments, from self-reflection to gradually educating others as the sphere of influence is widened. Grundy (1982) goes further by positing three modes of action research, 'technical', 'practical', and 'emancipatory', which correspond to the instrumental, pluralist-intuitionist, and critical-emancipatory approaches to evaluation. This conceptual device is useful in looking at what actually happens during an action-oriented enquiry, especially as it may change from one orientation to another as it evolves.

We need to study how educators perform as both evaluators and practitioners. McAlpine (1985), for example, used retrospective accounts of her own action-research enquiry. Several issues, in the form of tensions, came out of her interpretation: tension between action and reflection; between job as practitioner and role of evaluator; between practical and formal knowledge; between conception and reality; among the relationships of the curricular commonplaces of teacher, learner, subject matter and milieu; and between practical knowledge of evaluation and formal knowledge of evaluation. I believe that much can be learned about pedagogical and curricular beliefs and the actions of practitioners in evaluation situations that would be of importance to those who see their role as professional evaluators.

Other enquiries (Harvey, 1981; Mansfield, 1984; Wideman, 1981) have studied how individuals (learners) interact with the text of the evaluation and sometimes with the evaluator-as-educator. The field of evaluation is starting to pay attention to effects of text on readers. Stake (1984) has written passionately about naturalistic generalization and case-study reports. So we are starting to communicate about communication. But is it enough for us to know how people might interpret unless we know about what interpretations we are communicating to others? Evaluators create text in what they choose to look at, the language they use, and the way in which they interact with people. How do evaluators come to know about this text and its origins and influences? What was missing for me was the element of power — that reinforced by, created by and addressed by evaluators. How do we come to understand the power of evaluation in any situation? How can evaluation be used to look at the subtext of experiences?

Critical Ethnography

The analysis of social relationships as part of the enquiries we conduct is hardly an original idea. A large body of writings has accumulated which define and elaborate a critical perspective. A few, such as Apple in the US and Lundgren and Kallos in Sweden, were among the earliest to provide a critique of evaluation practices. In a critical-emancipatory approach to evaluation, Apple (1980) suggests that evaluators should situate their efforts within an evaluation of the relationships that an institution (such as a school) has with other institutions, as a means of unpacking latent commitments, e.g., at work and school. They should start from a theory of social relations which is distinctly non-liberal in orientation, and which at heart, questions 'who benefits most from our social, cultural and economic arrangements' (House, 1980). The method used is a form of ethnography that interrogates the social reality of schools to find out how sets of institutional relationships are constituted in everyday lives, and to look for contradictory elements, especially those which demonstrate resistance to a reproductive apparatus. The outcome of such study should be an understanding of power relationships and the emancipatory possibilities inherent in knowledge of not only how individuals are implicated in what happens to them but also the possible forms that personal agency might take.

Apple uses Willis' well-known *Learning to Labour* (1977) as an example of the kind of ethnography that evaluation should consider. Willis' work is seminal, in part because it serves as a useful model of critical ethnography, of which one element is the production of accounts that help readers to deconstruct the very social practices being studied. If this criterion is to be taken seriously then it is not enough to write reports, but rather to produce conditions so that those whose practices are being studied can engage in a dialogical encounter with the account. Willis provides this opportunity by engaging the working-class 'lads' in discussion to encourage them to come to know how they are implicated in what happens to them and to challenge them as to how things might be otherwise. This emancipatory intent is an example of what Lather (1986 a) calls catalytic validity, 'the degree to which the research process reorients, focuses, and energizes participants toward knowing reality in order to transfer it' (p. 272).

The Ideal Learning Community

Another approach that has been influenced by critical theorists is even more directly relevant to my concerns with the pedagogy of evaluation. Arising from their work as evaluators, Marshall and Peters (1985) from New Zealand speculated 'about a form of evaluation which took educational problems seriously, to the extent that they should form the theoretical framework of any model of evaluation' (p. 264). Influenced by Wittgenstein's ideas of rule following, they have developed a theory of evaluation which makes central the role of an 'ideal learning community'. Without being able to do much justice to the complexity of their ideas, let me sketch a few features of their work. The notion of rule applies to conformative behaviour and is inextricably tied to concepts of community and practice. Following rules must be explained with reference to some community; learning to follow a rule and rule-following are interpretive and creative acts; they are created through time in practices of people; there is no justification for a rule beyond what constitutes shared practice; judgments about rules are reiterations of agreements in practice; that they are subject to change, and rules as agreement in practice are the basis for evaluation. The implications of such a definition and description of rule-following are that it must be done in a community, indeed a community of learners, that formal evaluation of program or policy takes place in an evaluative context, that knowledge is a form of praxis, where the norms involve equality and shared responsibility for decision-making, and that community-learning process is at the heart of evaluation.

Marshall and Peters (1985) suggest that there must be a voluntary subordination of vested interests within a community (e.g., community might be of (a) professional evaluators, (b) those actually undertaking the evaluation, or (c) all stakeholders, i.e., the community in general) where evaluation is proposed, to the process of learning. It requires a commitment to the community and not just individual or sectional interests. Among the features of the learning community are a commitment to dialogue that is reflective and self-reflective, a communal-collaborative context emphasizing dialogical equality and shared decision-making, a commitment to praxis, and an openness to creative and transformative possibilities. Ultimately, these lead to, and are structured by, a focus on emancipation. In this context, 'evaluation becomes the systematic community learning process for the collaborative review, improvement and development of policies, programmes and practices' (p. 284).

A Proposed Educational Agenda

I look for evaluation to allow for reflective and reflexive opportunities in which there may be real opportunity for individuals (and by extension, institutions) to question the 'taken-for-granted' as a means of understanding the possibilities and their limits. My particular prescription for what ails evaluation is a dose of self-healing — that is, use our own knowledge and knowledge of our practice to better understand our condition. Specifically, we should look behind and through our educational practices. Here is a partial agenda of educational considerations for evaluators.

1. *Study our studies.* As a field, we study others and what they do. Perhaps we should study what we do when we are studying others, rather like a movie within a movie. Such a study may give us some insights about what we do, why we do it — possibly to look at the contradictions inherent in the enterprise. I have tried it, with painful results (Weiss, Reynolds and Simon, 1983). Most people do not have the audacity to

live up to their principles. However, such activity may provide insights about how things may have been different and what it would take for that to happen.

2. *Study ourselves*. In addition to studying our studies, we may consider knowing ourselves better. Perhaps a form of life history may be appropriate for understanding an evaluator's underlying ideology and reasons for making certain professional decisions, and, in general, trying to understand personal modes of knowing. Perhaps studying evaluations from different types of institutions, from different epistemological perspectives or from different educational backgrounds may help us to learn how to look at ourselves and the institutions we interact with over our professional lives. I can imagine Studs Terkel's next book: *Working Evaluators*?

3. *Study our curriculum*. I have previously suggested that part of the professionalization of evaluation has been the development of university graduate-school programs of study. Evaluators, however, usually come from universities which do not have formal programs. I am suggesting that we study the intended, actual, hidden and perceived curricula of the field; social philosophy and cultural analysis belong in our curriculum.

4. *Study others' perceptions of evaluation and evaluators*. I believe that there is cultural capital associated with evaluation, a cultural impediment to our being able to employ a variety of practices. Of course we must do a better job of disabusing educators, administrators, policy-makers and lay persons that evaluation is a narrowly-conceived affair.

5. *Study the teaching and curriculum fields*. Educational evaluators are fortunate in that we are not only expert in evaluation, but knowledgeable about education as well. Or are we? What do we know about the various forms of teaching and learning? What can we learn from a study of our own teaching and curricular practices? What can we learn from other educators?

Teachers and their Curriculum-Change Orientations

Dennis Thiessen

Introduction

In recent years, scholars and administrators have written prescriptions for effective curriculum change. Although organizational analyses and recommendations dominate much of their work, they have shown particular interest in the position of teachers in the curriculum-change process. This chapter contributes to this emerging interest by examining how some teachers construe those curriculum-change experiences for which they are responsible.

A curriculum-change orientation is a position an educator takes to explain why curriculum change ought to occur in particular ways. It includes both *assumptions* that frame how the educator views curriculum change, and *values* that justify why certain actions and interpretations are more important than others to bring about curriculum change. Such phenomena require careful study by curriculum researchers.

To study such orientations, I visited four Ontario school boards to examine how thirty educators responsible for the development and implementation of an intermediate-English curriculum guideline construe curriculum change. Using personal construct theory as a conceptual and methodological foundation (Kelly, 1955; Fransella and Bannister, 1977; Pope and Keen, 1981), I developed a qualitative form of enquiry that simultaneously focused on the person and on the phenomenon of curriculum change as interrelated units of importance. Each educator engaged in a retrospective construction of his or her unique view of curriculum change. The comparative tension between singular and collective constructs within and across biographies was an important aspect of the study.

In the following section, I focus on eight teachers from the King County Board of Education. I outline their construed context, differentiate between those teachers with a teacher-centered adaptation orientation and those teachers with a professional-renewal orientation, and compare what is most meaningful and important to the teachers in each orientation group. I then briefly introduce two additional curriculum-change orientations, structured-direction and strategic-influence, both of which are evident in the other educators in King County and in the remaining three school boards of the study. I conclude with discussions of the diversity within and across the four curriculum-change orientations and the implication of these multiple realities for teachers involved in curriculum change.[1]

The King County Teachers

The King County Board of Education is situated in the north-eastern region of Ontario. Its structure, size and operational pattern are similar to many middle-size school boards (student population of 10,000) outside major cities of the province. In the study, the King County educators include the superintendent of curriculum and the intermediate-English committee consisting of two elementary-school teachers, three secondary-school teachers, three secondary-school department heads, one language-arts consultant, and one intermediate-English consultant. The following segments focus on the teachers only, represented by the five elementary- and secondary-school teachers and the three secondary-school department heads.

The mandate of the committee is to evaluate the level of implementation of recommended intermediate-English curriculum practices (Ontario Ministry of Education, 1977). Earlier committees, over a five-year period, defined a philosophy of personal meaning for the intermediate-English curriculum, formulated a teaching format to guide intermediate-English teaching, designed a staff manual to support curriculum writing, negotiated the appointment of an intermediate-English consultant, developed numerous professional development strategies, and surveyed, observed, and interviewed intermediate-English teachers to determine how the format and staff manual were being used. For teachers on the committee, these events provided historical, administrative and political references to explain the objective context of curriculum change. To understand the relationship of these events to their curriculum-change orientations, however, it is necessary to address their construed context.

The construed context is the subjective view of the educational environment each teacher uses to elaborate the particular importance of the major curriculum-change events. To varying degrees, the King County teachers describe their construed context according to three issues in transition. Competing perspectives about what English education should emphasize, varied reactions from teachers to ideas that outside agencies prescribe for their classrooms, and mixed judgments about how curriculum-change strategies are structured, persist as issues which affect their views about curriculum change. When the King County teachers generate curriculum-change constructs from their experiences in committee deliberations, their development of units and ideas for their classrooms, departments and schools, their observations and reflections from inter-school visitations, and their understanding of classroom realities, they draw on their construed context to demonstrate the uniqueness of their views about curriculum change. Inherent in this uniqueness are two curriculum-change orientations the teachers use to elaborate and justify why curriculum change ought to occur in particular ways. The next three sections examine the teacher-centered-adaptation orientation group, the professional-renewal orientation group, and the similarities and differences among the teachers in each group.

Teacher-centered Adaptation

Ken, a secondary-school teacher, Bill, a secondary-school department head, and Donna and Philip, two elementary-school teachers, argue that to bring about change teachers must control how the curriculum is implemented in the classroom. They accept the notion that official curriculum policy is defined by bodies outside the school such as the Ministry of Education, the board of education, or committees representing the board of education. However, they argue that teachers have the right to mediate between what curriculum is official and what curriculum is practised in their intermediate-English classrooms. New curriculum practices must be scrutinized, reformulated, and altered so that teachers can determine the best way they can integrate the changes into their classrooms. These beliefs assume the right of teachers both to evaluate what works on criteria they define, and also to develop their own versions of the change in their classrooms. Conditions, strategies and tasks designed to bring about curriculum change are important if they support the initiatives of teachers to translate the change into meaningful classroom practices.

Teachers and their Curriculum-Change Orientations

The four teachers in this orientation group share similar assumptions about curriculum, curriculum change, and the teacher's role, and have similar positions about what values are important. They view curriculum as the practices teachers use in the classroom. Curriculum change then is a classroom phenomenon dependent on those actions teachers take in their classrooms. The classroom is separate from the political and administrative sources of the change but central to the decisions teachers make to implement their adaptations of the change.

Bill, Ken, Donna and Philip construe teachers as both the technicians of, and protectors against, curriculum change. Once the classroom door is closed, teachers are separated from the authorities who instigated and defined the change. With this presumed independence comes a more reactive image of teachers engaged in classroom trials of the change. The hesitation that teachers bring to curriculum change makes them change assimilators rather than change agents.

To bring about curriculum change, Bill, Ken, Donna and Philip recognize the values of instrumentalism, independence and collegiality. Instrumentalism is a conserving value that supports the efforts of teachers to mould the change into a form compatible with their existing practices. Independence translates into a self-interest argument in which the right of teachers to decide or at least mediate what curriculum practices they adopt takes precedence over what is defined in the official curriculum. Similarly, collegiality in the form of cooperative attempts among teachers to generate alternative approaches to the change at hand, also protects the community of teachers from unwanted directions from school board or Ministry of Education authorities. Together the values of instrumentalism, independence and collegiality give priority to a decentralized and teacher-directed approach to curriculum change.

Nevertheless, many variations in meaning and emphasis exist. Table 1 lists the teachers and their constructs. Constructs that focus on personalizing the change predominate, with those related to using time, providing support, establishing responsibilities and expectations, and maintaining superintendent involvement, stressed by only one or two teachers in the teacher-centered-adaptation group. They do not attach much importance to defining the philosophy of the change.[2]

Ken supports the importance of teacher choice in curriculum change. If he has the opportunity to develop units for use in his courses, then he can maintain what works best for him. He does not generalize beyond his self-interest in finding his own way to conform to the curriculum guidelines. Bill's views, on the other hand, are summed up in the construct, 'teachers must work and experience success with the change'. Drafting the staff manual, sharing the unit writing, and visiting classrooms are

Table 1: Curriculum change constructs of teachers with teacher-centered-adaptation orientation

Ken

The curriculum committee is compatible, has a common desire to make things work, yet includes people with different points of view.

Teachers must develop their own ideas and units, try them in their classrooms, and decide which ideas and units work best for their students.

Bill

Teachers must work and experience success with the change.

Drafting the staff manual provides the department head with the necessary understanding of the change.

The consultant and the department head or chairperson must build a network which supports teacher involvement in the change.

Philip

Members on a curriculum committee must generate and share new teaching ideas with the teachers responsible for the change.

The membership of the curriculum committee must change regularly.

Teachers in a school must work through their own units.

The superintendent guides and directs what the curriculum committee does.

Donna

In each school, those teachers responsible for the change must work together to interpret and to adapt the change.

The consultant spends much time in the school, working with students and discussing alternative teaching ideas with teachers before, during, and after they teach.

Chairpersons in elementary schools must have formal authority to coordinate and to evaluate curriculum change.

The curriculum committee must determine how to translate the framework into a form that teachers understand in practice.

---

part of the larger phenomena of teachers working with teachers to understand and to implement the philosophy of the change.

Donna, however, detaches herself from her role as a teacher and comments more as a supervisor of teachers. She feels teachers can be effective change agents through school-based development strategies that meet certain conditions. A structure for planning, an appointment of a chairperson responsible for curriculum change in the school, an organization of school priorities, and a linkage with key resource people are prerequisites to the effective engagement of teachers. To Philip, what is best for the classroom is what teachers know best. Consequently, the worth of any curriculum-change experience, unit writing, curriculum-committee suggestions, or superintendent interventions, is related to the degree to which they complement what the teachers perceive as meaningful for their classrooms. As an advocate of the rights of teachers, Philip argues that his activities as a committee member must enable the teachers to implement the new ideas he wants for his classroom.

At a more abstract level, Ken, Bill, Donna, and Philip agree on the framework of assumptions and values that underlie their curriculum-change orientation of teacher-centered adaptation. Yet the meaning and importance of these assumptions and values diverge as they elaborate their particular curriculum-change constructs. Although these differences are important, their insistence that teachers must have the right to determine how a change will work best in their classrooms unites them as a teacher-centered-adaptation orientation group.

Professional Renewal

In the professional-renewal orientation group, Allison and Bruce, two secondary-school teachers, and Pamela and Ruth, two secondary-school department heads, defend a position in which teachers, through collaboration with those directly influenced by the change, develop personally and socially responsible curriculum experiences for the classroom. What the change is, who defines the change, and how the change is put into practice, are interrelated and dynamic processes within any curriculum-change initiative. Each teacher is involved continuously in interaction with other stakeholders to negotiate what should or should not happen in the classroom. Participation in curriculum committees, in school or department planning, or in classroom trials of units or teaching ideas, promotes the type of reflection that encourages a teacher, in concert with both the students and other' teachers, to examine the working relationship between the changing curriculum as intended and the changing curriculum as experienced. Neither the compatibility with existing classroom practices nor the observable impact on students, is as central as the reflexive value of what happens for both the teacher and the students. Reflecting on the change-in-use creates an ongoing cycle of translation, evaluation, and transformation in curriculum change. What works in the instrumental sense is incorporated into the broader question of what informed actions are of most value. Curriculum change in the professional-renewal orientation is the reflective search for practical answers to this fundamental question of value.

Allison, Bruce, Pamela, and Ruth portray similar assumptions about curriculum, curriculum change, and the role of the teacher and have similar positions about what values are important (see Table 2). In their view, curriculum is what happens in the classroom—the complex and dynamic interrelationships of teacher, students and resources. Curriculum change is a personal phenomenon in which teachers make judgments about what should happen in the classroom based on their understanding of the classroom situation and on the external social, political and economic conditions that influence the classroom. Teachers collaborate with those who have a stake in the change to make sense of it and to evaluate its worth. Their ongoing involvement influences the curriculum-change process both inside and outside the classroom.

Interdependence, reflective evaluation and professional responsibility are interrelated values critical to the four teachers in the professional-renewal group. Interdependence is a uniting and holistic value. Efforts to interrelate curriculum documents and practices, guidelines and experiences, perspectives and action, and structures and outcomes are dynamic and problematic—and lead to curriculum change. By working interdependently with others involved in the curriculum change, teachers have the opportunity for reflective evaluation. The stakeholders interact to consider which positions and actions best represent their curriculum-change priorities. Finally, whatever curriculum-change actions are taken must be judged by the stakeholders as professionally responsible. Teachers are required to be the conscience of curriculum change. The values of interdependence, reflective evaluation and professional responsibility support a reflexive, intersubjective and evaluative approach to curriculum change.

Nevertheless, the teachers are different (see Table 2). Allison, for example, integrates many of her positions on curriculum change with her view of professional learning. Professional learning comes from a valued understanding of the change, based on comparative reflections that occur when teachers listen to, observe and discuss their views about the change with other educators.

Sensitive to the political dimensions of curriculum change, Bruce sees reflection and interaction as critical experiences that teachers must have to understand the change, to perceive its implications for their classrooms, and to define it in ways that are meaningful for their classrooms. Teachers provide a form of quality control to resist those changes that require conformity to administratively expedient but educationally questionable practices. It is the political and professional right of teachers to determine how curriculum change is 'personalized'. Included in this right is the power of teachers either to render inoperative imposed curriculum changes or to transform what the change prescribes into practices of value to teachers.

Table 2: Curriculum change constructs of teachers with professional-renewal orientation

Allison

Teachers must find in the philosophy of the change those themes or practices in which they can believe.

Concrete experiences in which teachers interact to build units or to discuss teaching help them to understand the practical implications of the change.

The timing of and the use of time for the change are problems teachers face.

Maintain the interest in the change by involving more teachers in the curriculum committee.

A curriculum committee must include people who bring both diverse and vested interests in the change.

Bruce

Teachers need time to understand the change, to see its implications for their classrooms, and to determine whether there are ways the change will be meaningful for their classrooms.

Change must come from 'within' the teacher and not from 'without'.

Teachers must engage in implementation experiences which focus on their own classroom priorities and concerns.

The consultant is sensitive to the individual differences of the curriculum committee members.

Ruth

The superintendent must be open and responsive to the considered opinions of those teachers who will implement the change.

If teachers are to change, they must focus on those strategies they use in their classrooms.

Both teachers and students learn in a humanistic environment that is personally meaningful.

Change must emerge from the consciousness-raising and the sense of mutuality that human interaction generates.

Pamela

Focus on the practical implications of the change in the classroom, how and why the change makes a difference to the students.

Teachers use their time to allow ideas to emerge and to explore new ways to improve the change.

Both teachers and students must 'personalize' the change, make it meaningful and important to their lives.

What is practical, what is personal, and what is meaningful about the change are factors that Pamela uses to explain what and how curriculum change happens. Her priorities are clear. Only the philosophy-in-use and the consequent curriculum students experience are important. Curriculum change must touch what teachers share with their students in the classroom.

For Ruth, the intersubjective principles of what it means to be human integrate her curriculum-change constructs. Ongoing experiences of human interaction become the medium for curriculum change. Barriers between people must be broken so that a comfortable and secure environment develops. The security, learning, and mutual understanding that arise from genuine collaboration make curriculum change happen.

Allison, Bruce, Pamela, and Ruth maintain essentially similar assumptions and values amidst significant differences in specific curriculum-change constructs. The ways in which the constructs interact reveal the distinct configuration of values that differentiates one teacher from another. Yet as professional-renewal teachers, they are drawn together by the continuous, constructive and critical examination of the reasons for curriculum change.

Comparison Between Teacher-Centered-Adaptation and Professional-Renewal Orientations

Numerous commonalities are evident among the eight teachers in these orientation groups. They share a view of curriculum change that focuses on the intense involvement of teachers, the importance of their interpretations and actions, and the necessity of their adaptations of the change in the classroom. Similar planning, professional development and evaluation activities are recommended forms of teacher participation. As a major force in what happens in schools, teachers are perceived in both orientations as pivotal sources of support, modification or resistance in any efforts to bring about change.

In the elaboration of their curriculum-change constructs, teachers in both orientation groups agree on the value of developing meaningful uses of the change. When teachers are able to test, alter, or create innovative teaching ideas or units, they determine what works best in their classrooms.

Nevertheless, there are important differences. What works best for the teachers with a teacher-centered-adaptation orientation is a functional exercise to find those practices that teachers can readily accommodate into their present techniques. Substantial or radical change is unlikely.

Consequently, curriculum change is a matter of adjusting, but not significantly altering, what teachers presently do. The professional-renewal teachers leave the question of what works best open for practical examination, informed discussion, and critical debate. No bounds are placed initially on the extent to which the curriculum should change. Although conscious of the instrumental dimensions of curriculum change, teachers with a professional-renewal orientation base their judgments about what works best on those values negotiated for the curriculum change.

Another difference between the orientation groups relates to the focus and the nature of teacher power implied in their positions. The teacher-centered-adaptation group argues for methodological independence, maintaining the exclusive right of each teacher to make decisions about how the change is implemented in the classroom. This micro-form of autonomy separates the philosophy and the people who define the philosophy from teachers and their applied practices. As the implementers, teachers must maintain control over how things work during the process of classroom curriculum change. Teacher power for the professional-renewal group permeates every curriculum-change experience. In curriculum-change decisions in the classroom, teachers may be strategically the most influential stakeholders. However, the degree of influence depends on the dynamics of engagement and not on the presumptions of position. This micro-macro perspective on autonomy recognizes the interdependence of the personal and social responsibilities of teachers. Power for teachers according to the professional-renewal group comes from belonging to, deliberating within, and affecting those situations, conditions and structures important to curriculum change.

The assumptions and values of each orientation provide a framework for the teachers both to explain the uniqueness of their curriculum-change constructs and also to justify why curriculum change happens or should happen in particular ways. Similarities between the two orientation groups exist at a general level, but when the fundamental differences of the curriculum-change orientations are included in the comparison, the similarities are significantly diminished.

Other Curriculum-Change Orientations

No other King County educators in the study articulate either a teacher-centered-adaptation or a professional-renewal orientation to curriculum change. Instead, the principal demonstrates a structured-direction orientation, and the superintendent of curriculum, the language arts consultant, and the intermediate-English consultant reveal a strategic-influence orientation. Among the remaining eighteen educators from the other three school boards in the study, there are three teachers with a teacher-centered-adaptation orientation, one consultant with a professional-renewal orientation, three teachers or department heads, three principals or vice-principals, one consultant, and one superintendent with a structured-direction orientation, and one teacher, three consultants, and two superintendents with a strategic-influence orientation. Across the four school boards, the teacher-centered-adaptation orientation is the only one exclusive to teachers although the professional-renewal orientation is predominantly teachers. Teachers are part of every orientation group sharing similar assumptions and values with some principals or vice-principals, consultants and superintendents.

Table 3 compares the assumptions and values of the teacher-centered-adaptation and professional-renewal orientations with the structured-direction and strategic-influence orientations. The structured-direction teachers are concerned that prudent curriculum strategies prevail. For structured-direction teachers, curriculum change is dominated by the development of products — curriculum documents that illustrate what the change is and guide teachers through the necessary steps to implement the change in their classrooms. Explicit directions and structured procedures promote an organized and sequential completion of the development and subsequent dissemination tasks. Harnessing the forces that maximize efficiency ensures the implementation of the curriculum documents. Structured-direction then is the preference for systematic and functional control by educators in positions of authority over the ways in which curriculum change occurs in the school board and schools.

In the strategic-influence orientation group, the teachers argue that one or more key educators who have recognized authority from the central office and are strategically situated within the social system of the school board will understand what the change is and which approaches best suit the implementation of the change. The key educators become an integral part of the communication network within the school, among schools, and between the schools and the central office. The central focus of this network for key educators is the school's primary responsibility for implementation. With this school-centered focus, activities such as document development or formal professional-development events become less important. Instead, activities that stimulate knowledge utilization in the classroom dominate what the key educators do to promote implementation. Curriculum change occurs when the key educators determine and affect those personal, interpersonal, and

Table 3: Assumptions and values in curriculum change

Orientation	What is curriculum change?	What is curriculum?	Who is the teacher?	What values are important?
Structured Direction	Organizational phenomenon	Commodity (document) to be implemented	Recipient, bottom point of the hierarchical structure	Power Efficiency Order
Teacher-centered Adaptation	Classroom phenomenon	What teachers do in their classroom	Technicians of and protectors against curriculum change	Instrumentalism Independence Collegiality
Strategic Influence	Environmental phenomenon	Norms that determine how students and educators think and act	One of the socio-cultural groups that occupy the environment	Intervention Alterability Development
Professional Renewal	Personal phenomenon	What happens in the classroom	Collaborator and evaluator	Interdependence Reflective Evaluation Professional Responsibility

environmental conditions and factors that most cause individuals and groups to adopt the beliefs and practices of the change.

Conclusion

Among the King County teachers, there are two curriculum-change orientations: teacher-centered-adaptation and professional-renewal. When all four school boards in the study are considered, some teachers also portray either a structured-direction or strategic-influence orientation to curriculum change. The underlying similarities in assumptions and values establish the parameters for and differentiations between each orientation. In comparison to the existing range of change approaches, models, or perspectives from other fields, the curriculum-change orientations offer alternative interpretive frameworks to facilitate an understanding of how teachers construe what is unique to bringing about change in schools and school boards. In sum, the existence of these orientations argues for a significant re-examination of what bringing about change means for teachers in particular, and for schools and school boards in general.

With this beginning in grounded curriculum-change orientations, we are better able to participate as informed and equal partners in any comparative attempts to build multi-disciplinary theories of change and changing (Fullan, 1985). Once the interrelatedness among the construed context, construct meaning and importance, and orientation of the teachers is considered, the distinctiveness of the curriculum-change orientations becomes clearer. Consequently, comparisons between the curriculum-change orientations and the approaches, models and perspectives currently available from other fields serve more to establish the uniqueness of the orientations, especially for the teachers, than to confirm the universality of existing frameworks.

This sense of uniqueness does not stop with the identification of the curriculum-change orientations but extends as well to the individuals. The teachers construe the significance of their contexts in different ways, convey different meanings for their constructs, have different configurations for and distributions of key constructs, and work with different assumptions and values to explain their constructs. How they view the dynamics of curriculum change varies in explicitness, relatedness, complexity and reference points. This does not deny the defensibility of orientations as interpretive frameworks. But it does caution against ignoring those differences that remain in any framework when curriculum change is construed at a personal level.

Finally, and more speculatively, the membership of some teachers in each of the four orientation groups raises the issue about how the teachers may view their involvement in curriculum change. It is difficult to generalize about what best represents their views. The teachers articulate different positions on who should control curriculum change, what form support for curriculum change should take, and what criteria should determine the effectiveness of curriculum-change approaches. This, in turn, demands a reconsideration if not dismissal of the numerous implementation strategies that work from an assumption of similarity among teachers. Instead, exploring how each teacher construes how he or she is situated in relation to other key educators in the school and school board may be essential to renewed efforts to bring about change. Given the increased emphasis on curriculum change in the school (Fullan, 1985), understanding the complex and diverse curriculum-change orientations among teachers will be important to creating informed and justifiable curriculum-change experiences. Future efforts must be sensitive and responsive to the multiple realities of teachers and be prepared to reconceptualize how and why particular curriculum-change practices are most effective for each teacher.

Notes

1 Given the space restrictions of the present volume, this chapter offers only highlights of an extended research study. All names of Boards and teachers are pseudonyms. For a further discussion of the research approach and an elaboration of the curriculum-change orientations for the thirty educators in the study, see the unpublished doctoral dissertation of the author (Thiessen, forthcoming).
2 Personalizing the change, using time, providing support, establishing responsibilities and expectations, maintaining superintendent involvement, and defining the philosophy of the change are the six curriculum-change construct areas portrayed by the twelve King County educators.

An Integrative Function for Teachers' Biographies[1]

Richard L. Butt

Background

The purpose of this chapter is to describe and comment upon an 'autobiographical' graduate course that integrates learning, teaching and professional development.[2] I shall characterize briefly the flavour of the course within the historical context of the use of autobiography in education, provide a specific image of the course through a description of its structure, content and process, and give the rationale for autobiography in graduate education by examining its potential for integrating teaching, learning, professional development and research.

The course invites experienced teachers to use an autobiographical approach in understanding how they think and act within the realities of their teaching contexts. Instructor and students interchange teaching and learning roles as they educate and become educated through individual and collective descriptions of experience. The course is based upon co-operative learning, peer-teaching and a particular model of social learning at the adult level.

> Social learning necessarily implies relationship with others; not only as an object of knowledge but as companions on the road in the same process—to think with others; to decide with them; to act in an organized way with them. It is a horizontal pedagogical relationship in which all are considered capable to give and receive; therefore all are masters and disciples, parents and children. The group is the educator who leads the members along the road to permanent maturity. It is no longer a vertical relationship in which the teacher monopolizes knowledge and decisions. (Diaz, 1977)

An Integrative Function for Teachers' Biographies

I would like the reader to know at the outset that despite the many reservations one might have about engaging in autobiography in graduate coursework in education, students emerge with some greater sense of coherence and direction as person-teachers than before. Participants are overwhelmingly positive, although one-in-twenty finds it difficult to be personal about his or her life and teaching career. This type of response to the educative potential of autobiography has been noted by others. For example, Ditisheim (1984) noted that autobiography serves cathartic, structural, cognitive and energizing functions, all of which are important for teachers. A self-guided analysis of the data revealed by autobiography enables students to express their feelings with respect to teaching, to deal with them explicitly (*cathartic function*), and to give *conscious* form and *explicit structure* to their experience; whereas before, the daily routines, stresses and immersion in teaching had submerged the sense of their experience. This form-giving is enabled by and enables the *discourse and communication* among teachers about their practice, serving the *cognitive function*. A personal synthesis of one's approach to teaching through individual effort and collective discourse enables us to countervail the devaluation of teachers' practical knowledge that has occurred during the last several decades (Schon, 1983) and lessens the alienation that teachers have experienced (Trempe, 1984). Ditisheim (1984) has found, as have I, that this personal derivation *energizes* teachers, giving them renewed commitment through the personal and collective empowerment generated by the autobiographical exercise.

The use of autobiographical approaches within education courses is not new. I can recall its benefit from personal experience some twenty years ago when I was studying at a teachers' college in England (Abbs, 1974). It was not a widespread approach in Britain, and had little presence in North American education programs. Given the power of empirical, behavioral, positivistic approaches in teacher education, it is not surprising that biography faded almost to oblivion during the last ten or more years. Two groups, however, kept biography and autobiography alive in North American education. First, reconceptualist curriculum theorists have emphasized autobiography and biography in pursuit of the essentially *personal* and *experiential* nature of teaching, and maintained the important emancipatory interest that characterizes personal-professional development (Grumet, 1980; Pinar, 1980, 1981, 1986). Secondly, scholars at the University of Alberta have drawn on phenomenology and critical theory that emphasize an understanding of the intentions, thoughts and feelings of participants in the process of education (Aoki, 1983; Aoki, Jacknicke and Frank, 1986; van Manen, 1978, 1979). In addition, Schon's (1983) research has emphasized how professionals of all sorts, including teachers, develop knowledge through reflection-in-action. Case studies of school-based change (e.g., Butt, 1981), case studies of individual teachers (Clandinin, 1985; Elbaz, 1983; Janesick, 1981), and biographical studies of how teachers think and act and how they came to be that way (Butt, Raymond and Ray, 1986), illustrate how *personal* and *experiential*, both in terms of present and past, a teacher's way of practising his or her profession can be. One may argue that autobiographical approaches provide teachers in training with the means of recovering, critically assessing and 'desocializing' their experiences *as learners* (Grumet, 1980). Further, one may advocate the use of autobiography by experienced teachers for the purpose of examining their thoughts and actions as professionals, and for furthering their own self-initiated professional development.

Course Assignments

There are four major course assignments, which, through a process of autobiographical writing, class presentation, discussion and rewriting, address the following topics: a depiction of current working reality; a description of current pedagogy and curriculum-in-use; an account of reflections on past personal and professional lives insofar as they relate to an understanding of present professional thoughts and actions; and a projection of preferred personal/professional futures as related to a critical appraisal of the previous three accounts. Each assignment is accompanied by a series of questions that the student may choose to address.

In order to minimize steering effects on what students choose to say or write, I am deliberately comprehensive in my suggestions. In struggling with what to say and how to write it, we have to make conscious choices as to what best characterizes our careers and lives. We may choose among daily journals, retrospective descriptive notes, tapes of lessons, or any other means, to begin our task. Another method is to identify what makes us most angry, sad, satisfied, afraid — or other such emotional extremes. Within our accounts, we identify particular preoccupations, worries, concerns, paradoxes, or problems, and describe examples of classroom activity that illuminate how these concerns are manifested in terms of lived experiences. Identifying sources of stress and conflict on the one hand, or sources for satisfaction on the other, may help respondents to understand their particular contexts. Other suggestions include narratives of a day in our professional lives, illustrative vignettes, significant events, or critical incidents. One student has used a beat-writing and stream-of-consciousness mode, another devised a dialogue between a judge and himself as a defendant, and another has written a play. All students are requested to engage in both description and some form of reflection and analysis, identifying themes and patterns if and when they emerge.

I ask students to do exploratory writing on a particular assignment using any of the suggestions, questions and forms given in each assignment. Having distanced themselves from these rough notes for a few days, they re-examine what they have written to identify significant ideas, events, issues, critical events or themes. These provide a structure or focus for a second draft that communicates the authentic flavor of their professional life to others. To encourage discussion, students select from their rough sketches a brief excerpt that they think best characterizes their teaching lives. Other participants are encouraged to attempt to understand the perspective, and the feelings and reality of the presenter, by asking questions for clarification. Comments of presenters and participants stimulate recall or strike resonant personal chords in others' stories. I encourage participants to make note of these occurrences to assist their own writing. Presenters are asked to use discussion of their accounts as a basis for elaborating their stories.

My first role in the process is to be a participant. I present aspects of my autobiography so that the relationship is more collegial. Secondly, I encourage through example the type of disclosure and dialogue most conducive to interpersonal understanding. I try to model some non-threatening conversational questions or act as a mirror for useful insights for others. Gradually, we move towards the model of social learning referred to above. I monitor the proceedings as unobtrusively as I can, intervening only when it is important to do so. Following a round of presentations on a particular assignment, the class attempts to identify patterns and themes that characterize not only individuals, but also commonalities among individuals, if they exist. This activity culminates each class assignment. Related readings are distributed *after* the class process for each assignment is completed. Then we elaborate, modify, redraft and polish our autobiographical pieces. After I have read each autobiographical piece, I write a response to each teacher. These responses can vary from half-a-page to four or five pages. My comments are discussed with each student where possible and where warranted. Sometimes students will redraft parts of their writing.

At the outset of the course I outline several interrelated conditions essential to ensuring the quality of our deliberations. Many students are used to writing university papers that are couched in objective and non-personal terms. I explain that a course that emphasizes subjective interpretation usually requires prose written in the first-person.

Sometimes, however, in order to write about certain aspects of themselves, students find it more comfortable to use the third-person (Abbs, 1974, pp. 20–21).

Being able to express, identify and describe feelings is an important aspect of our course. First, teachers experience and perhaps disregard many feelings that need to be expressed. Secondly, feelings provide fruitful routes to attitudes, values, thoughts and actions. Thirdly, when dealing with memory, feelings tend to be more accessible. They are affective labels for key incidents or understandings. If we identify and describe a feeling, ask why or how we come to feel that way, we can usually follow a trail back to the incident or paradigmatic situation with which it is associated. Finally, feelings are indicators of positive or negative experiences that need to be examined for personal or professional growth.

We need to identify and describe teachers' knowledge authentically, accurately, honestly and frankly. Posturing, or saying what we think is *expected* or *right*, will give a false basis for knowledge. It is important for class participants to say and write what they actually feel, think and do. To encourage personal exchange, it is vital that class participants are not afraid of sanctions from others as to the perceived quality of thoughts, feelings, actions and practices. I encourage participants, therefore, to accept others in a non-critical manner. Our focus, rather being judgmental, is on understanding the perspective of others and how they come to be the way they are. The tone of our questions, then, is geared to understanding, not criticism.

To encourage personal disclosure, participants are informed that what is said in class is completely confidential unless otherwise negotiated. *We each decide what personal distance and degree of disclosure is comfortable.* There is a minimal level of disclosure, however, related to professional life that is essential for the course. Beyond this level, there is no compulsion to reveal anything of a personal nature unless the student so desires. Usually, the collective support and a mutually created climate of trust enables participants to be personal. This enriches our understanding of the *teachers' perspective* with respect to the knowledge they hold. There are various aspects of the course for which different levels of disclosure might be appropriate. First, there is the course that occurs within our own heads that deals with very personal issues. Nobody is privy to this knowledge. Secondly, a collegial course may occur with a friend in the class through exchange and discussion of autobiographical pieces. Thirdly, there is the dialogue that occurs between me and each student which we do not necessarily reveal to this class. Finally, there is the public course that occurs through oral presentation and discussion in class.

An epistemological and practical rationale

The nature of the course may also be justified from epistemological and practical perspectives. Biographical enquiry may overcome blocks to educational change. These blocks are related to several current crises: reform, professional knowledge and scholarly enquiry (Butt and Raymond, 1987). The crisis of educational reform has caused researchers to examine assumptions about the theory, practice and human interactions that underlie the process of change. The crisis in professional knowledge relates to a lack of appropriateness and compatibility of prescriptive theory about teaching for the specificity of teaching situations and the practical knowledge held by teachers. The crisis of scholarly enquiry, which relates to the failure of research to solve some significant educational problems, has led to a reconsideration of basic issues of theory and method in research on teaching. Five arguments related to these crises support the use of biographical enquiry into the nature, sources and formation of a teacher's practical knowledge.

1 A first argument involves the issue of the relationship between knowledge and power. The image of teachers as semi-professionals who lack control over their own work and as persons who do not contribute to the creation of knowledge has permeated education (Elbaz, 1983; Lather, 1984). These views limit teachers' opportunities to exhibit, communicate and develop their practical wisdom which 'remains a largely untapped source of insights for the improvement of teachers' (Feiman-Nemser and Floden, 1986).
2 A second argument stems from the recent public concern with the quality of teaching. Accountability measures, such as standardized achievement tests, often ignore the critical role that personal and situation-specific knowledge plays in teaching. Day-to-day curriculum decisions and interactions are grounded in complex criteria that are not well known. These phenomena, if studied developmentally within their natural contexts, may shed new light on the issue of teacher accountability.
3 A third argument may be drawn from the field of professional development. Current staff development practices need to incorporate views of the teacher as an active adult learner (Guskey, 1985; Ingvarson and Greenway, 1981) involved in life-long learning and development. This position needs to be enriched through careful accounts of teachers evolving practical knowledge from teachers' perspectives.
4 A fourth argument is related to the need for expanded views of

curriculum development and implementation. Instead of only using perspectives of persons outside classrooms, we need to examine, directly, the central role of teachers' intentions and expertise in effecting significant classroom change (Aoki, 1983; Butt and Olson, 1983; Clandinin, 1985; Elbaz, 1983; Werner, 1982).
5   A fifth argument is grounded in basic theoretical assumptions about research on teaching. In teaching, as in other human interactions, people act in the light of their interpretations of the meanings of their surroundings (Erickson, 1986, pp. 126–127). Applied to the study of teachers' knowledge, this implies that the teacher's knowledge is not a fixed, or immovable entity; rather, it is shaped by personal and professional history and by the ecological circumstances of action in which a teacher finds herself.

Teachers' personal, professional and contextual histories, experience of classroom change, and the development of their own practical wisdom are not well documented by researchers, nor well understood by teachers themselves. This new type of knowledge, *as generated by biographical enquiry*, contributes significantly to new frameworks for overcoming the problem of classroom change. If we wish to have a decided impact on those whose role is central to improvement in the classroom, at least one major line of work should represent the teachers' perspective and work — how teachers perceive their realities. If outsiders and teachers understand teacher contexts, thoughts and actions, and how they evolved and adapted their professional knowledge, we may devise better ways not only of working with teachers, but also of teachers working with themselves, in a collective way, to improve education. Autobiography, better than biography, carries the teacher's voice; it also supports a more active and *self-initiated role* for the teacher in working with outsiders. Furthermore, this autobiographical enquiry *requires*, and evolves out of, *collaborative* endeavours that serve the multiple functions of teaching, learning, professional development and research. This collective approach suggests that coursework may be used as one vehicle for autobiographical enquiry. There are, however, more pragmatic reasons for autobiographical coursework.

Reasons for Autobiography as Coursework

One reason for using autobiographical courses relates to the role of a university professor. If one attempts to meet all the expectations of the role — teaching, research, publications, in-service work, projects, consulting, fieldwork, community service, etc. — the task becomes impossible. Throughout my career, I have tried to integrate as many functions as possible to alleviate the problem of overload. I spent, for example, ten years working with teachers in school-based improvement projects trying to understand teaching realities, and to discern ways of facilitating successful classroom change (Butt, 1981). Through this practice we were able to integrate many of a professor's functions. The major teaching function, however, through the traditional mode of coursework, was still separate as to time, place and people. Granted, the case studies from school-based endeavours served to improve the pertinence of coursework, but teaching was still not fully integrated. Moving on, for pedagogical and research reasons, to autobiographical coursework served to bridge that final gap of integrating teaching with the other endeavours. It provides a synergistic vehicle for all of a professor's functions.

Similarly, the overload to which teachers can be exposed has been well documented, as has the isolated nature of professional life. Surviving classroom reality and being seen to be competent under current conditions of accountability are arduous enough without the added imperative of continued personal/professional development, classroom change and educational improvement. This is especially true if one has to deal in an isolated fashion with *other people's* agendas for change that may not be congruent with one's own. School-based projects may, however, integrate most of these needs, particularly if focused on the personal, in-class, in-school needs, concerns and realities of teachers. Experience and research has shown these school-based efforts do facilitate change and growth. Another vehicle, however, for integrating more of these concerns is autobiographical coursework. It has the added advantage over the school-based project of emphasizing the unique personal-professional needs of each teacher. An autobiographical course provides for intensive reflection on contexts, renders thoughts and actions explicit, and allows for critical appraisal and the enunciation of future plans for the individual teacher. This individual empowerment and conscientization is probably basic to self-initated professional development.

A further reason for using autobiographical coursework is the collective endeavour within the class that provides a desirable context for individual work. It breaks down the isolation teachers feel, provides support for the autobiographical task, and generates energy and renewed commitment to teaching. As well, it provides a formal course of study for which the teacher can receive credit towards another credential. A final reason for using autobiography in coursework is related to the demands of research. It is very difficult to find a teacher with the time, commitment and energy to engage in spending eighty or more hours generating autobiographical data unless there is a reward—such as a research thesis or other such endeavour. Autobiographical coursework provides a way of overcoming this problem; generating data that offers rich potential for collaborative research.

The Synergistic Functions of Autobiographical Coursework: Teaching and Learning

A major criticism of education courses concerns the nature of knowledge presented to students regarding both educational theory and professional knowledge (Hilliard, 1971). The form of that knowledge (predominantly prescriptive theory) and the way in which it is conveyed, reflects certain assumptions about the nature of the relationship of theory to practice (McKeon, 1951). This, together with persistence of the lecture, gives rise to comments that courses are too professor-centered and the students' role too passive. Students see themselves as having little input as to what courses address and what pedagogy is utilized. Courses are criticized as being too 'theoretical'—that is, practical implications, concrete examples, and personal professional problems are neglected. Students perceive courses as not being related to their work-life and the improvement of their skills as teachers. They see neither a pedagogy that is exemplary of what one could expect of a first-rate professional educator, nor a pedagogy that respects the knowledge and skills they bring to class as adult learners and teachers. These problems are particularly telling at the level of a graduate student who is an experienced teacher.

The framework of the autobiographical course, however, deliberately focuses participants on what is personal, pertinent, practical and professional. Students are encouraged not only to be preoccupied with the detail of action (what is concrete or relevant) but also to be intellectual about being practical. Initially, teachers are encouraged to make sense of their own experience in individual ways; subsequently, they enquire collectively as to what might be commonalities across teachers' lives. The substance of the course, then, may be specific, as well as general, and may be related to individual *and* common concerns, problems, dilemmas and paradoxes. The course is 'the teacher'. Each teacher discerns content within the framework of the course; individuals and the group discern what is important about that content. The process is one of documentation, reflection and interpretation of experience so that we may think about where we are, where we have been, and where we wish to go. Equally important is the fact that I, as a *learner,* am constantly exposed to teachers' classroom realities, lives, and the evolution of their practical knowledge.

Professional Development

Curriculum implementation, classroom change and the improvement of teaching depend ultimately upon professional development. Inevitably, if reforms, changes, and improvements are couched *only* in terms of criteria enumerated by people outside the classroom, professional development efforts appear dysfunctional—top-down, logistical, or 'outside-in'. Such professional development is characterized by technical, teacher-proofing, marketing, or deficit models of implementation, all of which are disempowering and alienating for classroom teachers (Butt, 1985). The type of short-term, short-sighted, *in-service* efforts characteristic of this approach have been compared to *artificial insemination* (Sharma, 1982). As clearly documented by the Rand Corporation (1978), these approaches are demonstrably ineffective, whereas the same studies showed that when mutual approaches were used the likelihood of successful change was much higher. If we unfold the meaning of mutualism, we can see the implications for professional development. As innovative projects are evolved, a mutual approach requires equal opportunity for involvement and participation by both teachers and reformers from outside the classroom. The shape of the innovative project is adapted to meet contingencies of the situation as well as the personal dispositions of participants. These adaptations are negotiated from the requirements of both insiders and outsiders. The key ingredient of mutualism is the nature of the relationship between insiders and outsiders (Butt and Olson, 1983). This relationship is not logistic, whereby outsiders are perceived as experts who have the answers to insiders problems; it is dialectic, whereby insiders have equal status with outsiders (McKeon, 1951). Outsiders may be said to possess valuable conceptual knowledge; insiders may be well versed in practical knowledge, problems and needs. Both practical and conceptual/theoretical knowledge need to be seen as important aspects of problem solving for the improvement of education. Outsiders need to be students of insiders' perspectives, practical knowledge and the context of classroom reality; insiders need to be open to the conceptual knowledge of outsiders. Both, as co-learners and problem-solvers, need to negotiate and create appropriate praxis that accounts for and transcends both perspectives. This places teachers' authorship and ownership of classroom changes at the center of the improvement enterprise. Their personal, practical, classroom, school-based professional-development needs are essential to the derivation of improvement procedures.

To embark on an approach to professional development that carries with it these concerns, we have to begin with the individual teacher. To be able to engage most effectively in mutualistic approaches to improvement and change requires that teachers be students of their own realities, problems and practical knowledge. This knowledge cannot remain intuitive if it is to be communicated to and shared with both peers and outsiders. From an outside perspective, the clear implication is that practical teacher-knowledge is valuable and must be respected. The source of this knowledge must be acknowledged as being primarily derived from an interaction of the teacher, as person and professional, with experience of the context of the classroom. Acknowledging the teacher's development of practical knowledge as ensuing from a person learning from experience clearly involves a *biographic* conception of experiential education (Berk, 1980; Butt and Raymond, 1987; Dewey, 1963). To contribute to the collective project of educational improvement, each teacher must gain access to his or her biographic education and practical knowledge. As others have demonstrated (Schon, 1983), teachers need to evolve powers of reflection-*in*-action, and as importantly, as Dewey (1963) has maintained, gain access to the educative power of experience through reflection-*on*-action and the reconstruction of experience. This is the crux of the argument for the autobiographical course as professional development. It provides for most of the above conditions, especially the process of reflection-*on*-action that is a weak link in current professional development efforts. The autobiographical course enables individual teachers to make explicit how they think and act in particular contexts and to recover the biographical sources of this practical knowledge. They can confirm and document the personal and professional self, identifying the areas of coherence of that knowledge and its discontinuities with regard to both substance and evolution through past, present and into the future. This activity is not only cognitive in character; teachers express their affective selves, their beliefs, values, attitudes and feelings. This process of self-discovery and mutual confirmation builds an explicit concept of self-as-teacher.

The elucidation of self-as-teacher provides each participant with a comprehensive descriptive context and strong affective basis for making informed decisions about a future which may be self-chosen and self-initiated. But, as one of Flanders' (1983, p. 147) informants in a study of professional development said 'Who knows what you need? Yourself. But you need help, leadership'. The ideal professional development context provides for self-initiation, but within a supportive framework of peers and outsiders who can work and relate to each other in a dialectic way. The autobiographical course offers one such structure of mutual support that provides a comparative view of each person's interactions with varied contexts. This allows peers to act both as insiders for themselves and as outsiders for others, as theory and practice are integrated, and as the intellectual and practical worlds become one. These activities create both individual and collective professional knowledge that carries the teacher's perspective and voice in a language that speaks to practitioners and scholars alike. This may improve the status of the professional knowledge held by teachers in general.

A major contribution of the autobiographical course, besides documenting the present and past, is to project individuals into professional futures that are personally authentic. By critical appraisal of self and by comparison and contrast with others, individual strengths and points of growth may be identified. These strengths may overcome discontinuities, weaknesses and problems. Individual teachers may use personal knowledge of their own positions and prospective futures to make sense of, interpret, participate in, and *personalize* school-based projects, prescribed curricula, innovations, and other reforms that emanate from outside their classrooms. In this way, the ghettoization of teachers through non-reflective practice may be broken up, and their role given new direction by individual and collective *future-focused role images* (Polak, 1961). Having a clear and coherent picture of one's teaching self, derived through autobiographical study, provides explicit criteria by which a teacher can make judgments about what professional development opportunities in which to engage or create. What in the past has been a patchwork quilt of conferences, in-service workshops, clinics, visits and university courses with little unity and direction, may become a coherent and highly personal curriculum for continued professional development. If the elements and experiences of this curriculum are carefully selected, significant personal education, characterized by continuity, wholeness, interaction, and experience (Dewey, 1963), may result. If teachers engage in peer-supervision activities within the school system following a period of collaborative autobiographical inquiry, they may be clear themselves, and make it clear to their supervisor, what intentions they wish to pursue. The autobiographical course, then, may repatriate teachers to the center of the praxis of teaching as authentic creators of their own knowledge and action. The course places me back into my basic role of being a student of the phenomena of teaching and teachers—the best source of my own professional development.

Research

Epistemological arguments made earlier in this chapter clearly support autobiographical enquiry as research in education. The autobiographical course enables us to relate to the major actor in the educational process—

the teacher. It provides a structure that facilitates the evolution of new relationships in undertaking research. In fact, the structure of the course ensures that the teacher is given time, space and a context of peer support to become a researcher, particularly as regards teaching reality, and teacher knowledge. By this I mean that the outsider, the one whose preoccupation has been research, does not pre-empt the teacher as researcher. I do not cause the death of the teachers' investigation into self by imposing my premature conceptualizations on their data. Only after being a participant-observer, with the teacher doing his or her own research in the autobiographical manner throughout the course, can I understand sufficiently to be able to participate in collaborative interpretation. In this way, in contrast to other approaches to collaborative research, the autobiographical course enables the teachers' perspective, interpretation, language and metaphors to mature and prevail.

One hopes also that the skills and attitudes of thinking and enquiry developed during the course will become part of the teachers' professional repertoire and disposition. The substantive research, however, which has been commenced during the course can be pursued in a more formal way in order to discern the nature, sources and evolution of the practical knowledge of individual teachers and commonalities that exist among teachers. Danielle Raymond and I have collaborated with a number of teachers to pursue autobiographical enquiry further. The process of elaboration of teachers' autobiographies through the course is considered as Phase I of the research process. As outlined in this chapter it is a *teacher-based activity* giving rise to preliminary autobiographical data, analysis, and interpretations. Phase II of the process could be called the *collaborative phase* whereby individual teachers work with myself and Danielle Raymond to try to elucidate a further expression and understanding of the teachers' personal practical, knowledge and how it was acquired (see Butt, Raymond, McCue, and Yamagishi, 1986; Butt, Raymond and Ray, 1986; Butt, Raymond and Ray, in press). These studies portray a detailed and in-depth characterization of individual teachers' knowledge, sources of such knowledge, and how it was acquired.

Summary

This chapter has attempted to portray how one set of activities related to autobiographical enquiry can be framed within graduate coursework in education to serve, in an integrated and synergistic way, the multiple functions of teaching, learning, self-initated professional development and research for both students and instructor. The core characteristic of the processes that serve these functions is their emancipatory human interest.

Note

1 This work has been funded by the Social Sciences and Humanities Research Council of Canada.
2 I wish to thank Pat Panchmatia and Joyce Ito for typing the original manuscript.

How Much Life is there in Life History?

Geoffrey Milburn

> My dear fellow, life is infinitely stranger than anything which the mind of man could invent. We would not dare to conceive the things which are really mere commonplaces of existence.
>
> Sherlock Holmes, in *A Case of Identity*

I intend in this chapter to question certain aspects of what is called 'life history' research in education (e.g., Goodson, 1983 b).[1] My point of departure is *Teachers' Lives and Careers*, a collection of empirical studies edited by Stephen Ball and Ivor Goodson (1985 a), who also provided a lengthy introductory essay (1985 b). The contents of this book were selected from papers presented at a 1983 Conference in Oxford attended by many of the most influential British academics interested in the application of ethnographic methods to educational research. Perhaps I cannot claim that this collection is 'representative' of life-history research in any scientific sense; but the contributors are clearly far from being relegated to the status of straw-men.

First, a brief note on some features of the ten papers in *Teachers' Lives and Careers*. In content, they are largely concerned with teachers' rites of passage in contemporary schools: the stages through which they proceed in their professional careers (Sikes, 1985), the identification of critical incidents within career patterns of teachers (Measor, 1985), the nature of their commitment to their jobs (Cole, 1985), the pressures felt by particular groups within the teaching force (Webb, 1985; Bennet, 1985), differences in career patterns in different types of school (Nias, 1985; Burke, 1985), and the influences exerted by other groups within society and by students on teachers' careers (Beynon, 1985; Riseborough, 1985). The evidence upon which the articles were based was collected by means of interviews, questionnaires, participant observations and personal accounts—in other words, by customary ethnographic research techniques. Because the various authors are concerned with establishing generalizations in the traditional social scientific sense, they adopt a format that usually consists of a series of general statements, illustrated by quotations from field notes (which are, on occasion, fairly extensive).

I want to emphasize at the outset the high quality of the contents of *Teachers' Lives and Careers*. The generalizations offered by the various authors are both interesting and important, and their conclusions are based on some very energetic field work. As a result of their work, we possess a body of information and a set of research findings that shed a great deal of light on the condition of teachers in the United Kingdom, and, by comparative extension, in other countries as well.

My purpose herein, however, is not to draw attention to the obvious merits of the collection, but to discuss a number of questions that are prompted by its contents. Note, however, that my arguments herein are *not* intended to offer a critical review of the contents of the book; on the contrary, I intend to focus upon a limited number of issues related to the nature of life-history and life-history methods. In short, I am going to use the contents of *Teachers' Lives and Careers* as a case study for comment on problems related to (i) a definition of life history, (ii) the nature of data offered by life-history researchers, (iii) the presentation of life histories, and (iv) the interpretation of life histories.

(i) A definition of life history
I find the meaning of 'life history' elusive, despite the advice offered to me in standard methodology manuals (e.g., Bertaux, 1981; Plummer, 1983). It seems to be a term that is pulled in two directions by those who use it: on the one hand towards historical biography in the humanistic tradition, and on the other towards studies of collectivities in the social scientific tradition. This ambivalence may be one of the reasons why researchers have used other concepts to label what they are doing. The relationship of these other terms (such as life course, life story, life account, lived-experience, personal history, social-life history, and so forth—the examples are taken from Bertaux, 1981) to life history seems to depend at times on the whims of particular authors.

The difficulties persist in *Teachers' Lives and Careers*. The title itself may indicate the two traditions within life-history research. In their introduction to the book the editors set the scene (and perhaps promise more than they and their colleagues ultimately deliver) by indicating an interest in teachers' lives as a whole beyond the data generated within the classroom. They talk (Ball and Goodson, 1985 b, p. 13) of the need not only to set events in schools in the wider context of teachers' lives as a whole, but also to relate those lives to the history of their own times. Such a broad interpretation of life history encourages one of the contributors to speculate (in an interesting digression) on what he calls the functions of life history data in assisting us to understand the subjective reality of individual teachers, to relate teachers' lives to broader economic and social trends, and to serve as a means of checking older hypotheses or devising new generalizations (Beynon, 1985, pp. 164–165). These are certainly bold aspirations, which, if realized, may lead to a greater security in the meanings attached to life history.

I think that it is fair to say, however, that the authors in the collection do not come close to meeting these broad objectives. The contributors are almost exclusively concerned with 'career' questions that have a fairly narrow base: the pattern of life in schools, the stages through which teachers progress, the attitudes of subject groups towards their jobs, and so forth. The interest of the authors is to establish generalizations on these subjects, rather than to investigate the broader contexts required in the definitions of life history. A reader is left with the impression that the authors know the mountain is there, and glimpses of its contours appear in certain accounts, but the main climb is left for others.

This ambivalence is indicated in the frequency of the use of terms related to life history. As I have suggested above, 'life history' is certainly used in the book (and on one occasion [Smith, Kleine, Dwyer and Prunty, 1985, p. 181] even 'biographical life histories'), but not as often as a cluster of other terms: 'teachers' work and careers' (Ball and Goodson, 1985 b, p. 2), 'life cycle' (Sikes, 1985, p. 27), 'life structure' (Sikes, 1985, p. 29), 'life world' (Bennet, 1985, p. 120), 'professional identities' (Beynon, 1985, p. 158), 'daily lives' (Beynon, 1985, p. 176), 'life experiences' (Smith *et al.*, 1985, p. 181), 'richness of everyday school life' (Riseborough, 1985, p. 203), among others. The meanings of some of these terms (e.g., 'life world') are unclear, and the contributors have made few attempts to distinguish among them. (The situation becomes even more complex when terms are used in quote marks—' "life world" ' [Beynon, 1985, p. 120] —for no apparent reason.)

It is difficult to avoid the conclusion that proponents of life history are struggling with some very difficult problems. The central definitions of their task are in dispute, even among those committed to life-history approaches, and their arguments reveal tensions between various investigative positions. Consequently, the gulf between aspiration and implementation appears very wide.

How Much Life is there in Life History?

(ii) *The nature of the data offered by life-history researchers*

The text of *Teachers' Lives and Careers* is richly decorated with quotations. Without exception, the articles include lengthy extracts taken from tapes or field notes of discussions with teachers and students. The overwhelming proportion of the data presented in *Teachers' Lives and Careers* is of this type. The book's fabric is immeasurably enriched by these quotations, some of which are very funny (and likely will persist in instructors' lecture notes long after the book itself is consigned to the living death of University library depositories).

Reliance upon the actual words of 'subjects' is an integral part of life-history methodology. Researchers need what they continue to call 'data', and since teachers rarely write personal documents (and if they do, seldom publish them or even make them available), researchers have to generate the data they need. In the study of particular groups of teachers or students in particular schools, the interview is an obvious tool with which to generate the needed data.

I will argue herein that the use of such data ought to be handled much more gingerly than seems to have been the practice in *Teachers' Lives and Careers*; that the various authors often appear to have ascribed a greater certainty to the statements of their subjects than they ought to have done; and that, in consequence, the force of their conclusions is logically much weaker than may at first glance appear to be the case. (I should hasten to add that many of the contributors to the collection are aware of some of the difficulties to which I allude, although their doubts do not seem to have encouraged them to pause in their tracks.)

The problem to which I refer I have labelled 'a surfeit of objectification': a tendency to place greater faith in the certainty and accuracy of oral statements or interview responses than they warrant. This is more than just a point to be covered in passing, because many life-history researchers typically follow a pattern of, first, presenting generalizations and conclusions and, second, printing a quotation, or a series of quotations designed to illustrate, support, confirm or even prove the arguments that have already been made. If the certainty of the quotations is weakened, then the persuasiveness of the generalizations that they illustrate is similarly threatened. In short, the data that life-history investigators print in such profusion may not be able to bear the burden of the generalizations or conclusions that are drawn from them.

Reasons for questioning the certainty of the data are not difficult to catalogue:

a) The evidence of retired people recollecting the events of their career, or being able to interpret those events when they can recall, is highly suspect. (I am reminded of A.J.P. Taylor's comment [1965, p. 612] on *A Prime Minister Remembers*—'shows how much a prime minister can forget'.) The same note of caution ought to be expressed for practising teachers recalling the events of twenty years ago—or, indeed, in some circumstances, twenty minutes ago.

b) The format of the quotations of subjects in *Teachers' Lives and Careers* deserves some comment. Almost without exception they read very smoothly. My guess is that they have been edited, although the criteria for editing are not revealed. A minor point, perhaps; but it serves to introduce a much more serious issue: the difficulties involved in translating—perhaps 'transposing' is a better word—spoken words into written sentences. The possibilities for misunderstanding that exist in irony, emphasis, inflection, pauses, facial expressions and the like are well-known; and, to be fair, many of the contributors have tried to deal with the problem by adding stage directions (that, in their turn, create more difficulties). But most contributors simply offer their subjects' statements as though the meaning were readily available to, and commonly interpreted by, both them and their readers. Such confidence is surely misplaced.

c) There are occasions in which the warnings expressed in the previous paragraph are especially appropriate. When the respondents are subject to some emotional strain, difficulties in recording the data may increase (and the veracity of the final account may be diminished). Note, for example, a descriptive statement of a certain Mr Quilley, reported by Measor (1985, p. 64), on a traumatic episode in his career:

> And I've been bashed by kids about a quarter my size, and one of them got bashed back (laughter) and I ended up on the mat about it.

While this example in itself is trivial enough, it nevertheless is symptomatic of a much broader problem. As it stands, this testimony cannot be taken seriously. Its problematic nature is compounded by the difficulties the investigator experienced (which she was honest enough to admit) in recording the conversation:

> .... Mr Quilley had increased the pace of delivery of his sentences, so that I was able to take down only one phrase at a time .... He piled sentence upon sentence in a staccato fashion. (Measor, 1985, p. 64)

From the point of view of trustworthy evidence upon which to base generalizations or conclusions, the Quilleys of this world seem very unsatisfactory witnesses.

d) Most (probably all) of the statements of subjects are anonymous. One can easily understand why: the respondents will only speak under the cloak of confidentiality, and the researchers are anxious to avoid being dragged into court by their subjects of study. Notwithstanding these persuasive reasons, anonymity begets unreliability. Statements that can be cross-checked with other sources, comments about schools that can be 'triangulated', documents that independently support one another, are more convincing pieces of evidence upon which to base general statements. Note, for example, the effort made by Williamson (1982) to check in other sources the exclusively oral records of his grandfather, a north-country miner. Most of the evidence offered in *Teachers' Lives and Careers* cannot be cross-checked in this — or any other — way.

(iii) *The presentation of life histories*
Thus far, I have been considering fairly obvious questions about the technical quality of life-history methods; in the final two sections, however, I turn to issues of a more speculative nature. First, I shall examine some issues related to the presentation of life histories, and then turn to questions of interpretation.

During the last decade or so we have become particularly sensitive to issues related to the presentation of educational ideas, thanks largely to the work of Eisner (1979, 1985) and his associates. I am referring here to two features of that work: the notions that (a) the language in which the report is written, and (b) the presentation form in which the report is couched, to no inconsiderable extent affect the meanings conveyed to the reader. In other words, the artistic form of a report, and the language in which it is written, are not features that should be simply taken for granted (see on this point the recent work of Walker [1986]).

Few contributors to *Teachers' Lives and Careers* discuss this matter directly (it was not part of their mandate that they should). True, Beynon (1985, pp. 159, 165) bemoans the fact that teachers characteristically have been portrayed in previous research as 'cardboard cutouts without flesh or substance', and suggests that 'life histories are far more than "good stories" '; but he is far from specific in making any recommendations about the alternative form that such histories should take. Smith *et al.* (1985, p. 181) resort to metaphors to indicate what they are doing: describing their research on one occasion as a 'series of post holes drilled into our social and professional networks', and on another as learning about 'the thousands of frames which made up the full reel of our participants' life movie' (p. 183). Again, it is not clear how these images have affected the presentation of their work. Given this (not unexpected) lack of direction from the contributors, we are left with the task of drawing inferences from the text of the essays.

On a few occasions, this is easier said than done. What are we to make of the following sentence?

> Unconvinced teachers assuaged by self-doubt as to their efficacy while they go about the daily grind in the classroom are deluded. (Riseborough, 1985, p. 207)

And how do we deal with the cauldron of metaphors in these extracts?

> Teachers are erroneously conceived as automatons, reproduced reproducers simply and easily subjugating children because teachers are State functionaries, 'high priests of the ruling ideology' (Althusser, 1971, p. 246) and, as such, thoroughly pickled in it themselves.... In the monochrome of the overall structural analysis, in which *cowed* teachers are *cowing* pupils, irridescent existential variations in teacher and pupil activity are denied and of no consequence. (Riseborough, 1985, pp. 206–207)

Such prose suggests to me that the author is himself uncertain about the meaning of his data, and unclear about the interpretations to be derived from it. Nevertheless, notwithstanding this example, what the contributors in *Teachers' Lives and Careers* are trying to say is, in general, intelligible.

The first point I want to make is that the language is similar in important respects across all the entries in *Teachers' Lives and Careers*. Whatever the subject of study, the manner in which the authors report their findings tends to possess certain similarities that affect the reader's comprehension of the life histories being offered. That is not to say, of course, that the language is identical, or that the authors are mirror images of each other; but there is a noticeable similarity in the way that they present their findings.

This similarity is revealed in the extensive use of what I shall call (with little claim to originality) 'categorical language': the contents of *Teachers' Lives and Careers* depend for their structure on a framing of sociological categories. Here are just a few examples: 'life cycle' (Sikes, 1985, p. 28), 'career path' (Sikes, 1985, p. 48), 'critical incidents' (Measor, 1985, p. 61), 'self-estrangement' (Webb, 1985, p. 85) 'structures of schooling' (Cole, 1985, p. 89), 'strategic presentations of self' (Cole, 1985, p. 91), 'significant others' (Nias, 1985, p. 106), 'substantial selves' (Nias, 1985, p. 107), and so forth. These are not isolated terms wrenched from a context in which they appear as bit-part players: on the contrary, they are the featured actors on the collection's stage — and the readers, like the

How Much Life is there in Life History?

play's audience, have to sit through what is presented to them.

It may well be argued that the members of that audience knew what they were getting into when they bought a ticket. Perhaps some did — but many others may have come in for a show not comprehending what was going on. And a few may have been slightly misled — the contributors, after all, at least hinted that the show would be different: the editors talked of the 'symbolic power' (Ball and Goodson, 1985 b, p. 17) of the stories that teachers have to tell, and the authors bore witness to the 'richness' of life-history studies (Smith *et al.*, 1985, pp. 183, 203). Such high-flying claims surely need to be brought down to earth.

(In passing, note the effect — and contrast — of the relatively long narrative extract at the beginning of the book [Ball and Goodson, 1985 b, pp. 1–2], and the poem quoted at the beginning of Riseborough's article [1985, pp. 202–203]. Their presence — and location — is symptomatic of difficulties in the presentation of life histories in *Teachers' Lives and Careers*.)

(iv) The interpretation of life histories
Four or five English comedians — including John Cleese, although I cannot be certain that the group was *Monty Python* — offer a very funny sketch in which each participant attempts to better the preceding speaker in cataloguing the deprivations of his youth. You know the sort of exchange:

> I was brought up in a tar-paper shack pitched in the median of the M1 as it runs through Birmingham.

> What bloody luxury! My family stood in a queue for twenty years in the rain to rent one of those shacks.

With respect, I must admit that I began — very irreverently, certainly unkindly, and perhaps even unforgiveably — to recall that scene as I read through the sequence of potted biographies of the contributors to *Teachers' Lives and Careers* reproduced at the back of the book (Ball and Goodson, 1985 a, pp. 266–268).

What does it matter that many of the contributors have working-class backgrounds? Of course, it does not; unless that background pre-determines the results of an investigation. What does it matter that many of the articles have what may be called a left-wing view of education and society? Again, it does not; unless the authors brought with them to their studies a particular view of education and society, which exercised a determining effect on their research.

On this point, the evidence in *Teachers' Lives and Careers*, is uneven. In at least one major essay (Riseborough, 1985), the author makes few secrets of his political stance on educational issues, especially in what is

167

labelled the new barbarism of the Thatcher period (p. 262). He wears his anti-capitalism on his sleeve; so much so, indeed, that it is difficult to take his arguments seriously. If life historians follow this model, then I have no hesitation in suggesting that they will end up in intellectual culs-de-sac.

To be fair, however, most of the other authors in *Teachers' Lives and Careers* are guilty of nothing more serious than offering interpretations consonant with familiar sociological methods. They stress collectivities, search for generalizations, and write in social-scienteze — all perfectly acceptable academic pursuits, followed by scholars around the world. But it is worth stressing that such forms of research offer interpretations only (and particular kinds of interpretations at that), not objective truths, a truism that the contributors to the book neglect to emphasize. However, this is not the place to enter the campaign against the hegemony of social scientism in education — there are battalions (well, perhaps, platoons) of other academics willing to take the Queen's shilling on that issue.

In conclusion, then, I submit that if *Teachers' Lives and Careers* is in any way typical (and, indeed, it may not be), life-history research needs to be re-thought and perhaps re-structured. Questions of definition need to be explored, methods of gathering data re-assessed, alternative patterns of presentation designed, and customary interpretations reviewed. This is an extensive agenda that throws all the principal features of the work in *Teachers' Lives and Careers* into the hopper. I would not be surprised if one of the results of these re-considerations were that an academic paper constructed on traditional lines is not an appropriate format for recording life-history research.

It is at this point that the quotation of Sherlock Holmes at the beginning of this chapter becomes pertinent. Ordinary life — especially classroom life — is indeed 'strange', although that strangeness is often masked by the lens used to photograph it. In future, researchers may be required to pick up different kinds of cameras to record the 'commonplaces' of everyday life in classrooms.

Note

1 I benefited from the comments of Ivor Goodson on earlier versions of this chapter.

References

Abbs, P. (1974) *Autobiography and Education*, London, Heinemann.
Abrams, P. (1963) 'Notes on the uses of ignorance', *Twentieth Century*, **172**, 67–77.
Althusser, L. (1971) 'Ideology and ideological state apparatuses: Notes towards an investigation', in L. Althusser, *Lenin and Philosophy and Other Essays*, B. Brewster, Trans., pp. 121–73, London, NLB.
Altieri, C. (1981) 'Ecce: homo: Narcissism, power, pathos and the status of autobiographical representation', *Boundary II*, **9**(3–4), 389–413.
American Federation of Teachers (1987 a) *Education for Democracy*, Washington, DC, The author.
American Federation of Teachers (1987 b) *Democracy's Untold Story*, Washington, DC, The author.
Anderson, B.R. (1983) *Imagined Communities: Reflections on the Origin and Spread of Nationalism*, London, Verso.
Anyon, J. (1980) 'Social class and the hidden curriculum of work', *Journal of Education*, **16**(2), 67–92.
Aoki, T. (1983) 'Curriculum implementation as instrumental action and as interpretive praxis', in R.L. Butt, J. Olson and J. Daignault (Eds), *Insiders' Realities, Outsiders' Dreams: Prospects for Curriculum Change: Curriculum Canada IV*, pp. 18–29, Vancouver, Center for the Study of Curriculum and Instruction, University of British Columbia.
Aoki, T., Jacknicke, K. and Franks, D. (1986) *Understanding Curriculum as Lived: Curriculum Canada VII*, Vancouver, Center for the Study of Curriculum and Instruction, University of British Columbia.
Apple, M. (1979) *Ideology and Curriculum*, London, Routledge and Kegan Paul.
Apple, M. (1980) 'Analyzing determinations: Understanding and evaluating the production of social outcomes in schools', *Curriculum Inquiry*, **10**, 55–76.
Apple, M. (1982 a) *Education and Power*, London, Routledge and Kegan Paul.
Apple, M. (Ed.) (1982 b) *Cultural and Economic Reproduction in Education: Essays in Class, Ideology and the State*, Boston, Routledge and Kegan Paul.
Apple, M. (1986) *Teachers and Texts*, London, Routledge and Kegan Paul.
Armstrong, M. (1977) 'Reconstructing knowledge: An example', in Watts, J.

References

(Ed.), *The Countesthorpe Experience*, pp. 86–92 London, George Allen and Unwin.

ASHTON, P. and MERRITT, J. (1979) 'INSET at a distance', *Cambridge Journal of Education*, **9**(2), 153–64.

BAKHTIN/VOLOSINOV, V.N. (1973) *Marxism and the Philosophy of Language*, New York, Seminar Press.

BALL, S. (1981) *Beachside Comprehensive*, Cambridge, Cambridge University Press.

BALL, S.J. and GOODSON, I.F. (Eds) (1985 a) *Teachers' Lives and Careers*, London, Falmer Press.

BALL, S.J. and GOODSON, I.F. (1985 b) 'Understanding teachers: Concepts and contexts', in BALL, S.J. and GOODSON, I.F. (Eds), *Teachers' Lives and Careers*, pp. 1–26, London, Falmer Press.

BARNES, D. and SHEMILT, D. (1974) 'Transmission and interpretation', *Educational Review*, **26**, 213–228.

BARROW, R. (1984) *Giving Teaching Back to Teachers: A Critical Introduction to Curriculum Theory*, Brighton, Wheatsheaf.

BENNET, C. (1985) 'Paints, pots or promotion? Art teachers' attitudes towards their careers', in BALL, S.J. and GOODSON, I.F. (Eds), *Teachers' Lives and Careers*, pp. 120–1137, London, Falmer Press.

BERK, L. (1980) 'Education in lives: Biographic narrative in the study of educational outcomes', *Journal of Curriculum Theorizing*, **2**(2), 88–154.

BERNSTEIN, B. (1971) 'On the classification and framing of educational knowledge', in YOUNG, M.F.D. (Ed.), *Knowledge and Control,*, pp. 47–69, London, Collier-Macmillan.

BERNSTEIN, B.B. (1971–1977) *Class, Codes and Control* (Vols. 1–3), London, Routledge and Kegan Paul.

BERTAUX, D. (1981) *Biography and Society: The Life History Approach in the Social Sciences*, Sage Studies in International Sociology 23, Beverly Hills, CA, Sage.

BEYNON, J. (1985) 'Institutional change and career histories in a comprehensive school', in BALL, S.J. and GOODSON, I.F. (Eds), *Teachers' Lives and Careers*, pp. 158–79, London, Falmer Press.

BLOCH, E. (1986) *The Principle of Hope* (N. Plaice, Trans.), Oxford, Blackwell.

BOLAM, R. (Ed.) (1982) *School Focused In-service Training*, London, Heinemann.

BOURDIEU, P. (1977) 'Cultural reproduction and social reproduction', in KARABEL, J. and HALSEY, A.H. (Eds), *Power and Ideology in Education*, pp. 487–511, Oxford, Oxford University Press.

BOWLES, S. and GINTIS, H. (1976) *Schooling in Capitalist America*, New York, Basic Books.

BROWN, S., and McINTYRE, D. (1985) *Research Methodology and New Policies for Professional Development and Innovation*, Paper presented at the Scottish Educational Research Association, 1985.

BUCHMANN, M. (n.d.) *Problems of Practice and Principle in Research Communication*, Ann Arbour MI, Institute for Research on Teaching, Michigan State University.

BURKE, J. (1985) 'Concord Sixth Form College: The possibility of school without conflict', in BALL, S.J. and GOODSON, I.F. (Eds), *Teachers' Lives and Careers*, pp. 138–157, London, Falmer Press.

References

BURLINGAME, M. (1981) 'Superintendent power retention', in BACHARACH, S.B. (Ed.), *Organizational Behaviour in Schools and School Districts*, pp. 429–64, New York, Praeger.

BUTT, R.L. (1981) 'Classroom change and scientific literacy: A case study', in LEITHWOOD, K. and HUGHES, A. (Eds), *Curriculum Canada III: Canadian Research and Development and Critical Student Outcomes*, pp. 89–109, Vancouver, Center for the Study of Curriculum and Instruction, University of British Columbia.

BUTT, R.L. (1985) 'Curriculum: Metatheoretical horizons and emancipatory action', *Journal of Curriculum Theorizing*, **6**(2), 7–23.

BUTT, R.L. and OLSON, J. (1983) 'Dreams and realities: An approach to change through critical consciousness', in BUTT, R.L. and DAIGNAULT, J. (Eds), *Insider's Realities, Outsider's Dreams: Prospects for Curriculum Change: Curriculum Canada IV*, pp. 1–17, Vancouver, Centre for the Study of Curriculum and Instruction, University of British Columbia.

BUTT, R.L. and RAYMOND, D. (1987) 'Arguments for using qualitative approaches in understanding teacher thinking: The case for biography', *Journal of Curriculum Theorizing*, **7**(1), 62–93.

BUTT, R.L., RAYMOND, D. and RAY, (1986) 'Personal, practical and prescriptive influences on a teacher's thoughts and actions', in LOWYCK, J. (Ed.), *Teachers' Thinking and Professional Action*, pp. 306–328, Leuven, Belgium: University of Leuven.

BUTT, R.L., RAYMOND, D. and RAY (in press) 'Biographical and contextual influences on an 'ordinary' teacher's thoughts and actions', in LOWYCK, J., CLARKE, C. and HALKES, R. (Eds), *Teacher Thinking and Professional Action*, Lisse, Holland, Swets and Zeitlinger.

BUTT, R.L., RAYMOND, D., MCCUE, G. and YAMAGISHI, L. (1986, April) *Individual and Collective Interpretations of Teacher Biographies*, Paper presented at AERA, San Francisco.

BYRNE, E.M. (1974) *Planning and Educational Inequality*, Slough, NFER.

CARNOY, M. (1972) *Schooling in a Corporate Society*, New York, David McKay.

CARR, W. and KEMMIS, S. (1983) *Becoming Critical: Knowing Through Action Research*, Geelong, Aus., Deakin University Press.

CLANDININ, D.J. (1985) 'Personal, practical knowledge: A study of a teacher's classroom images', *Curriculum Inquiry*, **15**, 361–385.

CLANDININ, D.J. (1986) *Classroom Practice: Teacher Images in Action*, London, Falmer Press.

COLE, M. (1985) '"The tender trap?": Commitment and consciousness in entrants to teaching', in BALL, S.J. and GOODSON, I.F. (Eds), *Teachers' Lives and Careers*, pp. 89–104, London, Falmer Press.

COLLS, R., and DODD, P. (1986) *Englishness: Politics and Culture 1880–1920*, London, Croom Helm.

CONNELL, R.W. (1985) *Teachers' Work*, London, Allen and Unwin.

COOPER, B. (1985) *Renegotiating Secondary School Mathematics: A Study of Curriculum Change and Stability*, Lewes, Falmer Press.

COREY, S. M. (1953) *Action Research to Improve School Practice*, New York, Teachers' College, Columbia University.

CORRIGAN, P. (1975) 'Dichotomy is contradiction', *Sociological Review*, **23**, pp. 211–243.

References

CORRIGAN, P. (1977 a) *State Formation and Moral Regulation in Nineteenth-century Britain: Sociological Investigations*, Unpublished doctoral dissertation, University of Durham.

CORRIGAN, P. (1977 b) 'Feudal relics or capitalist monuments?: Notes on the sociology of unfree labour', *Sociology*, **11**, 435–463.

CORRIGAN, P. (1981) 'On moral regulation', *Sociological Review*, **29**, 313–337.

CORRIGAN, P. (1985, May) *The Context for Bovey; The Politics of the Educational State: A Concluding Comment*, Paper presented at the Toronto Higher Education Forum.

CORRIGAN, P. (1986) 'In/forming schooling', in D. LIVINGSTONE (Ed.), *Critical Pedagogy and Cultural Power*, pp. 117–39, Toronto, Garamond.

CORRIGAN, P. (in press-a) 'The body of the intellectuals', *Sociological Review*.

CORRIGAN, P. (in press-b), 'A day in whose life . . . .? Canada's IMAGE-nation', in MCGREGOR, G. (Ed.), *Canadian Art and Contemporary Theory*, Toronto, University of Toronto Press.

CORRIGAN, P. and CURTIS, B. (1985) 'Education, inspection and state formation: A preliminary statement', in JOHNSON, D. and OUELLETTE, L. (Eds), *Historical Papers: Montreal 1985*, pp. 156–171, Ottawa, Canadian Historical Association.

CORRIGAN, P., CURTIS, B., and LANNING, R. (1987) 'The political space of schooling', in WOTHERSPOON, T. (Ed.), *The Political Economy of Canadian Schooling*, pp. 21–43, Toronto, Methuen.

CORRIGAN, P. and SAYER, D. (1985) *The Great Arch: English State Formation as Cultural Revolution*, London, Blackwell.

CORRIGAN, P. and SAYER, D. (1987, May) *From the 'Body Politic' to the 'National Interest'*, Paper presented at the Mellon Symposium on Historical Anthropology, Pasadena, California.

CRONBACH, L.J. and Associates (1980) *Towards Reform of Program Evaluation*, San Francisco, Jossey-Bass.

CRONBACH, L. and SUPPES, P. (Eds) (1969) *Research for Tomorrow's Schools: Disciplined Inquiry for Education*, New York, Macmillan.

CURTIS, B. (1983) 'Preconditions of the Canadian state: Educational reform and the construction of a public in Upper Canada', *Studies in Political Economy*, **10**, 99–121.

CURTIS, B. (in press) *Building the Educational State: Canada West, 1836–1871*, London, Ontario, The Althouse Press.

DEPARTMENT OF EDUCATION AND SCIENCE (1983) *Teaching Quality*, London, HMSO.

DEWEY, J. (1963) *Experience and Education*, New York: Macmillan.

DIAZ, J. (1977, August) *Perspectives on Education in the Context of Peace Research*, Paper given at the World Council on Curriculum and Instruction, Istanbul.

DICKINSON, E. (1883/1984) 'Letter to Maria Whitney', in OLSON, T. (Ed.), *Mother to Daughter, Daughter to Mother*, p. 231, Old Westbury, NY, Feminist Press.

DIDION, J. (1961) 'On keeping a notebook', in DIDION, J. (Ed.), *Slouching Toward Bethlehem*, pp. 131–141, New York, Dell.

DITISHEIM, M. (1984, March) 'Le travail de l'histoire de vie comme instrument de formation en education', *Education Permanente*, **72–73**, 199–210.

DOUGLAS, A. (1977) *The Feminization of American Culture*, New York, Avon.

DURKHEIM, E. (1974) *Sociology and Philosophy*, New York, Free Press.
EARLE, W. (1972) *Autobiographical Consciousness*, Chicago, Quadrangle.
'Education for a happier life' (Theme issue), (1987, October) *The Plain Truth*, **52**(9).
EISNER, E.W. (1979) *The Educational Imagination: On the Design and Evaluation of School Programs*, New York, Macmillan.
EISNER, E.W. (1985) *The Art of Educational Evaluation: A Personal View*, London, Falmer.
ELBAZ, F. (1983) *Teacher Thinking: A Study of Practical Knowledge*, London, Croom Helm.
ELLIOTT, J. (1983) *Paradigms of Educational Research and Theories of Schooling*, Unpublished manuscript, Center for Applied Research in Education, University of East Anglia.
ELLIOTT, J. (1985) 'Some key concepts underlying teachers' evaluation of innovations', in TAMIR, P. (Ed.), *The Role of Evaluation in Curriculum*, pp. 142–161, London, Croom Helm.
ERICKSON, F. (1986) 'Qualitative methods in research on teaching', in WITTROCK, M.C. (Ed.), *Handbook of Research on Teaching*, 3rd ed., pp. 119–161, New York, Macmillan.
EVALUATION RESEARCH SOCIETY (1982) 'Standards of program evaluation', *New Directions for Program Evaluation*, **15**, 7–19.
FAY, B. (1975) *Social Theory and Political Practice*, London, Allen and Unwin.
FEIMAN-NEMSER, S., and FLODEN, R.E. (1986) 'The cultures of teaching', in WITTROCK, M.C. (Ed.), *Handbook of Research on Teaching*, 3rd ed., pp. 505–526, New York, Macmillan.
FISKE, E. B. (1986, September 3) 'Bennett urges overhaul of elementary curriculum', *New York Times*, A1, A11.
FLANDERS, T. (1983) 'Teachers' realities, needs, and professional development', in BUTT, R.L., OLSON, J. and DAIGNAULT, J. (Eds), *Insiders' Realities, Outsider's Dreams: Prospects for Curriculum Change: Curriculum Canada IV*, pp. 139–152, Vancouver, Center for the Study of Curriculum and Instruction, University of British Columbia.
FOUCAULT, M. (1981) 'Questions of method', *Ideology and Consciousness*, **8**, 3–14.
FOUCAULT, M. (1982) 'The subject and power', *Critical Inquiry*, **8**, 777–795.
FRANSELLA, F. and BANNISTER, D. (1977) *A Manual for Repertory Grid Technique*, London, Academic Press.
FROST, R. (1930/1950) 'Birches', in MATTHIESSEN, F.O., (Ed.), *The Oxford Book of American Verse*, pp. 559–561, New York, Oxford University Press.
FULLAN, M. (1985) 'Change processes and strategies at the local level', *The Elementary School Journal*, **85**, 391–420.
FULLAN, M. and CONNELLY, F.M. (1987) *Teacher Education in Ontario: Current Practice and Options for the Future: Position Paper*, Toronto, Ministry of Education and Ministry of Colleges and Universities.
GADAMER, H.G. (1975) *Truth and Method*, London, Sheed and Ward.
GIBSON, R. (1985) 'Critical times for action research', *Cambridge Journal of Education*, **15**, 59–64.
GIBSON, R. (1986) *Critical Theory and Education*, London, Hodder and Stoughton.
GLASER, B.G. and STRAUSS, A. (1968) *The Discovery of Grounded Theory*, London,

Weidenfeld and Nicolson.
GOFFMAN, E. (1962) *Asylums: Essays on the Social Situation of Mental Patients and Other Inmates*, Chicago, Aldine.
GOODSON, I.F. (1983 a) *School Subjects and Curriculum Change*, London, Croom Helm.
GOODSON, I.F. (1983 b) 'The use of life histories in the study of teaching', in HAMMERSLEY, M. (Ed.), *The Ethnography of Schooling: Methodological Issues*, pp. 129–154, Driffield, Nafferton Books.
GORMAN, C. (1987) *Strategic Planning in Education in Ontario*, Unpublished master's thesis, University of Toronto.
GRIFFIN, S. (1981) *Pornography and Silence*, New York, Harper and Row.
GRUMET, M. (1980) 'Autobiography and reconceptualization', *Journal of Curriculum Theorizing*, **2**(2), 155–158.
GRUMET, M. (1987) 'The politics of personal knowledge', *Curriculum Inquiry*, **17**, 319–329.
GRUNDY, S. (1982) 'Three modes of action research', *Curriculum Perspectives*, **2**(3), 23–34.
GUBA, E. and LINCOLN, Y. (1981) *Effective Evaluation: Improving the Usefulness of Evaluation Results through Responsive and Naturalistic Approaches*, San Francisco, Jossey-Bass.
GUSKEY, T.R. (1985) 'Staff development and teacher change', *Educational Leadership*, **42**(7), 57–60.
HABERMAS, J. (1970) 'Towards a theory of communicative competence', *Inquiry*, **13**, 360–375.
HABERMAS, J. (1979) 'What is universal pragmatics?' in HABERMAS, J., *Communication and the Evolution of Society*, pp. 1–68, London, Heinemann.
HALL, G. and LOUCKS, S. (1977) 'A developmental model for determining whether treatment is actually implemented', *American Educational Journal*, **14**, 263–276.
HALSEY, A.H., HEATH, A.F. and RIDGE, J.M. (1980) *Origins and Destinations*, Oxford, Oxford University Press.
HAMILTON, D. (1980) 'Adam Smith and the moral economy of the classroom system', *Journal of Curriculum Studies*, **12**, 281–298.
HAMILTON, D. and GIBBONS, M. (1980, April) *Notes on the Origins of the Educational Terms Class and Curriculum*, Paper presented at the AERA, Boston, MA.
HANSON, D. and HERRINGTON, M. (1976) *From College to Classroom: The Probationary Year*, London, Routledge and Kegan Paul.
HANSON, E.M. (1981) 'Organizational control in educational systems: A case study of governance in schools', in BACHARACH, S.B. (Ed.), *Organizational Behaviour in Schools and School Districts*, pp. 245–276, New York, Praeger.
HARGREAVES, A. (1978) 'The significance of classroom coping strategies', in BARTON, L. and MEIGHAN, R. (Eds), *Sociological Interpretations of Schooling and Classrooms: A Reappraisal*, pp. 73–100, Driffield, Nafferton Books.
HARGREAVES, A. (1982) 'The rhetoric of school-centred innovation', *Journal of Curriculum Studies*, **14**, 251–266.
HARGREAVES, A. (1986) *Two Cultures of Schooling*, Lewes, Falmer.
HARGREAVES, A. (in press) 'Teaching quality: A sociological analysis', *Journal of Curriculum Studies*.

HARGREAVES, D. (1982) *The Challenge for the Comprehensive School*, London, Routledge and Kegan Paul.
HARLAND, J. (1987) 'The new INSET: A transformation scene', *Journal of Education Policy*, **2**, 235–244.
HARRÉ, R. (1979) *Social Being: A Theory for Social Psychology*, Oxford, Blackwell, 1979.
HARRISON, J.F.C. (1984) *The Common People*, London, Flamingo.
HARVEY, C. (1981) *Practitioners' Perceptions of an Innovative School System in a Developing Country: A Qualitative Analysis*, Unpublished doctoral dissertation, University of Toronto.
HER MAJESTY'S INSPECTORATE (1977) *Curriculum 11–16*, London, HMSO.
HER MAJESTY'S INSPECTORATE (1983) *Curriculum 11–16: Towards a Statement of Entitlement*, London, HMSO.
HILLIARD, F.H. (1971) 'Theory and practice in teacher education', in HILLIARD, F.H. (Ed.), *Teaching the Teachers*, pp. 33–54, London, Allen and Unwin.
HOBSBAWN, E.J. and RANGER, T. (Eds) (1983) *The Invention of Tradition*, London, Cambridge University Press.
HOUSE, E.R. (1980) *Evaluating with Validity*. Beverly Hills, CA, Sage.
INGLIS, F. (1985) *The Management of Ignorance: A Political Theory of the Curriculum*, Oxford, Blackwell.
INGVARSON, L. and GREENWAY, P.A. (1981) *Portrayals of Teacher Development*, Unpublished paper, Monash University, Australia. (ERIC Document Reproduction Service No. ED 200 600).
INNER LONDON EDUCATION AUTHORITY (1984) *Improving Secondary Schools*, London, The author.
JACKSON, P.W. (1968) *Life in Classrooms*, New York, Holt, Rinehart and Winston.
JANESICK, V.J. (1981) 'Developing grounded theory: Reflections on a case study of an architectural design curriculum', in SCHUBERT, W.H. and SCHUBERT, A.L. (Eds), *Conceptions of Curriculum Knowledge: Focus on Students and Teachers*, pp. 15–22, Washington, DC, Creation and Utilization of Curriculum Knowledge, Special Interest Group of AERA.
JENKINS, D. and SHIPMAN, M. (1976) *Curriculum: An Introduction*, London, Open Books.
JOHNSON, R. (1970) 'Educational policy and social control in early Victorian England', *Past and Present*, **49**, 96–125.
JOINT COMMITTEE ON STANDARDS FOR EDUCATIONAL EVALUATION (1981) *Standards for Evaluation of Educational Programs, Projects, and Materials*, Kalamazoo, MI, Research Center, Western Michigan University.
JOSEPH, K. (1984, January) Speech to the North of England Education Committee.
KELLY, G. (1955) *The Psychology of Personal Constructs* (Vols. 1 and 2), New York, Norton.
KEMMIS, S. (1984 a) 'Introduction: Action research in retrospect and prospect', in KEMMIS, S. (Ed.), *The Action Research Reader*, pp. 11–31, Geelong, Aus., Deakin University Press.
KEMMIS, S. (Ed.) (1984 b) *The Action Research Reader*, Geelong, Aus., Deakin University Press.
KEMMIS, S. (1987) 'Critical reflection', in WIDEEN, M. and ANDREWS, I. (Eds),

Staff Development for School Improvement: A Focus on the Teacher, pp. 73–90, London, Falmer Press.

KODIKARA, A. (1986) *Schooling, Politics and the State*, Unpublished doctoral dissertation, University of Toronto.

LABOV, W. (1973) 'The logic of non-standard English', in KEDDIE, N. (Ed.), *Tinker, Tailor: The Myth of Cultural Deprivation*, pp. 21–66, Harmondsworth, Penguin.

LACEY, C. (1977) *The Socialization of Teachers*, London, Methuen.

LAMPERT, M. (1984) 'Teaching about thinking and thinking about teaching', *Journal of Curriculum Studies*, **16**, 1–18.

LATHER, P. (1984) *Gender and the Shaping of Public School Teaching: Do Good Girls make Good Teachers?*, Paper presented at the National Women's Studies Association, Douglass College, Rutgers State University, NJ.

LATHER, P. (1986 a) 'Research as praxis', *Harvard Educational Review*, **56**, 257–277.

LATHER, P. (1986 b) 'Issues of validity in openly ideological research: Between a rock and a soft place', *Interchange*, **17**(4), 63–84.

LAYTON, D. (1972, January) 'Science as general education', *Trends in Education*, **25**, 11–16.

LEWIN, K. (1946) 'Action research and minority problems', *Journal of Social Issues*, **2**, 34–46.

LINCOLN, Y. and GUBA, E. (1985) *Naturalistic Inquiry*, Beverly Hills, CA, Sage.

LORTIE, D. (1975) *Schoolteacher: A Sociological Study*, Chicago, University of Chicago Press.

MACDONALD, M. (1980) 'Schooling in the reproduction of class and gender relations', in BARTON, L., MEIGHAN, R. and WALKER, S., (Eds), *Schooling, Ideology and Curriculum*, pp. 29–49, London, Falmer Press.

MACINTYRE, A. (1981) *After Virtue: A Study in Moral Theory*, Notre Dame, IN, Notre Dame University Press.

MANNHEIM, K. (1936/1960) *Ideology and Utopia*, London, Routledge and Kegan Paul.

MANSFIELD, B. (1984) *Audience Reaction to Educational Accounts: A Case Study*, Unpublished doctoral dissertation, University of Toronto.

MARSHALL, J. and PETERS, M. (1985) 'Evaluation and education: The ideal learning community', *Policy Sciences*, **18**, 263–288.

MARX, K. and ENGELS, F. (1846/1976) 'The German ideology', *Collected Works*, Vol. 5, London, Lawrence and Wishart.

MCALPINE, L. (1985) *The Educator as Evaluator: Facilitating Professional Development*, Unpublished doctoral dissertation, University of Toronto.

MCCORMICK, R. and JAMES, M. (1983) *Curriculum Evaluation in Schools*, Beckenham, Kent, Croom Helm.

MCKEON, R. (1951) 'Philosophy and action', *Ethics*, **62**, 79–100.

MEASOR, L. (1985) 'Critical incidents in the classroom: Identities, choices and careers', in BALL, S.J. and GOODSON, I.F. (Eds), *Teachers' Lives and Careers*, pp. 61–77, London, Falmer Press.

MORGAN, R. (1987) *English Studies as Cultural Production in Ontario, 1860–1920*, Unpublished doctoral dissertation, University of Toronto.

NIAS, J. (1985) 'Reference groups in primary teaching: Talking, listening and identity', in BALL, S.J. and GOODSON, I.F. (Eds), *Teachers' Lives and Careers*, pp. 105–119, London, Falmer Press.

NIXON, J. (Ed.) (1981) *A Teacher's Guide to Action Research*, London, Grant McIntyre.
NODDINGS, N. (1984) *Caring*, Berkeley, CA, University of California Press.
NORWOOD REPORT (1943) *Curriculum and Examinations in Secondary Schools*, Report of the Committee of the Secondary School Examinations Council, appointed by the President of the Board of Education in 1941, London, HMSO.
O'BRIEN, M. (1981) *The Politics of Reproduction*, Boston, Routledge and Kegan Paul.
OLSON, J. (1982 a) 'Dilemmas of inquiry teaching: How teachers cope', in OLSON, J. (Ed.), *Innovation in the Science Curriculum: Classroom Knowledge and Curriculum Change*, pp. 140–178, London, Croom Helm.
OLSON, J. (Ed.) (1982 b) *Innovation in the Science Curriculum: Classroom Knowledge and Curriculum Change*, London, Croom Helm.
OLSON, J. (1984) 'Surrealistic tendencies in curriculum thought', *McGill Journal of Education*, **19**, 159–167.
OLSON, J. and EATON, S. (1986) *Case Studies of Microcomputers in the Classroom: Questions for Curriculum and Teacher Education*, Toronto, Ontario Minnistry of Education.
OLSON, J. and RUSSELL, T. (1984) *Science Education in Canada, Vol. III: Case Studies in Science Education*, Ottawa, Science Council of Canada.
OLSON, T. (Ed.) (1984) *Mother to Daughter, Daughter to Mother*, Old Westbury, NY, Feminist Press.
ONTARIO MINISTRY OF EDUCATION (1977) *Intermediate English*, Toronto, The author.
ONTARIO MINISTRY OF EDUCATION (1984 a) *Ontario Schools: Intermediate and Senior Division*, Toronto, The author.
ONTARIO MINISTRY OF EDUCATION (1984 b) *Review and Evaluation Bulletin: Towards the Year 2000: Future Conditions and Strategic Options for the Support of Learning in Ontario*, **5**(1), Toronto, The author.
ONTARIO MINISTRY OF EDUCATION (1986 a) *Discipline: Intermediate and Senior Divisions*, Toronto, The author.
ONTARIO MINISTRY OF EDUCATION (1986 b) *Behavior: Resource Guide*, Toronto, The author.
PARLETT, M. and HAMILTON, D. (1976) 'Evaluation as illumination: A new approach to the study of innovatory programs', *Evaluation Studies Review Annual*, **1**, 140–157.
Phenomenology and Pedagogy (1983–   ), Edmonton, AB, University of Alberta.
PINAR, W. (1980) 'Life history and educational experience', *Journal of Curriculum Theorizing*, **2**(2), 159–212.
PINAR, W. (1981) 'Life history and educational experience: Part Two', *Journal of Curriculum Theorizing*, **3**(1), 259–286.
PINAR, W. (1986, April) *Autobiography and the Architecture of Self*, Paper presented at AERA, San Francisco.
PLUMMER, K. (1983) *Documents of Life: An Introduction to the Problems and Literature of a Humanistic Method*, Contemporary Social Research Series 7, London, Allen and Unwin.
POIRIER, P. (1986, August 28) 'What's in a name?' *Globe and Mail*, A1.
POLAK, F.L. (1961) *The Image of the Future,* (Vol. 1), New York, Oceana.
POLLARD, A. (1984) 'Ethnography and social policy for classroom practice', in

References

BARTON, L. and WALKER, S. (Eds), *Social Crisis and Educational Research*, (pp. 171–199), London, Croom Helm.

POPE, M. and KEEN, T. (1981) *Personal Construct Psychology and Education*, London, Academic Press.

POULANTZAS, N. (1978) *State, Power, Socialism*, London, Verso.

RAND CORPORATION (1978) *Federal Programs Supporting Educational Change* (Vols. I–VIII), Santa Monica, CA, The author.

RAPOPORT, R.N. (1970) 'Three dilemmas in action research', *Human Relations*, **23**, 499–513.

REID, W.A. (1972) *The University and the Sixth Form Curriculum*, London, Macmillan.

REID, W.A. (1985) 'Curriculum change and the evolution of educational constituencies: The English sixth form in the nineteenth century', in GOODSON, I.F. (Ed.), *Social Histories of the Secondary Curriculum: Subjects for Study*, pp. 289–311, Lewes, Falmer Press.

RISEBOROUGH, G.F. (1985) 'Pupils, teachers' careers and schooling: An empirical study', in BALL, S.J. and GOODSON, I.F. (Eds), *Teachers' Lives and Careers*, pp. 202–265, London, Falmer Press.

ROTHBLATT, S. (1976) *Tradition and Change in English Liberal Education: An Essay in History and Culture*, London, Faber and Faber.

RUDDUCK, J. (in press) 'Accrediting teacher education courses: The new criteria', in HARGREAVES, A. and REYNOLDS, D. (Eds), *Educational Policy: Controversies and Critiques*.

SANFORD, N. (1984) 'Whatever happened to action research?' in KEMMIS, S. (Ed.), *The Action Research Reader*, pp. 72–80, Geelong, Aus., Deakin University Press.

SARTRE, J.P. (1954) *Kean*, London, Hamish Hamilton.

SCHECTER, S. (1987) 'Another turn of the screw: Educational reform in progress', in WOTHERSPOON, T. (Ed.), *The Political Economy of Canadian Schooling*, pp. 45–53, Toronto, Methuen.

SCHON, D. (1979) 'Generative metaphor: A perspective on problem-setting in social policy', in ORTONY, A. (Ed.), *Metaphor in Thought*, pp. 254–283, Cambridge, Cambridge University Press.

SCHON, D.A. (1983) *The Reflective Practitioner: How Professionals Think in Action*, New York, Basic Books.

SHAMAI, S. (1986) *Ethnic and National Identity among Jewish Students in Toronto*, Unpublished doctoral dissertation, University of Toronto.

SHAMAI, S. and CORRIGAN, P.R.D. (1987) 'Social facts, moral regulation and statistical jurisdiction: A critical evaluation of Canadian census figures on education', *Canadian Journal of Higher Education*, **17**(2), 37–58.

SHAPIRO, B.J. (1985) *The Report of the Commission on Private Schools in Ontario*, Toronto, Ministry of Education.

SHARMA, T. (1982, February) 'In-servicing the teachers: A pastoral tale with a moral', *Phi Delta Kappan*, **63**, 403.

SHARP, R. and GREEN, A. (1975) *Education and Social Control*, London, Routledge and Kegan Paul.

SIKES, P.J. (1985) 'The life cycle of the teacher', in BALL, S.J. and GOODSON, I.F. (Eds), *Teachers' Lives and Careers*, pp. 27–60, London, Falmer Press.

SIMON, R. and DIPPO, D. (n.d.) *On Critical Ethnographic Work*, Unpublished manuscript. The Ontario Institute for Studies in Education, Toronto.

SMELSER, N. (1968) *Essays in Sociological Explanation*, New Jersey, Prentice-Hall.
SMITH, D. (in press) *The Social Organization of Knowledge*, Boston, MA, Northeastern University Press.
SMITH, L.M., KLEINE, P.F., DWYER, D.C. and PRUNTY, J.J. (1985) 'Educational innovators: A decade and a half later', in BALL, S.J. and GOODSON, I.F. (Eds), *Teachers' Lives and Careers*, pp. 180–201, London, Falmer Press.
SMITH, N. (Ed.) (1981) *Metaphors for Evaluation*, Beverly Hills, CA, Sage.
STAKE, R.E. (1976) 'Program evaluation, particularly responsive evaluation', in DOCKRELL, W.B. and HAMILTON, D.F. (Eds), *Rethinking Educational Research*, pp. 72–87, London, Hodder and Stoughton.
STAKE, R.E. (1978) 'The case study method in social inquiry', *Educational Researcher*, 7, pp. 5–8.
STAKE, R.E. (1984, August) *An Evolutionary View of Educational Improvement*, Paper presented at the National Symposium on Evaluation, Federal University of Espirito Santo, Vitoria, Brazil.
STENHOUSE, L. (1975) *An Introduction to Curriculum Research and Development*, London, Heinemann.
STENHOUSE, L. (1980) *Curriculum Research and Development in Action*, London, Heinemann.
STRAUS, E. (1966) 'The upright posture', in NATANSON, M. (Ed.), *Essays in Phenomenology*, pp. 164–192, The Hague, Martinus Nijhoff.
TAUNTON REPORT (1868) *Schools Inquiry Commission: Report of the Commissioners*, London, HMSO.
TAYLOR, A.J.P. (1965) *English History 1914–1945*, Oxford, Oxford University Press.
THIESSEN, D. (forthcoming) *Curriculum Change Constructs and Orientations*, Unpublished doctoral dissertation, University of Sussex.
THOMPSON, E.P. (1968) *Education and Experience* (Fifth Mansbridge Memorial Lecture), Leeds, Leeds University Press.
TOMKINS, G.S. (1986) *A Common Countenance: Stability and Change in the Canadian Curriculum*, Toronto, Prentice-Hall.
TORONTO BOARD OF EDUCATION (1915) *Annual Report*, Toronto, The author.
TREMPE, P.L. (1984) 'Lavoisier: Science teaching at an Ecole Polyvalente', in OLSON, J. and RUSSELL, T. (Eds), *Science Education in Canada, Vol. III: Case Studies in Science Education*, pp. 209–256, Hull, Quebec, Science Council of Canada.
U.S. OFFICE OF EDUCATION (1986 a) *First Lessons*, Washington, DC, The author.
U.S. OFFICE OF EDUCATION (1986 b) *What Works: Schools without Drugs*, Washington, DC, The author.
UNIVERSITY OF CAMBRIDGE LOCAL EXAMINATIONS SYNDICATE (1958, 29 May) *One Hundredth Annual Report to University*, Cambridge, Cambridge University Press.
VAN MANEN, M. (1978) *A Phenomenological Experiment in Educational Theory: The Utrecht School*, Paper presented at AERA, Toronto.
VAN MANEN, M. (1979) 'The phenomenology of pedagogic observation', *Canadian Journal of Education*, 4, 5–16.
WALKER, R. (1986) 'Breaking the grip of print in curriculum research', *Journal of Curriculum Studies*, 18, 95–96.
WALLER, W. (1932) *The Sociology of Teaching*, New York, Wiley.
WEBB, R.B. (1985) 'Teacher status panic: Moving up the down escalator', in

References

BALL, S.J. and GOODSON, I.F. (Eds), *Teachers' Lives and Careers*, pp. 78–88, London, Falmer Press.

WEISS, J., REYNOLDS, C. and SIMON, R. (1983) *The Personal, Social and Material Bases of Research*, Paper presented at AERA, Montreal, PQ.

WERNER, W. (1982) 'An interpretive approach to curriculum implementation', in LEITHWOOD, K. and HUGHES, A. (Eds), *Curriculum Canada III: Canadian Research and Development and Critical Student Outcomes*, pp. 137–160, Vancouver, Center for the Study of Curriculum and Instruction, University of British Columbia.

WESTBURY, I. (1973) 'Conventional classrooms, open classrooms and the technology of teaching', *Journal of Curriculum Studies*, **5**, 99–121.

WESTON, P. and HARLAND, J. (in press) 'The lower attaining pupils' program: myths and messages', in HARGREAVES, A. and REYNOLDS, D. (Eds), *Educational Policy: Controversies and Critiques*.

WHITTY, G. (1985) *Sociology and School Knowledge: Curriculum Theory, Research and Politics*, London, Methuen.

WIDEMAN, H. (1981) *Using Portrayals in Formative Evaluation: A Case Study*, Unpublished Master's thesis, University of Toronto.

WILDEN, T. (1981) *The Imaginary Canadian: An Examination for Discovery*, Vancouver, Pulp Press.

WILLIAMS, R. (1961) *The Long Revolution*, London, Chatto and Windus.

WILLIAMS, R. (1981) *Culture*, London, Fontana.

WILLIAMS, R. (1983) *Towards 2000*, London, Chatto and Windus.

WILLIAMSON, B. (1982) *Class, Culture and Community: A Biographical Study of Social Change in Mining*, London, Routledge and Kegan Paul.

WILLIS, G. (1978) *Qualitative Evaluation: Concepts and Cases in Curriculum Criticism*, Berkeley, CA, McCutchan.

WILLIS, P. (1977) *Learning to Labour*, New York, Columbia University Press.

WILSON, B. (1962) 'The teacher's role: A sociological analysis', *British Journal of Sociology*, **13**, 22–36.

WILSON, J. (1979) *Fantasy and Commonsense in Education*, New York, Wiley.

WISE, R.I. (1980) 'The evaluator as educator', *New Directions for Program Evaluation*, **5**, 11–18.

WOODS, P. (1977) 'Teaching for survival', in WOODS, P. and HAMMERSLEY, M. (Eds), *School Experience: Explorations in Sociology of Education*, pp. 271–293, Lewes, Falmer Press.

YEO, S. (1979) 'Working class association, private capital, welfare and the state in the late nineteenth and twentieth centuries', in PARRY, N., RUSTIN, M. and SUTYAMURTI, C. (Eds), *Social Work, Welfare, and the State*, pp. 48–71, Leeds, UK, Arnold.

YEO, S. (1986) 'Socialism, the state, and some oppositional Englishness', in COLLS, R. and DODD, P. (Eds), *Englishness: Politics and Culture 1880–1920* pp. 308–369, London, Croom Helm.

YOUNG, M. (1971 a) 'An approach to the study of curricula as socially organized knowledge', in YOUNG, M.F.D. (Ed.), *Education and Control: New Directions for the Sociology of Education*, pp. 19–46, London, Collier Macmillan.

YOUNG, M. (Ed.) (1971 b) *Knowledge and Control: New Directions for Sociology of Education*, London, Collier Macmillan.

Notes on Contributors

CATHERINE BEATTIE (McMaster University) teaches courses on the theory and practice of curriculum development. She is interested in action research and the use of microcomputers in schools.

RICHARD BUTT (The University of Lethbridge) is interested in curriculum praxis, professional development, classroom change, science education and multiculturalism. He is also developing materials intended to reduce racism and prejudice.

ROBERT CLARK (The University of Western Ontario) is interested in curriculum history, the history of professionalization, local history, and political socialization.

PHILIP CORRIGAN (Ontario Institute for Studies in Education) has published many articles in the sociology of education, and is (with Derek Sayer) co-author of *The Great Arch: English State Formation as Cultural Revolution*, and co-editor of *Journal of Historical Sociology*.

BRUCE CURTIS (Wilfrid Laurier University) has published *Building the Educational State, Canada West, 1836–1871* and many other papers. With Philip Corrigan, he is co-director of the *Canadian State Formation Project*.

IVOR GOODSON (The University of Western Ontario) is author of *The Making of Curriculum* and *European Dimensions and the Secondary School Curriculum*. He is also founding editor of *Journal of Education Policy*.

MADELEINE GRUMET (Brook College, CUNY) is the author of *Bitter Milk: Women and Teaching*, and editor of the SUNY Press series on feminist theory and education.

ANDY HARGREAVES (Ontario Institute for Studies in Education) is author of *Two Cultures of Schooling: The Case of Middle Schools*, and numerous articles in learned journals.

GEOFFREY MILBURN (The University of Western Ontario) is interested in several curricular problems, including the use of alternative metaphors in curricular discourse.

JOHN OLSON (Queen's University) teaches courses in science methods and curriculum innovation. His current research interests focus on the relationship between the culture of the school and innovation.

DENNIS THIESSEN (The University of Toronto) is interested in school-based professional development and the perspectives that teachers and students use to portray their curriculum experiences in school.

JOEL WEISS (Ontario Institute for Studies in Education) is the founding editor of *Curriculum Inquiry*. He has contributed to the *Second Handbook of Research on Teaching* and *Review of Research in Education*, and written many articles in academic journals.

Index

Abbs, P. (1974) 147, 150
ability 19, 20
Abrams, P. (1963) 67
academic
   disciplines 18, 19
   power groups 3
academics 115, 118, 119
access: research communication 126-7
accountability 6, 72, 79, 104, 105, 151, 153
accounts, evaluation 129
   see also reports
achievement, educational 35, 36, 37, 68
action, professional
   and reflection 128
   science-based 103
action research 6-7, 124, 127
   control of 117, 118
   definition 111-12, 119-20n1
   theory and practice **110-20**
action researchers 7, 112
Action Research Network, The 111
adaption and flexibility 78
administrators, educational 5, 6, 8, 103, 105
adult education 21, 23, 24
adult learning 24, 125, 146, 151, 154
agencies, independent 79
agency 7, 101, 129
agents 101n3, 136
Akenson, D. H. (1971) 62n36, n38
Alberta, University of 101n4, 147
alternative practice 24
alternative research 10
alternatives, methodological **85-182**

Althusser, L. (1971) 68, 166
Altieri, C. (1981) 92-3
America 42, 59, 60, 110
   see also North America
American Evaluation Association 112
Anderson, B. R. (1983) 67
Anyon, J. (1980) 87
Aoki, T. (1983) 152
   and Jacknicke, K. and Franks, D. (1986) 147
Apple, M., 128, 129
   (1982a) 32
   (1982b) 87, 101n3
   (1986) 40
applied research 102
Armstrong, H., 61n10
Armstrong, M. 24
ascription 68
Ashton, P. and Merritt, J. (1979) 30
assessment constraints 31
assignments, course 8-9, 148-50
Australia, action research in 111
autobiographical
   course **146-59**
   enquiry 152
   research 146, 153-4, 157-8
autobiography **92-101**
autonomy 64, 76, 111, 141

'back-to-basics' 69
Bakhtin/Voloshinov, V. N. (1973) 67
Ball, S. (1981) 29
Ball, S. J. and Goodson, I. F.
   (1985a) 87, 160, 167
   (1985b) 162, 167
Barclay, Dr J. 41, 53, 62n52

183

Index

Barker, J. 61n10
Barnes, D. and Shemilt, D. (1974) 29
Barrow, R. (1984) 13
Beattie, C. 6-7, **110-20**
Becoming Critical 116
behaviour 59, 102, 103, 110, 129
behavioural approach 147
behavioural objectives 102
behaviours 68
belief: research communication 126, 127
Bennet, C. (1985) 160, 162
Bennett, W. J. 82n12
Bentham, J. 82n11
Berk, L. (1980) 156
Bernstein, B. 32, 33, 67
  (1971) 16, 28
  (1971-1977) 67
Bertaux, D. (1981) 161
Beynon, J. (1985) 160, 162, 165
biographical enquiry/studies 148, 151-2
biographic education 156
biography: life history 161
Black, C., 82n12
Bloch, E. (1986) 69
Bolam, R. (1982) 30
Bourdieu, P. 67
  (1977) 35
bourgeois concerns and society 48, 51, 56, 60, 66
Bowles, S. and Gintis, H.
  (1976) 101n3
Britain 59, 60, 147
  curriculum reform in 4, 42
  educational policy 26-40
British national curriculum 36-7
Brown, G. 46
Brown, S. and McIntyre, D. (1985) 30
Buchmann, M. 126
Bumstead, J. M. (1972) 62n32
Burke, J. (1985) 160
Burlingame, M. (1981) 27
Butt, R. L. 8-9, **146-59**
  (1981) 148, 153
  (1985) 155
  and Olson, J. (1983) 155
  and Raymond, D. (1987) 151, 156
  and Raymond, D. and McCue, G. and Yamagishi, L. (1986) 158
  and Raymond, D. and Ray (1986) 148, 158
Butts, J. C. 43, 61n13
Byrne, E. M. (1974) 18

Calvinism 3, 15, 25
Calvin, John 14
Cambridge Institute of Education 111
Campbell, J. 46
Canada 2, 14, 111
  curricular reform in **41-63**
  see also England
Canadas, the: state formation in 65
Canada West **41-63**
  see also Ontario
Canadian Evaluation Research Society 122
Canadian Series of Reading Books
  see 'Red Readers'
capitalism 67
capitalist relations of production 42, 59-60
capitalist system 4
career(s), teaching 6, 19, 23, 28, 103-4, 108-9
life histories 160, 162
Carlile, J., 58
Carmoy, M. (1972) 101n3
Carr, W. and Kemmis, S. 118
  (1983) 116, 117, 119, 120n
Carson, J. 43, 61n7
case-study 124, 128, 148
causal laws: classroom theory 117
centralization: school reform 64-5
certification of schooling 80-1
change, curricular 4, 6, **41-63**, 76, 78, 102, 103
  and evaluation 122-3
  orientations 8, **132-45**
  possibilities of: research 125
  school-based 148, 153
  strategies for 3-4, **29-39**
  theories 144
  see also classroom; teachers
child/children 29, 89, 90
Church, the: and education 21
Clandinin, D. J. (1985) 148, 152
  (1986) 30, 32
Clark, R. J. **1-10**
class, social 19, 24, 64, 69
  and curriculum 3, 13-14, 15, 17
  system 14
classes, notion of 13-14, 15
classroom 26, 33, 117, 134, 148
  action research 111, 112, 114, 115
  -centeredness, teachers' 27-8, 34, 38
  and curriculum change 138, 141, 152, 153, 155, 156
  isolation 27, 38, 40, 119, 153

and phenomenology 66
practice 30, 64-63, 114, 135
system 15, 16, 17
theory in 30, 114, 115
cognitive function: autobiography 147
Cole, M. (1985) 160, 166
collaboration 137, 140, 152
collaborative research 112, 153-4, 158
collegiality: curriculum change 135
Colls, R. and Dodd, P. (1986) 67
Common School 42
communication 32, 126-7, 128, 147, 156
network 142
community, ideal learning 129-30
compensatory education 69
comprehensive school reform 35
conclusion-orientated: research 121
confidentiality 150, 165
conflict 102, 103, 106
curriculum 18
Connell, R. W. (1985) 35
constraint 31, 34, 38, 40, 108
construct areas: curriculum change 145n2
constructs, teachers' 135, 136
construed context 134
consumer society 4, 64
control 117, 118, 119, 122, 127
curriculum 4-5, 14, 134, 138, 141, 142, 144
social 16, 22
teacher 7, 9, 112
see also knowledge
Cooper, B. (1985) 28
Cooper, J. 43, 61n12
co(operative)-learning 146, 155
Corey, S. (1953) 110
correspondence theories 89, 101n3
Corrigan, P. R. D. 4, **64-83**
(1975) 65
(1977a) 65, 82n13
(1981) 65
(1986) 67
and Curtis, B. (1985) 81n1
and Lanning, R. (1987) 65, 81n1
and Sayer, D. (1985, 1987) 66
and Shamai, S. (1987) 65
courses, graduate 8-9, 110, 111, 146-154
see also autobiographical
Craig, G. M. (1982) 62n52
'craft knowledge', teachers' 30
critical analysis 106

critical appraisal, teachers' 153
critical-emacipatory approach:
action research 127, 128
critical ethnography 128-9
critical perspective development 118
critical theory 7, 113, 114, 115, 116, 117, 118, 119, 124, 147
criticism, educational 5
Cronbach, L.
and Associates (1980) 124
and Suppes, P. (1969) 121
cross-curricular change 33
cultural
analysis 131
capital 35, 36, 37, 39-40
context: schools 5
—difference theorists 33
diversity 74
interruption 3, 26, 29-34, 39
issues: research 2-5
see also curriculum
culture 64, 76
of teaching 34, 36, 37, 38, 39, 40
curricular phenomena 7
curricular principles: evaluation 7
curricular reform **41-63**
curricular scholarship 1
see also change
curriculum 19, 21, 90, 103
academic influences 3, 18, 23, 335, 36
centralized 2, 36, 37, 38, 68, 81n9
class-based 3, 13-14, 15, 17, 23
cultural context 5, 23, **26-40**
definition 2-3, 13, 35, 75, 132, 138
developers 31, 111
development 26, 30, 74-5, 126, 151-2
differentiation/designation 15, 16, 17, 19
epistemology of 3, **13-25**
etymology: origins of term 1-2, 3, **13-25**
'hidden' 66, 68, 76, 77, 79
individualized 22
Irish: in Canada 42-7
materials 7, 32, 126
objectives 75
and pedagogy 15, 16, 17, 20, 21
and evaluation 16, 17, 21, 125-8, 137
policy 26-40
reform 3-4, 28, 33, 77, 102
review 36, 74-5

185

Index

social context   1–2, 3, 4, 14, 24, 56, 64, 67, 74–5, 82n12, 93
social organization and control   3, 14, 15, 22–3, 25, 134
and the state   4–5, 22–3
studies and investigations   1–2, 7–8, 9, 10, 67, 131
subject-centered   18, 19, 20, 34, 35, 36, 38, 75–6
theory   89, 90, **93–101**
whole school   27, 28
see also action research; Calvinism; change; classroom; conflict; economic; examination; knowledge; language; life experience; politics; 'Red Readers'; research; selection; standards; students; teachers; technical rationality; universities
Curriculum Policy: Review-Development-Implications (CRDI)   74
Curtis, B.   4, **41–63**
   (1983)   61n3
   (1985)   61n3
   and Corrigan, P. (1985)   81n1
   and Lanning, R. (1987)   81n1

data, research   162, 163–5, 168
decision-making   27, 64, 104, 117, 130
deconstructionists   93
Delhi, K.   81n7
Department of Education and Science:
   agenda of educational differentiation   36
   (1983)   37
designation and differentiation   15, 17
development strategies   136
Dewey, J. (1963)   156, 157
dialogue   23, 24, 130
Diaz, J. (1977)   146
Dickinson, Emily   92
didacticism   49–52, 55, 58, 59, 60
Didion, J. (1961)   92
differentiation   15, 16, 17, 67, 68
   educational   36, 37, 38
   gender   66, 100
   social   19, 37
discipline   14, 47, 51, 103
disciplines, subject   18, 21, 23, 24, 25
discourse   19
   and communication   147
discussion   149
Ditisheim, M. (1984)   147
diversity, problem of   77

Douglas, A. (1977)   90
Durkheim, E. (1974)   69

Earle, W. (1972)   92
economic
   conditions   2–3, 4, 138
economy   4, 57, 76
education   60, 108
   autobiographical coursework in   147
   change in: understanding   107
   and Church   21
   compensatory/supplementary   69
   evaluation as   125–8
   experiential   156
   hazards in   106, 107, 108–9
   history of   13–25
   home-based   15–16, 21
   and outside agencies   79
   post-secondary   75
   process of: implication   24
   programs, teacher   29–30, 34
   and reputation   107
   social/personal   37
   'new sociology of'   2
   and state   21, 22–3
   system   23, 67, 71, 73, 77, 78
   systems   2, 15
   and technical rationality   106–7
   working class   22–3, 35
   see also adult; biographic; economy; feminism; Jesuits; life experience; mutuality; pluralism; policy; politics; research; social control; social mobility; social tension; teacher
Education Act, (1870)   22
Education Act, (1944)   18
educational
   agenda: evaluators   7, 130–1
   change   34, 39–40, 75
   code, the   67
   differentiation   37
   issues: and teachers   33
   policy, 'givenness' of   1
   selection   36
   societies, British   57
   structures, change in   39–40
   theory   30, 90, 110, 154
   see also criticism; reflection; reform; reproduction; educators   131, 142
   as evaluators   124, 127–8
'effectiveness'   5
egalitarian practice   24
ego, the   89, 92

186

Index

Eisner, E. W.
  (1979) 124, 165
  (1985) 165
Elbaz, F. (1983) 30, 32, 148, 151, 152
'elect': social order 25
elementary education 21
elementary school(s) 17, 41, 57, 64, 75, 82n12, 110, 136
Elias, Norbert 60, 63n61
Elliot, J. 111
  (1983) 112, 118, 119n1
  (1985) 107
emancipation 7, 127, 129, 130
empirical approach 147
'ends and means' 102, 105, 106, 111
engenderization, process of 100
England 57–8, 110
  and curriculum 1, 3, 41, 42, 66
  schooling in 16–23
enquiry: educational process 124, 125
  see also biographical
entitlement 36, 37, 40
epistemological perspective 151
epistemology **13–25,** 114, 124
equality: evaluation 130
Erikson, F. (1986) 154
ethnography, critical 128–9
etymology (ies): curriculum **13–25**
Europe 3, 11
evaluation 4
  control 122
  and curriculum 8, 126, 131, 137, 138
  and pedagogy 15, 16, 17, 20, 21
  and education 7, 125–8
  historical forces 126
  'insider/outsider' 124
  professionalization 121–3
  reflective 138
  reporting 125, 126–7, 129
  studies 130–1
  as subversive educational activity **121–31**
  theoretical framework for 129
  see also program; research
Evaluation Research Society (1982) 122
evaluator
  educator as 7, 127
  as teacher 124, 125, 126, 128
evaluators 7, 30, 111, 122, 123, 125, 129, 130
  and curriculum 126, 131
  guidelines for 128–9
  illuminative/responsive 126

'insider/outsider' 124, 127, 155
  examination boards 16, 17, 18
examination constraints 31
examinations 16, 18, 33, 37, 103
excellence 76
experience 113, 122–3, 148
  in autobiographical course 147, 154, 156
expressivity 68, 107

family 15–16, 90, 91
Fay, B. (1975) 103, 107–8
Feimen-Nemser, S. and Floden, R. E. (1986) 151
female consciousness 89
female/male differentiation 100
feminism 6, **87–101**
  and the family 91
  and educational influences 89
feminist movement 66
feminist theory 87–8
Fiske, E. B. (1986) 82n12
Flanders, T. (1983) 156
flexibility 23, 78
Ford Teaching Project 119n1
form(s) 1, 23
formal grounded theory 114
Foucault, M. 81n2, 82n11
  (1981, 1982) 66
Fox, W. Sherwood (1972) 62n32
fragmentation 28, 36, 40
Frankfurt School 124–5
Fransella, F. and Bannister, D, (1977) 132
Freud, S. 89, 95, 100
Frost, R. (1950) 95
Fullan, M. (1985) 144
  and Connelly, F. M.: Report (1987) 80

Gadamer, H. G. (1975) 118
Galt, W. 61n10
gender 6, 66, 100
General Certificate of Education 18
General Certificate of Secondary Education 37
Gibson, R. (1985) 116, 117
  (1986) 111, 112–13
Glaser, B. G. and Strauss, A. (1968) 114
Godfrey, P. 82n12
Goffman, E. 105
  (1962) 103

187

Index

Goldstrom, J. M. 47, 57, 58, 62n34, n35, n40
Goodson, I. F. **1-10, 13-25**
  (1983a) 19, 28, 118
  (1983b) 160
  and Ball, S. J., (1985a) 87, 160
  (1985b) 160
Gorman, C. (1987) 81n6
governance 69, 73, 78
  and service delivery 74, 77
government 71, 78
  initiatives 38
  mandates 102
grades
  see standards
graduate-education courses 8-9, 110, 111, 154
grammar schools 18
'grand' theory 114
Graset, Rev. H., 41, 54, 62n52
Great Arch, The: English State Formation and Cultural Revolution (1985), 65, 66
Great Britain: culture of teaching 34
Griffin, S. (1981) 101n2
grounded theory, action research
  formal 114, 115, 116, 118
  'grand' 114
  of knowledge 114
  substantive 114, 115, 118
group-based pedagogies 16
group influences/pressures 160
Grove, T. J. 61n4
Grumet, M. R. 5-6, **87-101**, 147, 148
Grundy, S. (1982) 127
Guba, E. and Lincoln, Y. (1981, 1986) 124
guidelines: social/economic/political influences 2-5
Gunn, W. 61n14, n20
Guskey, T. R. (1985) 151

Habermas, J. 118
  (1970, 1979) 116
Hall, G. and Loucks, S. (1977), 102
Halsey, A. H., Heath, A. F. and Ridge, J. M. (1980) 35
Hamilton, D. (1980) 15, 16, 17
  and Gibbons, M. (1980) 13-14
Hanson, D. and Herrigton, M. (1976) 30
Hanson, E. M. (1981) 27
Hargreaves, A. 3-4, **26-40**
  (1978) 27

(1982) 30
(1986) 29
Hargreaves, D. (1982) 35, 40n1
Harland, J. (1987) 38
Harré, R. (1979) 103, 105, 107
Harrison, J. F. C. (1984) 22
Harvey, C. (1981) 128
Hegel, G. W. F. 89
Heidegger, M. 88
Her Majesty's Inspectorate 36, 57
  (1977) 35
  (1983) 28, 35
'hidden' curriculum 66, 68, 76, 77, 79
hierarchical structure: curriculum 24
highschool level teaching 28
high school 28
Hilliard, F. H. (1971) 154
Hobsbawm, E. J. and Ranger, T. (1983) 67
Hodgins, J. G. (1894-1910), 62n38
Hopkins, J. C. (1898) 62n52
House, E. R. (1980) 128
'Human Capital' 67
Husserl, E. G. A. 88
'hypothesis embodied': action research 111

idealism, repudiation of 92-3
identity 66, 68, 69, 73, 74
ideology and social relations 70
ignorance 60, 63n62, 67, 71
impact 5, 126, 127
independence 76, 135, 141
individual, the: and society 74, 75, 76
individual learners 78
individualization 74
industrial progress 59-60
information 73, 78, 126
'information age, the' 4, 73
Inglis, F. (1985) 63n62, 67
Ingvarson, L. and Greenway, P. A. (1981) 151
initial training: theory and practice gap 29, 30
Inner London Education Authority (1984) 35
innovation(s) 17, 28, 39, 31-2, 38, 107
innovative packages 102
in-service education 2-5, 29, 30, 34, 38, 155
'insider'/'outsider' evaluation 124, 127, 155
inspectors, state/school 22
instrumental approach 127, 137

Index

instrumentalism 135
integration 153, 158–9
intellectual criteria: selection 1
interdependence, teacher 138
interpretation 154
  of research findings 167–8
  see also phenomenal
interview techniques 164–5
Ireland 57
  see also Irish National Series
Irish Commission 48
Irish curriculum: Canada West 42–7
Irish National Series: school reading books 4, 41, 42–7, 57, 59
  and 'Red Readers' **47–52,** 55–6
isolation, teacher 27, 38, 40, 119, 153

Jackson, P. W. (1968) 27, 40n1
Janesick, V. J. (1981) 148
Jenkins, D. and Shipman, M. (1976) 20
Jesuit College, Quebec 14
Jesuits: curriculum 2, 14
Johnson, R. (1970) 66
Joint Committee on Standards for Educational Evaluation (1981) 122
Joseph, K. 65
  (1984) 35

Kallos, D.: evaluation 128
Katz, M. (1975) 62n33
Kelly, G. (1955) 132
Kemmis, S. (1984a) 110, 115, 116, 118
  (1984b) 124
  (1987) 108
  and Carr, W. (1983) 116, 117, 119, 120n
key educators 142, 144
Klotz, O. 44, 45, 61n22, 61n26, 61n27
Knowledge 7, 41, 57–60, 130, 148
  through action research 111, 115, 118, 119
  and control, social 1, 2, 3, 14
  and curriculum 3, 14, 16, 18, 24
  generation/production 121, 123, 124
  personal/practical 8, 9, 117, 128, 151, 155, 158
  and phenomenology 88, 91
  and power 151
  professional 9, 151, 154, 157
  pupils' 39–40
  school 42, 47
  academic, subject-based 1, 18, 35
  scientific 103, 117, 119
  social context of 1, 2, 3, 14, 24, 35
  of social science 104, 108
  teachers' 8, 9, 24, 150, 151, 152, 157, 158
  communicating/sharing 156
  theory of 114
Kodikara, A. (1986) 81n6

labor 66, 89, 90
  market prediction 73
Labov, W. (1973) 33
Lacan and Freud 100
Lacey, C. (1977) 28, 30
Lampert, M. (1984) 107
language
  'categorical' 166
  of curriculum change 32, 157
  evaluators' 128
  –game 68
  of research reporting 165–6
  teacher 31–3, 112, 158
  working class 32, 33
Lanning, R. 81n1
Lather, P. (1984) 151
  (1986a, 1986b) 125
Layton, D. (1972) 18, 20–1
learner, the 125, 128
learners 76, 78, 128
  adult 125, 148
learning 75, 76, 102, 110
  academic 36
  co-operative 146
  group-based 16, 78
  method of 23
  professional 9, 138, **146–59**
  sequence 13, 23
  social 146, 149
  special needs 73
  support 78
  and teaching roles 146, 154
learning community, ideal 129–30
Learning to Labour 129
lessons: classroom system 17
Lewin, K. 116
  (1946) 110
liberty, preservation of 71
life experience 21, 22
life history 8, 131
  research 9–10, **160–8**
  data 162, 163–5, 168
  definitions 9, 161–2, 168
life-world 88, 162
Lillie, T. W. 43, 61n9, n19

189

Index

Lincoln, Y. and Guba, E. (1981, 1984) 124
linguistic codes 32
'lived experiences' 122
Lortie, D. (1975) 27, 40n1, 87
Lovell, J. 46
Lundgren, U. P. 128

McAlpine, L. (1985) 127-8
McCabe, Jane 92, 93-100, 101n5
McCaul, Dr. J. 41, 54, 62n52
McColl, H. 61n15
McCormick, R. and James, M. (1983) 124
McCullough, W. 43, 61n8
Macdonald, M. (1980) 87
MacIntyre, A. (1981) 108
McKeon, R. (1951) 154, 155
McRae, H. 61n11
male/female consciousness: theorists 89
 differentiation 100
management 2, 78, 104, 105
 theory 6, 29
Management of Ignorance, The (1985) 63n62, 67
managerial class 64
managerial domination 31
Mannheim, K. (1936) 128
Mansfield, B. (1984) 128
Marshall, J. and Peters, M. (1985) 129-30
Marx, K. 66, 67, 89
 and Engels, F. (1846) 70
mastery learning 102
Mayo, E. (1851) 62n47
meaning and knowledge 91
'means and ends' 102, 105, 106, 108, 126
Measor, L. (1985) 160, 164, 166
media: evaluative conditions and content 7
'mentalities' (ability) 19
meta-theory 7, 114, 115, 116, 117, 118, 119
methodological alternatives **85-182**
methodology, research 5, 10, 103, 104, 151, 160, 161
middle class 36, 37, 51
middle class schools 16, 57
Milburn, G. **1-10, 160**-8
'milieu' 125, 126, 128
militarism: reading books 58
Mir, M.: 'classes' 13-14
mobility, social 74

model school 47, 60
Montaign, college of 13-14
Monteath, R. 61n11
morality 42, 48, 57, 59
moral regulation **64-80,** 81n9
Morgan, R. (1987) 67
Munro, A. A. 61n18
Murray, L. 43, 48
mutual approaches 155
mutal confirmation 156
mutual support 156
mutualism 155, 156
mutuality in education 24

narrative: reading books 54, 56, 58-9
 see also phenomenal
nationalism, developing 58
needs, ignoring 103
 see also special learning
Newcastle Commission (1861) 57
'new sociology of education' 2
Nias, J. (1985) 160, 166
Nietzsche, F. W. 92-3
Nixon, J. (1981) 119n1
Noddings, N. (1984) 101n4
normalization 42, 60, 77
normal school 43, 44, 47, 60, 73
North America; autobiography in education courses 147
Norwood Report (1943) 17, 18-19

objectivity/subjectivity 91, 93
object-relations theory 91
O'Brien, M. (1981) 89
observation: action research 117, 127
Olson, J. 6, **102-9**
 (1982a) 107
 (1982b) 30, 31-2
 (1984) 103
 and Eaton, S. (1986) 107
 and Russell, T. (1984) 107
Olson, T. (1984) 92
Ontario (Canada West) 4, 8, 122
 Towards the Year 2000 **69-79**
Ontario Ministry of Education, (1977) 133
 (1984b) 65, 70, 74
 (1986a, b) 83n13
Ontario Schools: Intermediate and Senior Divisions (OSIS), (1984a) 74
Ormiston, Dr. W. 41, 53-4, 62n52
OSIS
 see Ontario Schools: Intermediate and Senior Divisions

Index

outsider-insider dichotomies 9
  see also evaluators
Oxford Conference, (1983) 160

Parlett, M. and Hamilton, D. (1976) 126
'payment-by-results' 57
pedagogical matters 29, 40, 59, 60
pedagogy 16, 29, 101, 124, 126, 129, 154
  see also curriculum
peer-utilization: teaching/learning 146, 156, 157, 158
perception, influencing 107
personal
  interpretation 124
  practice, teaching 147, 148
  professional development 147
'person-teachers' 147
Pestalozzi, J. H. 51, 62n46
Pestalozzianism 51
phenomena 113, 114
  educational 117, 119
  personal 138
phenomenal interpretations of narrative 95-6, 97-8, 99-101
phenomenology 5, 6, 66, 147
  of the familiar: and feminism **87-101**
Phenomenology and Pedagogy 101
philosophical analysis 108
philosophy 29, 92-3, 131, 141
  of curriculum change 135, 136
Pinar, W. (1980, 1981, 1986) 147
Plummer, K. (1983) 161
pluralism 73
pluralist-intuitionist approach 127
pluralist society 76-7
Poirier, P. (1986) 81n8
Polak, F. L. (1961) 157
political
  economy: education 48, 49, 50, 51, 55, 56, 57, 58, 60
  ideologies 5
  ignorance 60
  influences 7, 138
  systems 2-5, 10
politics 73, 90
  and education 47, 51, 55, 59, 71, 76
  and curriculum 2-3, 4, 21, 38, 58, 74, 138
policy
  education 1, 106, 126, 130
  -making 122

Pollard, A. (1984) 31
Pope, M. and Keen, T. (1981) 132
positivism 88, 114, 147
Poulantzas, N. (1978) 67
power
  issues 31, 124-5, 128
  and knowledge 151
  relationships 4, 5, 129
  teacher 141
'practical' mode: action research 127
practice, school 30, 89
  and action research 110, 111, 112, 117
  and technical rationality 102, 103
  see also theory
practitioners, action research
  theory production 115
  evaluation 124
prescription 13
prescriptive theory 154
pressure groups 160
private schools 22, 80
problem-solving 155
process-orientated curriculum 75-6
production, capitalist relations of 42, 59-60
products, development of 142
professional development 9, 26, 40, 133, **146-59**
  self-initiated 148, 158
professional
  identities 162
  life 103, 153
  -renewal orientation 8, 133, 137-41, 142, 143
professional evaluation 121-3
program
  evaluation 7, 121-3, 130, 131
  individualization 76
  see also courses; education
psychoanalytic approach 6
psychoanalytic theory 91
psychologists, school 60
psychologists 29
public opinion: curriculum change 6, 77
public schools, English 23
pupil(s) 19, 20, 21, 24, 39-40, 58
  -teacher relationship 27, 114
  see also students

qualitative research 5, 7, 132
Quebec: Jesuit College 14

191

Index

Rand Corporation (1978)   155
Rapoport, R. N. (1970)   110, 119n1
rationality, technical
   see technical rationality
Ratio Studiorum   14
readers (school textbooks)   4, 57–60
   see also 'Red Readers'
reality   128, 152
Reagan, R.   82n12, 83
'Red Readers': and curricular change   4, **41–63**
   and Irish Readers   52–4, 55–6
reflection   128, 130, 148, 156
   in action research   117, 127
   autobiographical course   149, 153, 154
   constraints on   34, 38, 39
reflective evaluation   138
reflective practice   103, 107
reflexive value of curriculum change   137
reform, educational: crisis of   64, 65, 151
reformers, outside: and teachers   115
regulation, moral   68, 77, 81n9
Reid, W. A. (1972)   20
   (1985)   23
relationships   123, 128–9
   see also power; social
religion   68
   in reading books   47, 48, 51, 52, 55, 56, 57, 58
Report on a System of Public Elementary Instruction for Upper Canada
   (1846)   42
reports
   evaluation   125, 126–7, 129
   presentation   165
   research   165, 167–8
reproduction, educational   6, 89, 90, 129
reputation   103, 104–6, 107
research   9, 102, 121, 124, 125, 152
   case-study   124
   communication   126–7
   curriculum: cultural perspectives   2–5, 8, 10, 30, **85–182**
   educational   110, 112, 117, 118
   problems   151
   institutes   102, 104
ethnographic   161
female contribution   89
funding   115
methodologies   5, 10, 151, 160, 161

substantive   158
see also action; alternative; applied; autobiographical; cultural; data; life-history; qualitative; social science; teachers
researcher   2, 114, 158, 167–8
   teacher as   111, 158
research officers: evaluation   122
researchers   5
   teacher collaboration   30, 31
resistance to change   107–8, 129
resource allocation patterns   18, 19
resources, educational   19, 20, 23, 27, 79, 124–5, 138
responsibility   92, 93, 138, 141
Review and Evaluation Bulletin
   see Towards the Year 2000
Revised Code   57, 58
Richardson, J.   61n10
Riseborough, G. F. (1985)   160, 162, 166, 167
Robertson, T. N.   61n10
roles-as-rules   68
Rose, G. (1888)   62n52
Rothblatt, S. (1976)   21
Rudduck, J.   38
rules, basis for evaluation   69, 129–30
Ryerson, E.   44, 46, 47, 53, 61n19, n20, n21, n25, n26, 63n60, 71, 72, 73
   (1846)   42
   (1847)   61n2
   (1866)   62n30

Sanford, N. (1984)   110
Sartre, J. P. (1954)   87
Scarlett, E.   61n11
Schecter, S. (1987)   64–5, 80
scholarly enquiry, crisis of   151
Schon, D. (1983)   102, 103, 107, 126, 147, 156
school   10, 40, 57, 66, 68, 162
   −based projects   148, 153, 157
   −centered innovation   31, 142
   discipline   59
   organization   24
   subjects (disciplines)   3, 28
   system   17, 18, 104
   see also curriculum; knowledge; management; practice; reform
School Act, (1846)
schooling   1, 4, 13–14, 27, 59, 73, 112
   and ascription   68
   certification   80–1
   compulsory   66

192

Index

hazards: technical rationality 106
re-politicization 81n9
and society: social context 66, 67, 74
state 15–16, 17, 21, 22, 23, 59, 66
schools 14, 16, 20, 65, 105, 112, 128–9
   see also Common; comprehensive; elementary; grammar; middle class; model; normal; private; public; secondary; technical; working class
Schools Council Humanities Project 119n1
Schools Council Integrated Science Project (SCISP) 31
science 104, 105, 106, 124
scientific management theories 6
SCISP
   see Schools Council Integrated Science Project
secondary education 21
secondary modern schools 19
Secondary Regulations, (1904) 18
secondary school 16–17, 19, 28, 64, 75, 110
selection, educational 25, 35, 36, 37, 76
   and curriculum 1, 66
self: anxiety and resistance 108
self-appraisal, critical: teachers 157
self-discovery, teachers' 156
self-interest, teachers': career pursuit 28, 78–9, 135
self-initiation, teacher 156
self-justification 59
self-reflection: evaluators 7, 112, 127, 130
self-study: evaluators 131
service delivery and government 73, 77, 78
Shamai, S. (1986) 65
   and Corrigan, P. R. D. (1987) 65
Shapiro, B. J.: Report (1985) 80
Sharma, T. (1982) 155
Sharp, R. and Green, A. (1975) 27
Sikes, P. J. (1985) 160, 162, 166
Silber, K. (1973) 63n46
Simon, R. and Dippo, D. 123
skills, thinking 102
Smelser, N. (1968) 15–16
Smiles, S. 54
   (1859) 65
Smith, D. 66
Smith, L. M., Kleine, P. F., Dwyer, D. C. and Prunty, J. J. (1985) 162, 165, 167

Smith, N. (1981) 124
social
   analysis 110–11, 112
   cohesion 71
   conditions; classroom 138
   control 3, 15, 22–3
   curriculum 67, 74–5
   differentiation 16, 17, 19
   grammar 80
   hierarchy 24
   organization 64
   philosophy 131
   politics 5, 10
   programs 110
   relations 2, 5, 23, 24, 70, 124–5, 128–9
   science 7, 88, 106–8, 161
   methodology 10, 103, 104
   research 102, 116
   selection 35
   systems 28
   tension 22–3
   well-being 76
   see also curriculum; identities; learning; mobility; schooling
'Social, The': 'five Rs' 66, 67, 68
Social Content of Education, The 57
socialization: teachers 28
societal relationships 123
society 56, 72, 74, 75, 78, 125
   see also bourgeois; consumer; pluralistic
sociology of education 2, 29, 66
   categories 166
span of control: governance 78
specialism: curriculum change 28
specialization, subject 18
special learning needs 73
SPTG
   see Strategic Planning Task Group
Stake, R. E. (1976) 126
   (1978) 124
   (1984) 128
standardization 17, 72
'standards' (grades) 14, 89, 90, 122
   and curriculum 2, 16–17
state, the 64, 82n11, 89, 90
   control: curriculum 4, 106
   formation and classroom practice **64–83**
   see also schooling
status 18, 19, 20, 23, 37–8
Stenhouse, L. 111
   (1975) 119n1, 124
   (1980) 26

193

Index

strategic influence orientation 8, 133, 141–2, 143
Strategic Planning Initiative 80
Strategic Planning Task Group (SPTG) 69
Strachan, J. 54
Stauss, E. (1966) 89, 114
streaming (tracking) 17, 74
structural-functionalism, Parsonian 68
structural redefinition 26, 39–40
structural reinforcement 34–9
structured direction 8, 133, 141–2, 143
student(s) 2–3, 7, 13–14, 20, 23, 160
  adult/graduate 9, 24, 76, 147, 154
  and curriculum change 136, 137, 138, 139, 140
  see also pupil(s)
study, sequential programs of 15
subject(s), school 3, 17. 18., 19–21
  – centered curriculum/classroom pedagogy 28, 29, 34, 38, 76
  matter 125–6, 128
  restraints 28, 33
  specialization 4, 36, 39
    – status hierarchies 31
  and teacher 28, 38
  see also curriculum
subjective interpretation 150
subjectivities 69, 82n11
subjectivity 64, 68, 92, 93
subjectivity/objectivity 91
subordination 68, 69
substantive grounded theory 114
supplementary education 69
symbolic, the 68
system
  see education; school
system plans: implementation 104
system-reduction 78
stystems-based packages 105
systems theory 104

task(s) 24, 107
Taunton Report (1868) 16–17, 18
Taylor, A. J. P. (1965) 164
teacher, the 125, 128
  as adult/graduate learner 151, 154
  and evaluator 7, 126
  as researcher 158
  and student/pupil 27, 40, 138
teacher
  autonomy 111
  – based activity 158
  – centered-adaption-orientation 8, 133, 134–7, 142, 143

certification 78
competence 37
control 7, 9, 112
decision-making 117
education 8–9, 29–30, 34, 110, 111, **146–59**
effectiveness 2
interaction 137
  – proofing: curriculum materials 155
  – training 28, 38, 40, 47, 57, 58, 60, 80
teachers 75, 93
  biographies **146–59**
  constraints 31, 34, 38, 40
  and curriculum change **26–40,** 102, 108–9, 126, 151, 152, 156
  as agents 135, 136
  alienation 147, 155
  orientations **132–45**
  resistance 3, 107
  rights 134, 137, 138, 141
  and innovations 31–2, 38, 155
  pressures on 38, 60
  and research 7, 30, 31, 111, 112, 114, 115, 117, 118, 119–20n1
  self-interest 28, 78–9, 135
  status: specializations 19, 20, 37–8
  and technical rationality 6, 103–4, 105–6
  women 90, 101
  see also careers; classroom; in-service; knowledge; language; professional development
Teachers' Lives and Careers (1985) 87, 160, 161, 163, 164, 165, 166, 167, 168
teaching 6, 8, 9, 16, 26, 87, 107, 131
  career 108
  context of 34
  culture of: curriculum change 3, 8, **26–40**
  integrated 153
  and learning **146–59**
  methods 23, 24
  process 75
  profession: redefining 78–9
  quality 151
  and research 119, 124, 126
  styles 102
  see also classroom-centeredness; conservatism; fragmentation
technical
  – management 8
  mode: action research 127
  programs: teachers 34

194

Index

—rational approaches 9
schools 19
technical rationality 5, 6, 64, 69, **102-9,** 147
  and curriculum 102, 104
  defined 103
technology 72, 73
tension 22-3, 127-8, 132
Terkel, S. 131
testing, standardized 33, 37, 57-8, 151
textbooks, school 4, 47, 57, 72
  see also 'Red Readers'
texts for students: influences 2-5, 23, 128
theorists, academic 7
theory 5, 89, 91, 151, 152
  and action research 113, 115, 117
  construction 7
  language of 32-3
  personal construct 132
  and practice 7, 9, 30-1, 111, 112, 116 118, 154
see also critrical; curriculum; educational; grounded; knowledge; management; meta-theory; prescriptive; scientific management; systems
Thiessen, D. 8, **132-45**
thinking 93
  skills 102, 158
Thompson, E. P. (1968) 22-3, 24
Thompson of Fleet, Lord 65
time 19
  constraints, teachers' 33, 34
timetables: classroom system 17
tracking (streaming) 17, 74
transformation: curriculum change 137
Tremenheere, H. S. 82n13
Trempe, P. L. (1984) 147
Tomkins, G. S. (1986) 2, 14
Torrance, R. 61n25
Towards the Year 2000: Future Conditions and Strategic Options for the Support of Learning in Ontario, (1984b) 65, **69-79,** 80, 82n12
Turner, H. E. (1982) 62n52

understanding 124, 127, 130, 150
United States (US) 40, 82n12, 128
universities: disciplines and curriculum 18, 19-20, 23, 25, 122, 123
university examination boards 16, 17
university programs of study 131

Univeristy of Cambridge Local Examinations Syndicate (1958) 16
Upper Canada
  see Ontario
US
  see United States

validity, catalytic 129
value consensus 68
value judgments 126
value positions 103, 106
values: curriculum change orientation 132
van Manen, M. (1978, 1979) 147

Walker, R. (1986) 165
Waller, W. (1932) 26, 27, 40n1
Webb, R. B. (1985) 160, 166
Weiss, J. 7-8, **121-31**
  and Reynolds, C. and Simon, R. (1983) 130
Werner, W. (1982) 152
Westbury, I. (1973) 27
Weston, P. and Harland, J. 37
Whately, Archbishop 50
Whately, R. 61n23
Whitty, G. (1985) 2
Wideman, H. (1981) 128
Wilden, T. (1981) 67
Williams, R. 81n1
  (1961) 1, 22, 65
  (1981, 1983) 65
Willis, G. (1978) 124
Willis, P. (1977) 129
Williamson, B. (1982) 165
Wilson, B. (1962) 107
Wilson, J. (1979) 108
Wise, R. I. (1980) 124
Wittgenstein, L. J. J. 129
women 6, 89-90
  family and phenomenology 91-2
Woods, P. (1977) 27
Working class education, nineteenth century 21, 25, 36
  political economy 60
  private schools 22
  textbooks 47, 48, 51, 55, 57, 58, 59
working class language 33

Yeo, S. (1979, 1986) 69
Young, M. (1971a) 1
  (1971b) 65
young, the: socializing through education 76

195